First World War
and Army of Occupation
War Diary
France, Belgium and Germany

20 DIVISION
Divisional Troops
33 Sanitary Section
23 July 1915 - 31 March 1917

WO95/2110/2

The Naval & Military Press Ltd
www.nmarchive.com
Published in association with The National Archives

Published by

The Naval & Military Press Ltd

Unit 10 Ridgewood Industrial Park,

Uckfield, East Sussex,

TN22 5QE England

Tel: +44 (0) 1825 749494

www.naval-military-press.com

www.nmarchive.com

This diary has been reprinted in facsimile from the original. Any imperfections are inevitably reproduced and the quality may fall short of modern type and cartographic standards.

© **Crown Copyright**
Images reproduced by permission of The National Archives, London, England, 2015.

Contents

Document type	Place/Title	Date From	Date To
Heading	2110/2		
Heading	20th Division 33rd Sanitary Section Jly 1915-1917 Mar To 3 Army		
Heading	20th Division Summarised but not Copied From July To Nov 15 San Sect 33 Vol I		
Heading	War Diary Of Lieutenant N.A. Dore. R.A.M.C Officer Commanding Sanitary Section 33 1st London (City Of London) Sanitary Company R.A.M.C. (T) Attached XXth (Light) Division. B.E.F. France. From 23rd July To 30th November 1915 Volume I.		
War Diary	Rollestone Camp Salisbury Plain.	23/07/1915	23/07/1915
War Diary	Havre	24/07/1915	25/07/1915
War Diary	Wizernes	26/07/1915	27/07/1915
War Diary	Lumbres	28/07/1915	28/07/1915
War Diary	Lynde	29/07/1915	29/07/1915
War Diary	Merris	30/07/1915	09/08/1915
War Diary	Sailly	10/08/1915	10/08/1915
War Diary	Armentieres	11/08/1915	11/08/1915
War Diary	Estaires	12/08/1915	12/08/1915
War Diary	Merris	13/08/1915	26/08/1915
War Diary	Estaires	26/08/1915	24/09/1915
War Diary	Sailly	24/11/1915	30/11/1915
Heading	20th Div Dec 1915 33 San. Sect Summarised But Not Copied		
Miscellaneous	War Diary Of Lieutenant N.A. Dore R.A.M.C Officer Commanding Sanitary Section 33 (1st London City Of London Sanitary Company) R.A.M.C. (T.F) Attached XXth (Light) Division B.E.F. France From 1st To 31st December 1915 Volume II		
War Diary	Sailly Sur La Lys	01/12/1915	31/12/1915
Heading	20th Div 33rd Sany Section Jan Feb Mar 1916		
Miscellaneous	San Sect 33 Vol 3		
Miscellaneous	War Diary Of Captain N.A. Dore, R.A.M.C (T.F.) Officer Commanding Sanitary Section 33 1st London City Of London Sanitary Company) R.A.M.C. (T.F) Attached XXth Light Division B.E.F. France January 1916 Volume III		
War Diary	Sailly	01/01/1916	11/01/1916
War Diary	Morbecque	12/01/1916	22/01/1916
War Diary	Oxlaere	23/01/1916	27/01/1916
Heading	San Sect 33 Vol 34		
Heading	War Diary Of Captain N.A. Dore R.A.M.C (T.F.) Officer Commanding Sanitary Section 33 (1st London City Of London Sanitary Company) R.A.M.C. (T.F) Attached XXth Light Division B.E.F. France February 1916 Volume IV		
War Diary	Wormhoult	05/02/1916	12/02/1916
War Diary	Poperinghe	13/02/1916	29/02/1916

Heading	War Diary Of Captain N.A. Dore R.A.M.C (T.F) Officer Commanding Sanitary Section 33 (1st London City of London Sanitary Company) R.A.M.C. (T.F) Attached XXth Light Division B.E.F. France March 1916 Volume V		
War Diary	Poperinghe	01/03/1916	31/03/1916
Heading	B. 33 Sanitary Section April 1916		
Heading	War Diary Of Captain N.A. Dore R.A.M.C (T.F.) Officer Commanding Sanitary Section 33 (1st London City Of London Sanitary Company) R.A.M.C. (T.F) Attached XXth Light Division B.E.F. France April 1916 Volume VI		
War Diary	Poperinghe	01/04/1916	17/04/1916
War Diary	Wormhoult	18/04/1916	30/04/1916
Heading	War Diary Of Captain N.A. Dore R.A.M.C (T.F.) Officer Commanding Sanitary Section 33 (1st London City Of London Sanitary Company) R.A.M.C. (T.F) Attached XXth Light Division B.E.F. France May 1916 Volume VII		
War Diary	Wormhoult	01/05/1916	20/05/1916
War Diary	Poperinghe	21/05/1916	31/05/1916
Heading	War Diary Of Lieut. A.F. Girvan, R.A.M.C. (T.F.) Officer Commanding Sanitary Section 33 1st London (City Of London) Sanitary Company, R.A.M.C. (T.F) Attached 20th (Light) Division. B.E.F. France 19th. June, 1916 to 30th June, 1916 Volume 1		
War Diary	Poperinge	19/06/1916	30/06/1916
Diagram etc	Purification Plant For Soapy Water.		
Heading	War Diary Of Captain N.A. Dore R.A.M.C (T.F.) Officer Commanding Sanitary Section 33 1st London (City Of London) Sanitary Coy R.A.M.C. (T.F). attached 20th Light Division B.E.F. France 1st June to 23rd June 1916 Volume 8.		
War Diary	Poperinghe	01/06/1916	23/06/1916
Heading	War Diary Of Lieut. A.F. Girvan. R.A.M.C (T) Officer Commanding Sanitary Section 33 1st London (City Of London) Sanitary Company, R.A.M.C. (T.F) Attached 20th Light Division. B.E.F. France July 1916 Volume 2.		
War Diary	Poperinge	01/07/1916	16/07/1916
War Diary	Wormhoudt	17/07/1916	20/07/1916
War Diary	Bailleul	21/07/1916	23/07/1916
War Diary	St Sylvestre Capel	23/07/1916	25/07/1916
War Diary	Doullens	26/07/1916	26/07/1916
War Diary	Couin	27/07/1916	31/07/1916
Heading	War Diary Of Captain A.F. Girvan, R.A.M.C (T.F) Officer Commanding, Sanitary Section 33, 1st London (City Of London) Sanitary Company) R.A.M.C. (T.F) Attached 20th. Light Division B.E.F. France August 1916 Volume 3.		
War Diary	Couin	01/08/1916	17/08/1916
War Diary	Terramesnil	18/08/1916	18/08/1916
War Diary	Candas	19/08/1916	20/08/1916
War Diary	Treux	20/08/1916	21/08/1916
War Diary	Citadel	22/08/1916	22/08/1916
War Diary	Somme Citadel	23/08/1916	31/08/1916

Miscellaneous	Report For Week Ending Saturday 12th Appendix I		
Miscellaneous	List Of Disinfectants		
Miscellaneous	To. A.D.M.S., 20th Division.		
Miscellaneous	Report For Week Ending 26th August 1916 Appendix II		
Miscellaneous	List Of Disinfectants		
Miscellaneous	To A.D.M.S. 20th Division.		
Miscellaneous	To A.D.M.S. XXth Division.	20/08/1916	20/08/1916
Heading	War Diary Of Captain A.F. Girvan, R.A.M.C (T.F.) Officer Commanding Sanitary Section 33 1st London (City Of London) Sanitary Company) R.A.M.C. (T.F) Attached 20th Light Division B.E.F. France September 1916 Volume 4.		
War Diary	Citadel (F21 Central Albert Combined Sheet 1/40000)	01/09/1916	05/09/1916
War Diary	Forked Tree	05/09/1916	06/09/1916
War Diary	Corbie	07/09/1916	11/09/1916
War Diary	Forked Tree	11/09/1916	17/09/1916
War Diary	Citadel	18/09/1916	21/09/1916
War Diary	Forked Tree	22/09/1916	22/09/1916
War Diary	Meaulte	23/09/1916	30/09/1916
Miscellaneous	Report For Week Ending Sunday 3rd September 1916 Appendix A		
Miscellaneous			
Miscellaneous	To. A.D.M.S., 20th Division.		
Miscellaneous	To. A.D.M.S., XXth Division.	10/09/1916	10/09/1916
Miscellaneous	Report On Sanitary Condition Etc, For Week Ending 9th September 1916 Appendix B		
Miscellaneous	List Of Disinfectants	09/09/1916	09/09/1916
Miscellaneous	To. A.D.M.S., 20th Division.		
Miscellaneous	Report On Sanitary Conditions Etc. Of Units Of 20th Division During The Week Ending 7th September 1916	07/09/1916	07/09/1916
Miscellaneous	Report For Week Ending September 23rd. 1916	23/09/1916	23/09/1916
Miscellaneous	To Town Major. Meaulte Appendix E		
Miscellaneous	Report For Week Ending Appendix F		
Heading	War Diary Of Captain R.A.M.C (T.F.) Officer Commanding 33rd Sanitary Section 1st London (City Of London) Sanitary Company R.A.M.C. (T.F) Attached 20th (Light) Division B.E.F. France. October 1916 Volume 5.		
War Diary	Meaulte	01/10/1916	16/10/1916
War Diary	Corbie	17/10/1916	19/10/1916
War Diary	Vignacourt	20/10/1916	21/10/1916
War Diary	Belloy Sur Somme	22/10/1916	31/10/1916
War Diary	Sanitary Report Appendix A		
Miscellaneous	Weekly Report. Appendix B		
Miscellaneous	To A.D.M.S. 20th. Division. Appendix C		
Miscellaneous	Report For Week Ending 28th. October 1916	28/10/1916	28/10/1916
Heading	33rd Sanitary Section 20th Div 140/1862		
Heading	War Diary Of Captain A.F. Girvan R.A.M.C. (T.F.) Officer Commanding 33rd Sanitary Section 1st London (City Of London) Sanitary Coy R.A.M.C. (T.F) Attached 20th (Light) Division B.E.F. France. November 1916 Volume 6		
War Diary	Belloy Sur Somme	01/11/1916	01/11/1916
War Diary	Riencourt	02/11/1916	15/11/1916
War Diary	Corbie	16/11/1916	30/11/1916

Miscellaneous	Report Appendix A	01/11/1916	01/11/1916
Diagram etc	Baths Picquigny Rough Plan		
Miscellaneous	Report Appendix B	04/11/1916	04/11/1916
Miscellaneous	Report Appendix C	11/11/1916	11/11/1916
Miscellaneous	Report Appendix D	01/11/1916	01/11/1916
Miscellaneous	Report Appendix E	18/11/1916	18/11/1916
Diagram etc	Divisional Baths Proposed Laundry Corbie Appendix F		
Heading	War Diary Of Captain A.F. Girvan R.A.M.C (T.F.) Officer Commanding 33rd Sanitary Section 1st London (City Of London) Sanitary Company R.A.M.C. (T.F) Attached 20th (Light) Division B.E.F. France. December 1916 Volume 7		
War Diary	Corbie	01/12/1916	11/12/1916
War Diary	Montauban A2d 97 Albert Combined Sheet	12/12/1916	13/12/1916
War Diary	Montauban F2 D 97	14/12/1916	23/12/1916
War Diary	Corbie	24/12/1916	31/12/1916
War Diary	Report Appendix A	25/11/1916	25/11/1916
Miscellaneous	Report Appendix B	02/12/1916	02/12/1916
Miscellaneous	To A.D.M.S. 20th Division Appendix C.		
Miscellaneous	After Daily Order By Captain A.F. Girvan. R.A.M.C. (T.F.) Commanding 33rd. Sanitary Section Appendix D (1)	20/12/1916	20/12/1916
Operation(al) Order(s)	Daily Order No 40 By Captain A.F. Girvan, R.A.M.C. (T.F.) Commanding 33rd. Sanitary Section Appendix D (2)	11/12/1916	11/12/1916
Miscellaneous	Report Appendix E	15/11/1916	15/11/1916
Miscellaneous	Report		
Miscellaneous	Sanitary And Water Notes Of Forward Area Appendix F		
Miscellaneous	Extracts From 20th Divnl. Orders. No. 495 Dated 14/12/16 Para 1	14/12/1916	14/12/1916
Diagram etc	Rough Sketch Plan Showing Traffic Routes		
Operation(al) Order(s)	Daily Orders No. 44 By Captain A.F. Girvan. R.A.M.C. (T.F.) Commanding 33rd Sanitary Section.	21/12/1916	21/12/1916
Miscellaneous	Sanitary Section Report For Fortnight Ending Appendix H	16/12/1916	16/12/1916
Miscellaneous	Weekly Report Appendix I	23/12/1916	23/12/1916
Miscellaneous	Appendix J		
Heading	War Diary Of Captain A.F. Girvan R.A.M.C (T.F.) Officer Commanding 33rd Sanitary Section 1st London (City Of London) Sanitary Company R.A.M.C. (T.F) Attached 20th (Light) Division B.E.F. France. January 1917 Volume 8		
War Diary	Corbie	01/01/1917	04/01/1917
War Diary	Minden Post F 18 C Albert Combined Sheet	05/01/1917	06/02/1917
War Diary	Minden Post	07/01/1917	28/01/1917
War Diary	Heilly G.I. Sheet (Amiens)	29/01/1917	30/01/1917
War Diary	Heilly	30/01/1917	31/01/1917
Miscellaneous	Daily Orders No. 49 By Captain A.F. Girvan R.A.M.C. (T.F) Commanding 33rd Sanitary Section	01/01/1917	01/01/1917
Miscellaneous	Disposition Of 33rd Sanitary Section And Attached /Work In Forward and Reserve Areas		
Miscellaneous	Daily Order No. 59 By Capt. A.F. Girvan, R.A.M.C. (T.F) Commanding 33rd Sanitary Section Tuesday 2nd Jan. 1917	02/01/1917	02/01/1917
Miscellaneous	Weekly Report Appendix 3	30/12/1916	30/12/1916

Miscellaneous	Sanitary And Water Report Appendix 4	06/01/1917	06/01/1917
Miscellaneous	Sanitary And Water Report Of 33rd. Sanitary Section Appendix 5	13/01/1917	13/01/1917
Miscellaneous	To. A.D.M.S. 20th. Division Appendix 6		
Miscellaneous	Sanitary And Water Report For Week Ending	20/01/1917	20/01/1917
Miscellaneous	Notes On Sanitation Water And Baths In Forward Area Appendix 8		
Miscellaneous	Water Supplies. Appendix A		
Diagram etc	Water Supply Of Combles Rough Sketch Plan Showing Wells		
Miscellaneous	Appendix B Combles.		
Miscellaneous	Daily Order No. 27 By Captain A.F. Girvan R.A.M.C. (T.F) Commanding 33rd Sanitary Section	25/01/1917	25/01/1917
Miscellaneous	Dispositions of Sanitary Section and attached Personnel in Reserve Area		
Miscellaneous	To. A.D.M.S. 20th. Division Appendix 10		
Miscellaneous	War Diary Of Captain A.F. Girvan R.A.M.C (T.F) Commanding 33rd Sanitary Section 1st London (City Of London) Sanitary Section R.A.M.C. (T.F) Attached 20th (Light) Division B.E.F. France. February 1917 Volume 1917 Vol 16		
War Diary	Heilly	01/02/1917	09/02/1917
War Diary	Carnoy A2d 97	10/02/1917	10/02/1917
War Diary	Carnoy A2d 97 Albert Combined Sheet	10/02/1917	13/02/1917
War Diary	Carnoy A2d 97	14/02/1917	19/02/1917
War Diary	Carnoy A2d 97 Albert Combined Sheet	20/02/1917	21/02/1917
War Diary	Carnoy A2d 97	22/02/1917	27/02/1917
War Diary	Carnoy A2d 97 (Albert Combined Sheet)	27/02/1917	28/02/1917
Miscellaneous	Sanitary And Water Report Appendix A	02/02/1917	02/02/1917
Miscellaneous	Daily Orders No 59 By A.F. Girvan RAMC (T.F) Appendix B Commanding 33rd Sanitary Section	05/02/1917	05/02/1917
Miscellaneous	Disposition List Of Sanitary Section		
Miscellaneous	Sanitary Section Report For Period Of Ten Days Ending	17/02/1917	17/02/1917
Miscellaneous	Report on Latrines "A"		
Miscellaneous	Report on Incinerators		
Miscellaneous	Work Required To Be Done		
Miscellaneous	War Diary Of Captain A.F. Girvan R.A.M.C (T.F.) Officer Commanding 33rd Sanitary Section 1st London (City Of London) Sanitary Company R.A.M.C. (T.F) Attached 20th (Light) Division B.E.F. France. March 1917		
War Diary	Carnoy	01/03/1917	08/03/1917
War Diary	Corbie	09/03/1917	11/03/1917
War Diary	Carnoy A2d 9.7.	12/03/1917	15/03/1917
War Diary	Carnoy Rear 11 days A2d97 Albert Combined Sheet	16/03/1917	23/03/1917
War Diary	Carnoy A2d 97 Albert Combined Sheet	24/03/1917	26/03/1917
War Diary	Briqeterie A.4d. 5.2	29/03/1917	31/03/1917
Miscellaneous	Sanitary Section Report For Period Of Fourteen Days Ending 3rd March 1917	03/03/1917	03/03/1917
Miscellaneous	3rd. Sanitary Section. S165/4/17	06/03/1917	06/03/1917
Miscellaneous	Div Hoare. G.G.		
Miscellaneous	To 33rd Sanitary Section		
Miscellaneous	Standing Orders For Corbie Laundry	16/03/1917	16/03/1917
Miscellaneous	Fire Drill Regulations For Corbie Laundry.	16/03/1917	16/03/1917
Miscellaneous	Laundry Corbie Regles En Cas De Feu	16/03/1917	16/03/1917

Miscellaneous	Report Of 33rd Sanitary Section For Fortnight Ending	17/03/1917	17/03/1917
Diagram etc	Sketch Plan Of Laundry At Corbie		
Diagram etc	Rough Diagram Of Wash House		
Diagram etc	Sketch Plan. Of Drying Room		
Miscellaneous	33rd. Sanitary Section No. S198/2/17	24/03/1917	24/03/1917

2/10/12

20TH DIVISION

33RD SANITARY SECTION
JLY 1915 — ~~DEC 1916~~
1917 MAR

TO 3 ARMY

San: Sect: 33
Vol I

121/7534

30th Burdwan

Summarised but not copied

From July 16 Nov. 15

S/

July 1905
Aug
Sept
Oct
Nov

CONFIDENTIAL.

WAR DIARY

OF

LIEUTENANT N. A. DORE, R.A.M.C.

OFFICER COMMANDING

SANITARY SECTION 33

1ST LONDON (CITY OF LONDON) SANITARY COMPANY,
R.A.M.C. (T.)

ATTACHED

XX TH (LIGHT) DIVISION,
B.E.F. FRANCE.

FROM 23RD JULY TO 30TH NOVEMBER 1915.

VOLUME I.

ORIGINAL

Army Form C. 2118.

WAR DIARY

~~INTELLIGENCE SUMMARY~~

(Erase heading not required.)

Place	Date	Hour	Summary of Events and Information	Remarks and references to Appendices
	1915			
ROLLESTONE CAMP, SALISBURY PLAIN.	23 July	A.M. 10.30	Leave SALISBURY PLAIN. Raining heavily. Marched five miles to AMESBURY.	
		P.M. 7.15	Entrain at AMESBURY for SOUTHAMPTON.	
		4.0	Embark on "AFRICAN PRINCE."	
		5.0	Boat sailed. Picked up escort at PORTSMOUTH. Sea extremely rough.	
HAVRE	24 July	A.M. 4.0	Reached HAVRE. Anchored outside harbour.	
		7.0	Entered harbour and disembarked. Entrainment Orders received from A.L.O. to entrain at 4.30 p.m. but these Orders subsequently cancelled.	
		P.M. 2.30	Marched out to Rest Camp No. 5. Movement Order received and Motor Lorry despatched in charge of One N.C.O and two drivers to LUMBRES, DEPARTMENT DU NORD, via CANCHY, HESDIN, FRUGES, FAQUEMBERGUES and CLÉTY.	LUMBRES. Reference HAZEBROUCK 5B No.48. Scale 1/250000
HAVRE	25 July	A.M. 7.30	Orders received to entrain at GARE DE MARCHANDISES. Marched out of Rest Camp.	Do. 4.C.
		8.30	Entrained. Journey all day. Passed ROUEN, ABBEVILLE, BOULOGNE, CALAIS and ST. OMER.	
WIZERNES	26 July		Detrained. Marched to LUMBRES. Very hot day. Billeted in a farmhouse.	
	27 July		Rendered Official Returns B.2013 (Field Return) B.2069 (Offence Report) and B.103 (Casualty Return) to Adjutant-General's Office. 3rd Echelon Base. Drew weekly hay from Field Cashier. Movement Orders received to march out next	

Army Form C. 2118.

Instructions regarding War Diaries and Intelligence
Summaries are contained in F.S. Regs., Part II.
and the Staff Manual respectively. Title pages
will be prepared in manuscript.

WAR DIARY
~~INTELLIGENCE~~ SUMMARY
(Erase heading not required.)

Place	Date	Hour	Summary of Events and Information	Remarks and references to Appendices
	1915			
LUMBRES	28 July	1 a.m.	Morning and afternoon Divisional Column in line of march. Paraded bearing marching order, marched out and passed Divisional Column at WIZERNES. Reached LYNDE at 2 p.m. and billeted at EBLINGHEM. Section March well.	
LYNDE	29 July	6.30 a.m.	Leave LYNDE and march to MERRIS. Distance 20 kilos. Arrive 11.15 a.m. Very hot. Billets in farm close to church.	
MERRIS	30 July		Water supply supervised. Ample supply available. Weather fine.	
	31 July		Men filter inspecting and testing shallow wells with Horrock's Case. Two wells in MERRIS give good returns when absence of Nitrates.	
	(Day)		Divide Sanitary Section into three squads, one to each Brigade. A fourth is to remain at Headquarters to cover Headquarters Troops. Head of Civilians in MERRIS above average owing to infantile mortality below.	
	3 Aug		Think it advisable to make several resting lines Entrals for inspecting work. Supervise rebuilding of incinerators. As plenty of pea gravel is available the ordinary 3'x1'x2' deep trench latrine is adopted.	

2353 Wt.W3544/1454 700,000 5/15 D.D.&L. A.D.S.S./Forms/C. 2118.

WAR DIARY
INTELLIGENCE SUMMARY.
(Erase heading not required.)

Place	Date	Hour	Summary of Events and Information	Remarks and references to Appendices
MERRIS (cont).	Aug 3rd	—	Problem of how to deal with the large numbers of flies is one which gives us food for thought. Crude paraffin is effective but quantities not available. An emulsion of Soft Soap, paraffin, Cresol & water appears to be effective. The spraying of all manure heaps adjacent billets seems the only really sound method of killing ova & larva in them all manure 90% of the flies breed in manure. Used squad to disinfect billets + clothing & men with Scabies.	
	4th		Am supplying with parties drawn from salvage Coy & Cyclists Bn to deal with accumulations of refuse in and around billets. Also hire Carts + horse from Civilian at 7 frs per day to collect same. Have pointed out that all water is chlorinated before many heavy wells contain "Coli" in dangerous proportion.	
	5th		Formaldehyde is very ineffective as a fly deterrent. Weather still very warm. The biscuit tin urinal fat seems to be the most efficient & is being used generally throughout the Division. Also portable Trench latrines made from biscuit boxes are also adopted.	
	6th		Divisional Area includes OUDERSTEEN, VIEUX BERQUIN and STRAZEELE. Visited several shallow wells in divisional area which have been sunk by 2nd FORTRESS Coy. Supposed to yield 1000 gls per day at a depth of 25 ft average. Probably the true yield is about 250 gls pr diem. Well heads have not been built. Consequently in several cases water had washed down from horse lines & had infected the water all through. Consequently wells contained bad water + Coli. Carried out verified the...	

Army Form C. 2118.

Army Form C. 2118.

WAR DIARY

INTELLIGENCE SUMMARY.

(Erase heading not required.)

Instructions regarding War Diaries and Intelligence Summaries are contained in F. S. Regs., Part II. and the Staff Manual respectively. Title pages will be prepared in manuscript.

Place	Date	Hour	Summary of Events and Information	Remarks and references to Appendices
Aug 7th — MERRIS (Cont.)			Experience great difficulty in covering Divisional Area on a horse. Obviously a motor bicycle would be more suitable. Apply for one with A.D.M.S. approval but 3rd Corps will not permit. Infantry here are pretty good onto whose but several of the Artillery Units are bad particularly the 91st R.F.A. Visit VIEUX BERQUIN and STRAZEELE.	
	8th	10 o'ck am	Go into BAILLEUL and return via METEREN. Visit Royal Shropshires + R.I.B.S. Not as good as they should be. — Tell M.O's about them under the latter.	
	9th —		Hear that 37th Division is not available to us in CAESTRE. Visit Vieux Camplain —	
SAILLY	10th —	11 o'ck	Go to SAILLY for three days for instruction in first line duties. Billet with O.C. S.& B. Sanitary Section 8th Division. Turbo my have been out longer than O.C. S.& B. 8th Division.	
		2 o'ck pm	Ride round part of area with the officer.	
ARMENTIERES	11th	10.30 am	Go over to ARMENTIERES with Cap. Price. Town very much knocked about — Sanitary methods in 8th Division very similar to 28th Division ideas. Monastery Institute in 8th Division very similar to 28th Division ideas.	
ESTAIRES	12th	9.45	Ride over to ESTAIRES. Remarkably dirty place & apparently no Sanitary arrangements at all exist. Indian Division in occupation, probably account for this.	
		3 o'ck	Return to MERRIS.	

Army Form C. 2118.

WAR DIARY
INTELLIGENCE SUMMARY.
(Erase heading not required.)

Instructions regarding War Diaries and Intelligence Summaries are contained in F.S. Regs., Part II. and the Staff Manual respectively. Title pages will be prepared in manuscript.

Place	Date	Hour	Summary of Events and Information	Remarks and references to Appendices
MERRIS	Aug 13th		Disinfection carried out at billet occupied by 2 men in 10th K.R.R. Also clothing. 15 to men with scabies. This diseases seem rather to increase. Probably the use of the latrine seat is apt to spread it. It is advisable that it should not be permitted.	
	14th		No remarks.	
	15th		Visit lines of Shropshire + R B's. The found requires is without all satisfactory with regard to sanitation.	
	16th		Water in XX th Div. Area on the whole good but this will be probably satisfactory later on.	
	17th		No remarks.	
	18th		The MERRIS water Cart which has been made out of a barrel Cart, makes its appearance with success. Visit Warren lines in the area. Begin to show improvement.	
	19th		No remarks.	
	20th		No remarks.	

Army Form C. 2118.

WAR DIARY

INTELLIGENCE SUMMARY.

(Erase heading not required.)

Instructions regarding War Diaries and Intelligence Summaries are contained in F. S. Regs., Part II. and the Staff Manual respectively. Title pages will be prepared in manuscript.

Place	Date	Hour	Summary of Events and Information	Remarks and references to Appendices
Hdqrs Fy MERRIS	Aug 21st		Disinfection carried out at STRAZEELE. Weather fine & warm. The problem of burying all trainees in hovelines is being very difficult, but nevertheless units are doing their pretty well.	
	22nd		Scabies seems still on the increase.	
	23rd		No remarks	
	24th		No remarks	
	25th	11 oclock	Order received to leave present billets in ESTAIRES.	
		5.30 pm	Moved out of MERRIS with F.A.W.U.	
		6.15 pm	Arrived at ESTAIRES & taken over billets at Starch factory which is to be used as Divisional baths.	
ESTAIRES	26th		Send squad to clean & disinfect Headqrs & Q Office at NOUVEAU MONDE. Am ordered to assist O.C. F.A.W.U. is generally supervising work of alterations in Starch factory for Div: baths. Have to attend a meeting at Mairie with A.A Q.M.G. to submit estimate re rent, cost of alterations etc.	

Army Form C. 2118.

WAR DIARY
INTELLIGENCE SUMMARY.
(Erase heading not required.)

Instructions regarding War Diaries and Intelligence Summaries are contained in F. S. Regs., Part II. and the Staff Manual respectively. Title pages will be prepared in manuscript.

Place	Date	Hour	Summary of Events and Information	Remarks and references to Appendices
ESTAIRES	Aug 27th		Any amount of work before Factory can be used as baths. Proprietor seems the extremely inadequate & seems to think we are firm. Unless his boilers up. Two pumps are all that are necessary for the supply of baths. Laundry itself will be worked by existing compound engine at a huge cost as this engine which is about 150 h.p. runs 3 shafts enormous pulleys. Motor to ARMENTIERES in afternoon to buy press, fixings etc. for boilers. Boilers are in very bad order & will require wholetaking up.	
	28th		Drainage & general Sanitary scheme in ESTAIRES as usual very primitive. Attend another meeting at Mairie. Proprietor of Starch factory seems very annoyed about military scheme to divert to Capville of the XX Division. Sent to man from Sanitary Section to live at NOUVEAU MONDE. The returned by 62nd Field Ambulance.	
	29th		Go over to MERVILLE in search of water cart- without success yet. Ride over to LAVENTIE in afternoon. Town very much knocked about. It is in a very dirty state. New division arr in area very large one & much work will have to be done to make it less insanitary.	
	30th		Water supply in ESTAIRES seems the fairly good. Three shafts wells are available. Works proceeding satisfactorily at Starch Factory.	

Army Form C. 2118.

Instructions regarding War Diaries and Intelligence
Summaries are contained in F.S. Regs., Part II.
and the Staff Manual respectively. Title pages
will be prepared in manuscript.

WAR DIARY

INTELLIGENCE SUMMARY.

(Erase heading not required.)

Place	Date	Hour	Summary of Events and Information	Remarks and references to Appendices
ESTAIRES	Aug 31st			
	Sept 1st		Baths increased at NOUVEAU MONDE, ESTAIRES and LAVENTIE. for use of troops billeted in neighbourhood. Badly used permanent fatigue party to assist in cleaning up. Arrange to pay up to 10/- per day for Civilian labour in ESTAIRES. All billets in ESTAIRES used by troops have to be supplied with latrine buckets. Civilian undertake the cleaning up of all refuse, the carting away of faeces etc. this day. Seems the endless amount of work at Starch factory. Go up to trenches in afternoon everything very quiet. new Trench latrines seem to be successful. Wet day. Used to have men to work at NOUVEAU MONDE & LAVENTIE. Am able to get fatigue parties whenever to clear up LAVENTIE.	
	2nd		Still very wet. No further remarks.	
	3rd	10am	Another meeting with Proprietor of Starch factory at Maine. Perused Balterau going the path to terminer. Probably two about it to morrow day.	
	4th		Still very wet. Ride over to ROUGE DE BOUT and LAVENTIE.	
	5th		Alteration at battershill progressing slowly. Sanitation in XX D division improving	

Army Form C. 2118.

WAR DIARY
INTELLIGENCE SUMMARY.
(Erase heading not required.)

Instructions regarding War Diaries and Intelligence Summaries are contained in F. S. Regs., Part II. and the Staff Manual respectively. Title pages will be prepared in manuscript.

Place	Date	Hour	Summary of Events and Information	Remarks and references to Appendices
ESTAIRES	Sept 6th		Very warm and fine. The lice question is beginning to make itself felt in trenches. Kerosene arrive soon. Baths working at last. R.E.'s have drainage partwork refinish & so soon. The cost of running them will be pretty high. Ride up to EPINETTE FARM in afternoon.	
	7th		No remarks.	
	8th		Fine day. Things still quiet on the frontline. Compound linquid cobalt for young troubles. Cadavers all wrong. Values want up are wig. Units in the Division are showing much improvement in sanitation.	
	9th		No remarks	
	10th		Lice are becoming prevalent now. Petrol rubbed on the skin is excellent. Fumes of Sulphur seems to be a good deterrent but not changes. Paraffin soaps is good only for officers or in cases of infected clothing. This suffocates the louse when he emerges from the egg. Sanitary Section at NOUVEAU MONDE are doing very good work.	

Army Form C. 2118.

Instructions regarding War Diaries and Intelligence
Summaries are contained in F. S. Regs., Part II.
and the Staff Manual respectively. Title pages
will be prepared in manuscript.

WAR DIARY

INTELLIGENCE SUMMARY.

(Erase heading not required.)

Place	Date	Hour	Summary of Events and Information	Remarks and references to Appendices
Staff ESTAIRES	Sept 14		Fine very windy – Sanitary Condition at LAVENTIE very bad. Water supply bad also –	
	Sept 14		Visit first WESTOUTRE which is just over Belgian Frontier. 28th Division in occupation.	
	Sept 15		No remarks.	
	Sept 16		Arrange to further inspect civilian trenches at LAVENTIE. Inspect various infantry lines & find drains inadequate.	
	Sept 15 –16		Visit aid posts in neighbourhood of Rue Boiselle and PETILLON.	
	17th		No remarks – This day. Several German Aeroplanes near LAVENTIE. Motor to BETHUNE in afternoon to buy spare parts for Surgeon and (orders at Inilka).	
	18th		Men working well inspecting billets. Sanitation generally in XX Division is unpromising.	
	19th		No remarks.	

#353 Wt. W544/7454 700,000 5/15   D. D. & L.   A.D.S.S./Forms/C. 2118.

Army Form C. 2118.

WAR DIARY
INTELLIGENCE SUMMARY.
(Erase heading not required.)

Instructions regarding War Diaries and Intelligence Summaries are contained in F. S. Regs., Part II. and the Staff Manual respectively. Title pages will be prepared in manuscript.

Place	Date	Hour	Summary of Events and Information	Remarks and references to Appendices
ESTAIRES	September		No remarks —	
	21st		Fine. Inspect Artillery lines. Notice gastroenteritis. Take over all supply of Disinfectants from A.S.C. so that Sanitary Section can redistribute to the troops.	
	22nd		Fine morning. Civilians in ESTAIRES clean out main drain which has choked. Reassembly trade drains are all laid with angles at different points.	
	23rd		Our artillery rather busy. Expect the long promised attack. Withdraw men from Sanitary work to assist at Field Ambulances if necessary.	
	24th		Artillery still more active. Send men from section to report to 61st & 62nd Field Ambulances.	
	25th		Attack made all along the line. Take my lorry up to LAFLINQUE. The 61st Advanced dressing Station collect wounded. Pick up nearly 140 wounded — Very wet day. Good men however there.	

#353 Wt. W2544/1454 700,000 5/15 D.D.&L. A.D.S.S./Forms/C. 2118.

Army Form C. 2118.

WAR DIARY
INTELLIGENCE SUMMARY.
(Erase heading not required.)

Instructions regarding War Diaries and Intelligence Summaries are contained in F. S. Regs., Part II. and the Staff Manual respectively. Title pages will be prepared in manuscript.

Place	Date	Hour	Summary of Events and Information	Remarks and references to Appendices
ESTAIRES	Sept 26th		Everything quiet again. Our Cavalry not heavy. Ride to Rouge de Bout in afternoon. Head Sanitary Section back to divisionary duty.	
	27th		No remarks	
	28th		French victory reported with 20,000 prisoners. Very wet day.	
	29th		Shall probably have to make arrangements for the disinfection of Division Hutments. This will mean 20,000 per month. Interesting.	
	30th		Inspect various lines which affect whole armies & Govt garden.	
Oct.	1st		No remarks	
	2nd		Our troops in all kinds from air very troublesome but not probably unhealthy. When possible however their abodes be cleared out. Lice seem to be on increase in the Division.	

Army Form C. 2118.

WAR DIARY

~~INTELLIGENCE~~ SUMMARY.

(Erase heading not required.)

Instructions regarding War Diaries and Intelligence Summaries are contained in F.S. Regs., Part II and the Staff Manual respectively. Title pages will be prepared in manuscript.

Place	Date	Hour	Summary of Events and Information	Remarks and references to Appendices
ESTAIRES	Oct 3rd		Have to arrange to dry up some filter disinfection Petrolmineral blankets. Fix me up at LAVENTIE to 6th Brigade.	
		4th	Arrange this morning for blankets at LAVENTIE to Ordnance Shed and ESTAIRE'S. Find that the most efficient way of dealing with vermin on blankets is to spray with 10% Formaldehyde between hay. Afterwards sprinkle with N.C.I. Powder. Naphthalene (96%). Iodoform (2%) Naphthalene (2%) This is easily the best Lice destroyer we can find. Practical demonstration proved it on 24 lice placed in contact with this were all dead in 6½ minutes.	
	5th		No remarks	
	6th		No remarks	
	7th		Inspect billets at PONT DE HEM on LA BASSEE Road which the Division has just taken over. Bill eta very troublesome.	

#353   Wt. W2544/1454   700,000   5/15   D. D. & L.   A.D.S.S./Forms/C. 2118.

WAR DIARY

INTELLIGENCE SUMMARY

Place	Date	Hour	Summary of Events and Information	Remarks and references to Appendices
ESTAIRES	Oct 9th		Artillery action by our & German batteries. Discovered a 2 gun Minen batt of opposite and tried by Armour made a very fine shoot, direct hits on the position. This morning is needed badly for discovering more positions. All trenches & billets for 3 minutes in Z.7. saturated Correct.	
	Oct 10th		Artillery doing precision destruction in all fixed wire billets. The only difficulty will be food. Industry small quantities will be needed daily. In the rear (Sup/Cemy Infantry) Ranjordo the question (hanny or extra is important.	
	10th		No remarks.	
	11th		Artillery action again. Inspect Pillets at PONT DE HEM. Showing some improvement.	
	12th		No remarks —	

Army Form C. 2118.

WAR DIARY
or
INTELLIGENCE SUMMARY.
(Erase heading not required.)

Instructions regarding War Diaries and Intelligence Summaries are contained in F. S. Regs., Part II. and the Staff Manual respectively. Title Pages will be prepared in manuscript.

Place	Date	Hour	Summary of Events and Information	Remarks and references to Appendices
ESTAIRES	Oct 13th			
	14th		Artillery active again. In advice small attack at 12 o'clock (midday). Two cases of Enteric (civilian) reported. Disinfection carried out & patients removed. Both taken to LABASSEE Road.	
	15th		Now disinfecting about 5000 blankets per week. Scabies & lice seem to be on the decrease again. Building the piece detention at R.E. billets. Striving no working pay satisfactorily. Inspected billets in ESTAIRES Latrine accommodation will have to be improved. No Cavalry.	
	16th		No Cavalry.	
	17th		Units practically all using the portable bucket box trench latrines. During winter months latrine buckets will have to be used in all fixed W.C.s.	
	18th		Weather much colder but dry. Inspection areas of entries refused in LAVENTIE. Disinfection carried out. (civilian)	

Army Form C. 2118.

WAR DIARY

INTELLIGENCE SUMMARY.

(Erase heading not required.)

Place	Date	Hour	Summary of Events and Information	Remarks and references to Appendices
ESTAIRES.	12/1/16		Inspect billets at LAVENTIE and aid posts	
	20th		Bring O.C. Dosages work while here inclusive – weather fine and fuel. Inspect billets at Rouge de Bout	
	21st		No Remarks	
	22nd		Civilian depend at LAVENTIE increased to 25. Ditch cleaning work proceeded with.	
	23rd		No remarks	
	24th		Inspect billets at LA FLINQUE. Weather cold & fine	
	25th		Ride to LAVENTIE. no particulars.	
	26th		Send samples of Pump water to be examined at Canadian Lab. MERVILLE. Inspect billets at ESTAIRES.	

Army Form C. 2118.

WAR DIARY

INTELLIGENCE SUMMARY.

(Erase heading not required.)

Instructions regarding War Diaries and Intelligence Summaries are contained in F.S. Regs., Part II. and the Staff Manual respectively. Title pages will be prepared in manuscript.

Place	Date	Hour	Summary of Events and Information	Remarks and references to Appendices
ESTAIRES	Oct 27th		Nouveau	
	28th		Wet day. Ditch cleaning finished at LAVENTIE Centaine at NOUVEAU MONDE. Inspect turn tulle etc on LABASSEE Road.	
	29th		On leave — Train leaves LA GORGUE 1.45 PM. Arrive Victoria (London 2.45 PM)	
Nov.	7th		Return Victoria 1.30 PM. Motor from BOULOGNE to ESTAIRES and arrive 2.30 PM.	
Nov	8th		Return to find work carried on satisfactorily during absence. Authorised to hire more civilian labour in ESTAIRES.	
	9th		LAVENTIE gets shelled during the morning — Inspect various civil shelters.	
	10th		Inspect Willette tram at EPINETTE. Several casualties this during morning. Motor to BETHUNE in afternoon with S.S.O to try various posts for supposed in fall.	

Army Form C. 2118.

WAR DIARY

INTELLIGENCE SUMMARY.

(Erase heading not required.)

Place	Date	Hour	Summary of Events and Information	Remarks and references to Appendices
ESTAIRES	Nov 11th		Meeting at Mairie ESTAIRES with A.A.Q.M.G. + others to arrange in cases of civilian labour in ESTAIRES to carry on Sanitation of the town in properties. GUARDS Division Cav. into LA GORGUE.	
	12th		Disinfecting room at LAVENTIE hit by a shell. No one hurt. Evacuate the position in consequence.	
	13th		Inspect lines at NOUVEAU MONDE	
	14th		Ride to LAVENTIE in morning. Carry on with disinfection of blankets at Railway Shed. Her numerous journey to SAILLY shortly this day.	
	15th		Ride over to SAILLY arrange to take over 8 mD Divisin Sanitary Section. (Write in to make the move — March to FLEURBAIX in afternoon.	

Army Form C. 2118.

WAR DIARY

INTELLIGENCE SUMMARY.
(Erase heading not required.)

Instructions regarding War Diaries and Intelligence Summaries are contained in F.S. Regs., Part II. and the Staff Manual respectively. Title pages will be prepared in manuscript.

Place	Date	Hour	Summary of Events and Information	Remarks and references to Appendices
ESTAIRES	Nov 16th		Motor to brd A.D.S. at Rouge de Bout. Made all arrangements there –.	
	17th		Motor to FLEURBAIX to fix up 61st A.D.S. Inter A.D.S.s.	
	18th		Inspected all A.D.S. at LAVENTIE. 1ui don. Guards Division here now taken over LaBASSEE Road –.	
	19th		Very cold. A.M. Prince of Wales visits Divisional (suttomil) ESTAIRES.	
	20th		No remarks –.	
	21st		Motor over to SAILLY & FLEURBAIX with A.D.M.S.	
	22nd		Probably move to SAILLY tomorrow. Pay off all civilian working in LAVENTIE. Shall continue with sanitation in ESTAIRES. Leaving N.C.O. + the two men to supervise.	

WAR DIARY

INTELLIGENCE SUMMARY

Place	Date	Hour	Summary of Events and Information	Remarks and references to Appendices
ESTAIRES	Nov 23rd		Sent to men totals me billets & must to Division to demand authority put into grease trouzy extent. Very few cases of true to trench feet - Still cold. Units that seem to extent.	
SALLY	Nov 24th	10 o'clock	Move to SALLY. Section all billeted together. 8th Division leave billets in very bad state. Many complaints made. Major disinfecting apparatus laundry SALLY bath. Apparently taken over by Div. bath orders running ESTAIRES as well.	
	25th		Plenty French the done in new area. Billets left in dirty condition in nearly every case. Tide we cu clean. Opened kitchen cents. from 6th Division. Weather very cold.	

Army Form C. 2118.

WAR DIARY

INTELLIGENCE SUMMARY.
(Erase heading not required.)

Instructions regarding War Diaries and Intelligence Summaries are contained in F.S. Regs., Part II. and the Staff Manual respectively. Title pages will be prepared in manuscript.

Place	Date	Hour	Summary of Events and Information	Remarks and references to Appendices
SAILLY	26 Nov		Inspected Billets at BAC ST MAUR and SAILLY. Snow on the ground during the morning.	
	27 Nov		Move to FLEURBAIX. Much work to be done. Carry out disinfection of several verminous billets. Weather very cold.	
	28 Nov		15th of frost during the night. Move to ESTAIRES to inspect billets there. Very large area to cover here. SAILLY seems to be cleaner than the usual French town.	
	29 Nov		Some more to FLEURBAIX to inspect Artillery + Infantry Billets and billets.	
	30 Nov		No remarks. Much warmer.	

McDole Lieut R.A.M.C.
O.C. SANITARY SECTION 33,
ATTACHED XXth (LIGHT) DIVISION.

San. Sect: 33
Vol: 2

121/7931

20th/5/15

33 SAN. SEC. E

Recommended but not acted

S
Dec 1915

CONFIDENTIAL.

WAR DIARY

OF

LIEUTENANT N. A. DORE. R.A.M.C.
OFFICER COMMANDING

SANITARY SECTION 33
(1ST LONDON [CITY OF LONDON] SANITARY COMPANY)
R.A.M.C. (T.F.)

ATTACHED

XXTH (LIGHT) DIVISION
B.E.F.
FRANCE.

FROM 1ST TO 31ST DECEMBER 1915.

VOLUME II.

ORIGINAL

Army Form C. 2118

WAR DIARY
or
INTELLIGENCE SUMMARY.
(Erase heading not required.)

Instructions regarding War Diaries and Intelligence Summaries are contained in F. S. Regs., Part II. and the Staff Manual respectively. Title pages will be prepared in manuscript.

Place	Date	Hour	Summary of Events and Information	Remarks and references to Appendices
SAILLY SUR LA LYS	1915 Dec 1st		Inspect lines at BAC ST MAUR. Beginning to shew signs of improvement. Wet day.	
	" 2nd		Have 25 civilians working in SAILLY with two refuse carts and one mud cart.	
	" 3rd		Inspect lines at FLEURBAIX and RUE BRUGES. New Vermin powder (Oxford Powder) sent out by A.S.C. No good at all. Have tried in Hospitals.	
	" 4th		Very wet. Sent sanitary Squad (3 men) to meet one 61st Fd Amb. A.D.O.S. Ambulance is to report from SAILLY to FLEURBAIX tomorrow. Inspect A.S.C. lines at ESTAIRES.	
	" 5th		Visit 191st Coy R.E. lines and make alterations re water supply here which is being obtained from an old ditch. Snow day.	
	" 6th		Inspect lines at BAC ST MAUR.	
	" 7th		Inspect lines at FLEURBAIX.	
	" 8th		Inspect lines at ROUGE DE BOUT and FLEURBAIX.	
	" 9th		Wet day. Alterations at Bac finished	

#353 Wt. W2544/1454 700,000 5/15 D. D. & L. A.D.S.S./Forms/C. 2118.

Army Form C. 2118

WAR DIARY
or
INTELLIGENCE SUMMARY.
(Erase heading not required.)

Instructions regarding War Diaries and Intelligence Summaries are contained in F.S. Regs., Part II and the Staff Manual respectively. Title pages will be prepared in manuscript.

Place	Date	Hour	Summary of Events and Information	Remarks and references to Appendices
SAILLY	Dec 10th		Wet day. Inspect lines at BAC ST MAUR. Floods	
	11th		Wet again. River LYS in. Disinfecting Shed. Manage to save a drowning horse.	
	12th		Fine day. Inspect lines at FLEURBAIX. + Signal Coy lines. Trace Typhoid Carriers at ROUGE DE BOUT	
	13th		Inspect 91st R.F.A. lines. Very good. Disinfect 800 blankets during the week. Fine day.	
	14th		Ride over to DOULIEU. Rather heavy bombardment in morning. Inspected smoke helmets. FLEURBAIX Shelled. Arrest a deserter from 12th R Bn in SAILLY. Fine day	
	15th		Fine. Go over to ESTAIRE'S in morning to supervise drainage scheme at both field Amb.	
	16th		Inspect lines in FLEURBAIX area. Fine day	

WAR DIARY
or
INTELLIGENCE SUMMARY.
(Erase heading not required.)

Army Form C. 2118

Place	Date	Hour	Summary of Events and Information	Remarks and references to Appendices
SAILLY	Dec 17th		Wet day. No remarks.	
	18th		Wet day.	
	19th		Billets all in very satisfactory condition. Disinfect 7000 blanks during week.	
	20th		Fine. Gehenny 30 cwt lorry badly ditched. Have to get Repair workshop from St OMER to get it out. Sixteen's removing.	
	21st		Wet day. 90 men to MERVILLE to Advanced Medical Base to stores.	
	22nd		Wet. River Lys fell tremendous water level. Curry out a system of testing all water certain division for free chlorine. Several units not chlorinating their water.	
	23rd		Fine day. Attend conference of men attached to 12th R.B's. Ride to ESTAIRES in afternoon.	

WAR DIARY
or
INTELLIGENCE SUMMARY.
(Erase heading not required.)

Army Form C. 2118

Place	Date	Hour	Summary of Events and Information	Remarks and references to Appendices
SAILLY	24th		Ride to FLEURBAIX, & inspect Cuis. Weather showery.	
	25th		Christmas day. Gave Sanitary Section a holiday. Weather fine. A fairly strong thunderstorm during the day.	
	26th		Showery day. Ride to ESTAIRES.	
	27th		Inspect Cuis. at FLEURBAIX. Wet day.	
	28th		Probably moving to new area very shortly. Go over to MORBECQUE near HAZEBROUCK to arrange to take over billets for 8 Divns on Sunday next. Fair to day.	
	29th		Ground area & inspect billets. Wet day.	
	30th		No remarks.	
	31st		Forder Lorry Thresh Disinfector has arrived about 600 Blankets in 6 hours. Disinfect 5600 Blankets thus. Go over again to MORBECQUE.	Capable of disinfecting

M.D. Orchard Reeve
O.C. SANITARY SECTION 33,
ATTACHED XXth (LIGHT) DIVISION.

26th Div

33rd Sam Sichor

Jan
Feb 1916
Mar

San: Sect. 33
Vol 3

CONFIDENTIAL

WAR DIARY

— OF —

CAPTAIN N. A. DORE, R.A.M.C. (T.F.)
OFFICER COMMANDING

SANITARY SECTION 33.
1ST LONDON (CITY OF LONDON) SANITARY COMPANY,
R.A.M.C. (T.F.)

ATTACHED

XXTH LIGHT DIVISION,
B. E. F.
FRANCE.

JANUARY 1916.

VOLUME III

ORIGINAL

WAR DIARY
or
INTELLIGENCE SUMMARY.
(Erase heading not required.)

Army Form C. 2118.

Place	Date	Hour	Summary of Events and Information	Remarks and references to Appendices
SAILLY	1916 Jan 1st		Inspect Billets at FLEURBAIX. Locate two Typhoid carriers this day.	
	2nd		Wet Day. Inspect Billets at BAC S' MAUR & ESTAIRES.	
	3rd		Fine. Test various water carts in the division.	
			All nineteen reacted with Chloride of Lime & fine for drinkable.	
	4th		Not examined –	
	5th		Probably warm interest shortly to MORBECQUE. Visit un[?]ed huts at BOISGRENIER.	
	6th		Motor to MORBECQUE tramway track over billets.	
			Parties 8th Division. Inspect Artillery lines & dug outs – Instruction	
	7th		this day. Write paper on "pediculi" to be given at the 3rd Corps Medical Society.	
	8th		Send advance party to MORBECQUE.	
	9th		Organising to clean clothe depot at MORBECQUE this day.	

Army Form C. 2118.

WAR DIARY
or
INTELLIGENCE SUMMARY.
(Erase heading not required.)

Instructions regarding War Diaries and Intelligence Summaries are contained in F. S. Regs., Part II. and the Staff Manual respectively. Title pages will be prepared in manuscript.

Place	Date	Hour	Summary of Events and Information	Remarks and references to Appendices
SAILLY	Jan 10th		Motor to MORBECQUE & take over billets from 8th Division. Sent Foden lorry Thresh Disinfector to MORBECQUE.	
	11th		No remarks.	
MORBECQUE	12th		Move to MORBECQUE. Fine day. Sent out section & Disinfector to BELLE "HOSTESSE"	
	13th		BLARINGHEM & STEENBECQUE. Inspect Divisional rest area which consists for the most part of camps. 8th Division left many dirty billets. Fix on site for Bath in disinfecting works.	
	14th		Clean cloth depot - now in working order. Fine. Ground frozen very hard - ditches full & muddy in cinematos. Water supply in this area very short.	
	15th		Necessary to have water from ditch by Repair Workshops to OMER. Arrange for horse cart to ular to work in town in divisional area or refuse removal.	

T2134. Wt. W708—776. 500000. 4/15. Sir J. C. & S.

Army Form C. 2118.

WAR DIARY
or
INTELLIGENCE SUMMARY.
(Erase heading not required.)

Instructions regarding War Diaries and Intelligence Summaries are contained in F.S. Regs., Part II. and the Staff Manual respectively. Title pages will be prepared in manuscript.

Place	Date	Hour	Summary of Events and Information	Remarks and references to Appendices
MORBECQUE	Jan 15 (cont)		Motn over to BAC St MAUR with ADMS & gave paper on "Pediculi" to Medical Society 3 interp.	
	16th		Fine. Visit STEENBECQUE + BLARINGHEM. Leave stopped officially	
	17th		Visit Camps in area. All in good order.	
	18th		Cinema. Intr men to being late into billets. Visit Steenbecque + Blaringhem. A good deal to work in regards to clean up these villages.	
			Men were moving in a day or two.	
	20th		Fine day. Official Wine that he were on 22nd. Ride near to STEENBECQUE	
	21st		Review orders to have Father lorry at MORBECQUE. Hand it over to 24th Division	
	22nd	10.15am	Were in car to 62nd Field Ambulance. Arrive OXLAERE at 1.40 P.M. Fine day	

Army Form C. 2118.

WAR DIARY
or
INTELLIGENCE SUMMARY.
(Erase heading not required.)

Place	Date	Hour	Summary of Events and Information	Remarks and references to Appendices
OXLAERE	Jan 23rd	2pm	Fine day. No news. Visit Review at St SYLVESTRE CAPPEL + ECKE and CAESEL in afternoon	
	25th		No news	
	26th		Not much news as we are apparently moving again in a few days.	
	27th		O.C leave to England	

Visit Capt Reeve

C. Dainty Lechin 33
O.C. Dainty Section 33

San: Sect: 33
Vol: 4

CONFIDENTIAL

WAR DIARY

OF

CAPTAIN N.A. DORE, R.A.M.C.(T.F.)
OFFICER COMMANDING

SANITARY SECTION 33,
1ST LONDON (CITY OF LONDON) SANITARY COMPANY,
R.A.M.C. (T.F.)

ATTACHED

XXTH LIGHT DIVISION,
B.E.F.
FRANCE.

FEBRUARY 1916.

VOLUME IV.

ORIGINAL

WAR DIARY
or
INTELLIGENCE SUMMARY.

Army Form C. 2118.

Place	Date	Hour	Summary of Events and Information	Remarks and references to Appendices
	February			
WORMHOULT	Feb 5th		During absence on leave Division moved to ESQUELBEC and WORMHOULT. Fine day.	
	6th		Visit ESQUELBEC in morning + WATOU in afternoon. Horses broken down at ABEELE. Wet.	
	7th		Inspect lines at WINNEZEELE.	
			Having to POPERINGHE in a day or two several cartloads of refuse removed during day + burned.	
	8th		Visit POPERINGHE in morning. 2/0 round area with OC 1st(?) Div Sanitary Section. Much work to be done, whereas were were moved to POPERINGHE + arrange for billets.	
	9th		Move. Norlemarch	
	10th		Moved to POPERINGHE, met OC Sanitary Section	
	11th		le Dunain. he and two in the No 14 th Café which served as guards Division in 6th Divn in + 20th Division.	
			About Advance Party to take over billets.	

WAR DIARY
or
INTELLIGENCE SUMMARY.
(Erase heading not required.)

Army Form C. 2118.

Place	Date	Hour	Summary of Events and Information	Remarks and references to Appendices
WERN HOULT POPERINGHE	Feb 13th		Fine. No news. Move to POPERINGHE	
	13th		Move to POPERINGHE to another part of the town as original billets were out of the Divisional Area.	
	14th		Fine. Moved on to WESTOUTRE to arrange washing & clothing for troops in three air raids during the night.	
	15th		Have have air raids during the day. Go over to ELVERDINGE & inspect bain day huts. Water supplies particularly seem bad.	
	16th		Go to ELVERDINGE again. The Sanitary conditions of POPERINGHE seem particularly bad. Arrange with town Sanitary office to organise a system of refuse & urinary carts. Two men detailed to CHATEAU Churove for duty at Corps headquarters. Two men sent to A. + B. Camps & 4 men to Camps 1.2.3 + 4 for permanent Orderly duties.	

Army Form C. 2118.

WAR DIARY
or
INTELLIGENCE SUMMARY.
(Erase heading not required.)

Instructions regarding War Diaries and Intelligence Summaries are contained in F.S. Regs., Part II. and the Staff Manual respectively. Title pages will be prepared in manuscript.

Place	Date	Hour	Summary of Events and Information	Remarks and references to Appendices
POPERINGHE	Feb 17th		Have to organise laundry train for division. Send men to head qrs for permanent duty there.	
	18th		Move bounds during the night to. Think interim taken up with laundry train. Weather getting colder.	
	19th		No remarks.	
	20th		Disinfection of clothes now organised & are doing about 1500 per day. Order today that disinfectors will be from [?] Division.	
	21st		Disinfection Hut at Camp Carried out. Troops seem to be very much infected with Pediculi probably owing to the fact that isolation huts or tents have been available while in the [?] move.	
	22nd		Laundry nearly completed. Other hut in the chinese late Ofoteur and to be installed in 2 camps this day.	

T2134. Wt. W708—776. 500000. 4/15. Sir J. C. & S.

WAR DIARY
or
INTELLIGENCE SUMMARY.

(Erase heading not required.)

Army Form C. 2118.

Place	Date	Hour	Summary of Events and Information	Remarks and references to Appendices
POPERINGHE	Feb 23rd		Fine & cold. No renewals.	
	24th		Showing laundry now printed except for materials coming from Dunkirk.	
	25th		Men baths during the day. Sanitation at various camps much improved.	
	26th		Fine. Go to ELVERDINGHE is running & arrange to fix up shower baths there. Rain later.	
	27th		Open laundry. Question of water supply being sufficient (due or to the available stream drying up in hay). Inspect lines at VLAMERTINGHE. Howfall destroyed the inlet scaries still show increase. Water supply at STEEN JS	
	28th		Mill report shows good results. Fine. Inspect camp at ELVERDINGHE. Water supply on canal bank very bad.	
	29th		Fair. Necessary to action steps taken in POPERINGHE to improve sanitary conditions.	W.D.N. Capt Rouse to Sanitary Sectn 33.

T2134. Wt. W708—776. 500000. 4/15. Sir J. C. & S.

33 San Sec
Vol 5

CONFIDENTIAL.

WAR DIARY

—— OF ——

CAPTAIN N.A. DORE. R.A.M.C. (T.F.)
OFFICER COMMANDING

SANITARY SECTION 33,
1st LONDON (CITY OF LONDON) SANITARY COMPANY,
R.A.M.C. (T.F.)

ATTACHED

20TH LIGHT DIVISION
B.E.F.
FRANCE.

MARCH 1916.

VOLUME V

WAR DIARY
or
INTELLIGENCE SUMMARY.
(Erase heading not required.)

Army Form C. 2118.

Place	Date	Hour	Summary of Events and Information	Remarks and references to Appendices
POPERINGHE	1st	Headqrs.	Continue work at Divisional Baths & Laundry. Put forward suggestions with regard to Baths at Headquarters A.23.6.	
	2nd		Sept 28. Commence work on water supply of various areas. Made arrangements to fix Keel patent Sherelette at EVERDINGE CHATEAU for use of Battalion in rest. Visit "J" Camp. Sanitary condition fairly good.	
	3rd		Visit EVERDINGE in morning. Bath finished during visit by Chateau & Shelled laundry. Visit "G" Camp.	
	4th		Enlargement of laundry noted. Work of Isolated men. POPERINGE shelled during the day. Canadian troops dispersed Headquarters. Snow during the day.	
	5th		Baths at POPERINGHE now heavily employed. Rode to WESTOUTRE in afternoon. Fine day.	
			Left for POPERINGE. Finished work line to front at EVERDINGE. Complete the building of the Pantech. At Headquarters Snow during the day.	

Army Form C. 2118.

WAR DIARY
or
INTELLIGENCE SUMMARY.
(Erase heading not required.)

Instructions regarding War Diaries and Intelligence Summaries are contained in F. S. Regs., Part II. and the Staff Manual respectively. Title pages will be prepared in manuscript.

Place	Date	Hour	Summary of Events and Information	Remarks and references to Appendices
	March			
POPERINGHE	7th	-	Heavy rain morning + afternoon. Decide on site for bath at Headquarters A.23. Building to be constructed where necessary to well the sand + water supply true. Send men up to Canal Bank to work under N.C.O.	
	8th		Much work to be done there. Also send squad up to ELVERDINGHE to disinfect clothes there. Labouring thus	
	9th		two days. Inspect Camps at VLAMENTINGHE. Return very tired by division.	
	10th		Work slow. G.O.C. inspects baths laundry at POPERINGHE & is satisfied with same. Report to field state of signal by lines. 6500 blankets disinfected during week.	
	11th		Inspect lines at ELVERDINGHE. Continue with survey of water supply. Work started on new bath at A.22 b.- bell also very drunk	

T2134. Wt. W708—776. 500000. 4/15. Sir J. C. & S.

Army Form C. 2118.

WAR DIARY
or
INTELLIGENCE SUMMARY.
(Erase heading not required.)

Instructions regarding War Diaries and Intelligence Summaries are contained in F. S. Regs., Part II. and the Staff Manual respectively. Title pages will be prepared in manuscript.

Place	Date	Hour	Summary of Events and Information	Remarks and references to Appendices
	March			
POPERINGHE	12th		Arrived & reported to town Sanitary Officer of POPERINGHE re: bad state of Wells & insanitary condition of town in general. Go over to New Camps we are taking over from 6th Division at A 30. Check 28 Infantry Wells in Poperinghe & find them in bad order.	
	13th		Continue with water survey work.	
	14th		Fine day. Go over to Camps at A 30 with 6th Division Sanitary Officer. New Latrines at Headquarters progressing slowly.	
	15th		Send N.C.O. + two men section to Camps at A 30. Take men latrines there. Find very bad water supply there.	
	16th		Headquarters all the morning with A.D.M.S. Inspect 9. Camp in afternoon. Find drainage work improving.	
	17th		Get motor pump to wash out laundry. This saves crowds at Labour & Ulean two hour for other duties. Infantry lines at ELVERDINGE	

WAR DIARY
or
INTELLIGENCE SUMMARY.
(Erase heading not required.)

Army Form C. 2118.

Place	Date	Hour	Summary of Events and Information	Remarks and references to Appendices
POPERINGHE	March 18th		This day - Take over A30 Camps officially. Put Sergt + 6 men in charge Matls. Camp Quartermasters appointed to be responsible for camps.	
	19th		This day - Inspect D.C.+ E. Camps in morning. Complete work of bringing ELVERDINGHE in afternoon. Laundry.	
	20th		This day - Inspection at Headquarters	
	21st		Inspect D.C+ E Camps + find them in good order. Baths working well. Continue with water survey work. 14" Culvs who cut subway well (Arkview) are now down 600 ft with out striking water.	
	22nd		Wet day - Inspect Camp at ELVERDINGE. Go up to Canal Bank in the evening sleep at 6.15" Field Amb. O.A.S.	
	23rd		Inspect dug outs + Sanitary conditions generally at Canal Bank	

WAR DIARY
or
INTELLIGENCE SUMMARY.
(Erase heading not required.)

Army Form C. 2118.

Place	Date	Hour	Summary of Events and Information	Remarks and references to Appendices
POPERINGHE	March 23rd inst.		Contact wire much improved. Water supply schedule improved. Leave in afternoon.	
	24		Take on Brig in Col. Ardl; workshop work for a week while O.C. is on leave. Worked JAN ST BIEZEN Ti morning. Own dump (to-day). Headquarters during the afternoon and also inspect C.R.E. camps.	
	25th		Headquarters talk was nearly finished. Leave is granted again. Erect destructs at new dates.	
	26"		Finding Med. meeting on water supply at Quad. Division Headquarters with A.A.Q.M.G.	
	27		Red. RELUEBINGE in afternoon & Survey ground to lay pipe & include to lead to use of units in the advanced area. Pipes also the laid from Dicke BUSCH lake to canal bank. Shewing large inspect Road at Hendyn return C.O. & Camps. Go to JAN ST BIEZEN in afternoon.	

Army Form C. 2118.

WAR DIARY
or
INTELLIGENCE SUMMARY.
(Erase heading not required.)

Instructions regarding War Diaries and Intelligence Summaries are contained in F. S. Regs., Part II. and the Staff Manual respectively. Title pages will be prepared in manuscript.

Place	Date	Hour	Summary of Events and Information	Remarks and references to Appendices
POPERINGHE	March 28/16		Inspect C.D. to Camps with D.D.M.S. Sketch line at BRIELEN in afternoon	
	29th		Commence work on water supply at EVERDINGHE. Battn. H⁴ Headquarters open. Well supply seen to be a good one.	
	30th		Continue work at EVERDINGHE.	
	31st		Two cases measles reported from Balloon Section G. Camp. Two days Inspect Camp "I" with A.D.M.S. and N.C.O.'s ready to t Camp which is occupied by Battalion. Go to EVERDINGE in afternoon.	

W D Bright
Capt
RAMC
O.C. SANITARY SECTION 33,
ATTACHED XXth (LIGHT) DIVISION.

No. 33 Sanitary Section

April 1916.

33 San. Sec.
Vol 6

CONFIDENTIAL

WAR DIARY
— OF —
CAPTAIN N.A. DORE. R.A.M.C.(T.F.)
OFFICER COMMANDING

SANITARY SECTION 33
1ST LONDON (CITY OF LONDON) SANITARY COMPANY
R.A.M.C.(T.F.)

ATTACHED

XXTH (LIGHT) DIVISION
B.E.F. FRANCE.

APRIL 1916.

VOLUME VI

ORIGINAL

Army Form C. 2118.

WAR DIARY
or
INTELLIGENCE SUMMARY.
(Erase heading not required.)

Instructions regarding War Diaries and Intelligence Summaries are contained in F.S. Regs., Part II. and the Staff Manual respectively. Title pages will be prepared in manuscript.

Place	Date	Hour	Summary of Events and Information	Remarks and references to Appendices
POPERINGHE	April 1st		Fine. Make arrangements for water supply from lake at ELVERDINGE CHATEAU. Inspect A + E Camps.	
	2nd		Fine. Inspect Transport lines + Carriers with supervision of work at ELVERDINGE. Go up to Canal Bank in evening.	
	3rd		Start laying pipe line from ELVERDINGE CHATEAU lake to road distance of 350 yards. Inspect Camps J + H. Fine day.	
	4th		Fine. Continue with work at ELVERDINGE.	
	5th		Inspect lines at BRIELEN. Work at ELVERDINGE continuing satisfactorily. Fit up two filter tanks covered for water cart tadraw from.	
	6th		Inspect Camps G.F.J. + H. Fit motor pump at ELVERDINGE in dugout to pump water through pipe line to road. Work nearly finished. Water supply up STEENJE MILL getting short. Inspect billets at POPERINGHE.	

Army Form C. 2118.

WAR DIARY
or
INTELLIGENCE SUMMARY.
(Erase heading not required.)

Instructions regarding War Diaries and Intelligence Summaries are contained in F. S. Regs., Part II. and the Staff Manual respectively. Title pages will be prepared in manuscript.

Place	Date	Hour	Summary of Events and Information	Remarks and references to Appendices
POPERINGHE	April 7th		Work at ELVERDINGE completed but water pump not strong enough to pump into tanks. Larger pump necessary. Inspect several Kampementerie with A.D.M.S. Fine day.	
	8th		Inspect Transport lines. Complete water survey map of divisional area.	
	9th		No remarks	
	10th		Inspect Camps C.D.E. Make arrangements to take over billet at WORMHOUT when division moves.	
	11th		Go over to WORMHOUT & ZEGGERS CAPPEL with O.C. Sanitary Section 6th Division.	
	12th		Very wet. Inspect camps J. H. G. F.	
	13th		Inspect lines at ELVERDINGE & VLAMERTINGE.	

Army Form C. 2118.

WAR DIARY
or
INTELLIGENCE SUMMARY.
(Erase heading not required.)

Instructions regarding War Diaries and Intelligence Summaries are contained in F. S. Regs., Part II. and the Staff Manual respectively. Title pages will be prepared in manuscript.

Place	Date	Hour	Summary of Events and Information	Remarks and references to Appendices
POPERINGHE	April 14th		Go round K.L.M.N. Camps with O.C. Sanitary Section. 6 Bns: Camps in good order but many improvements possible.	
	15th		Inspect K.L.M.N. Camps with A.A.Q.M.G.	
	16th		Inspect transport lines. Send advance party to WORMHOUT to take over billet.	
	17th		No remarks	
WORMHOUDT	18th	3.P.M.	Leave POPERINGHE & arrive WORMHOUDT about 4.30 P.M. Complete move from POPERINGHE. Inspect baths at WORMHOUDT	
	19th		ZEGGERS CAPPEL & suggest certain improvements to A.A.Q.M.G.	
			Make further arrangements with regard to improvements at baths at WORMHOUDT & bath & laundry at ZEGGERS CAPPEL	
	20th		Attend 14th Corps water meeting at POPERINGHE with A.A.Q.M.G. Several suggestions made with regard to increasing water supply in YPRES district.	
	21st			

T2134. Wt. W708—776. 500000. 4/15. Sir J. C. & S.

Army Form C. 2118.

WAR DIARY
or
INTELLIGENCE SUMMARY.
(Erase heading not required.)

Instructions regarding War Diaries and Intelligence Summaries are contained in F. S. Regs., Part II. and the Staff Manual respectively. Title pages will be prepared in manuscript.

Place	Date	Hour	Summary of Events and Information	Remarks and references to Appendices
WORMHOULT	April 22nd		Very wet. Complete work of improvements to laundry and baths ZEGGERS CAPPEL.	
	23rd		Inspect Camps R.L.M.N. made arrangements for the building of delousing huts, filter beds & the sanitary improvements.	
	24th		Inspect lines at OUDEZEELE & WINNIZEELE	
	25th		Inspect Camps R.L.M.N. work then continuing satisfactorily	
	26th		Give papers on Sanitation to the Pioneer battalion which recently joined the Division	
	27th		Inspect Artillery lines at ZEGGERS CAPPEL. Inspect Camps R.L.M.N. & find work progressing normally.	
	28th		Inspect Camps at WATOU & HERZEELE. also at ZEGGERS CAPPEL	
	29th 3.0ᵃ		Leave granted to England	

Will. D.T. Clayton Capt R.A.M.C.
O.C. SANITARY SECTION 33,
ATTACHED XXth (LIGHT) DIVISION.

T2134. Wt. W708—776. 500000. 4/15. Sir J. C. & S.

33 San Sec Vol 7

CONFIDENTIAL.

WAR DIARY

OF

CAPTAIN N.A. DORE. R.A.M.C.(T.F.)
OFFICER COMMANDING

SANITARY SECTION 33

1st LONDON (CITY OF LONDON) SANITARY COMPANY
R.A.M.C. (T.F.)

ATTACHED

XXTH (LIGHT) DIVISION
B.E.F.
FRANCE.

MAY 1916.

VOLUME VII.

ORIGINAL May 1916

COMMITTEE FOR THE
MEDICAL HISTORY OF THE WAR
Date 26 JUN. 1916

WAR DIARY
or
INTELLIGENCE SUMMARY.
(Erase heading not required.)

Army Form C. 2118.

Place	Date	Hour	Summary of Events and Information	Remarks and references to Appendices
WORMHOULT	May 1st-9th		On leave in England.	
	10th		Inspect Artillery lines at ZEGGERS CAPPEL.	
	11th		Inspect K.L.M.+N Camps at WATOU.	
	12th		Inspect-lines at WORMHOULT HERZEELE & ZEGGERS CAPPEL.	
	13th		Made suggestion with regard to alterations to Battery laundry at ZEGGERS CAPPEL. Divisional Horse show in afternoon. Rainy day.	
	14th		Met O.C. Sanitary Section Guards Division at POPERINGHE in morning & made arrangements with regard to taking over billets when Division were to Inspect Camps K + L in afternoon.	
	15th		Inspect various Head quarter billets at ESQUELBEC.	
	16th		Meet D.M.S. 2nd Army & go round Camps K.L.M.N. etc D.M.S. very satisfied with Sanitary Condition of Camps	

Army Form C. 2118.

WAR DIARY
or
INTELLIGENCE SUMMARY.
(Erase heading not required.)

Instructions regarding War Diaries and Intelligence Summaries are contained in F. S. Regs., Part II. and the Staff Manual respectively. Title pages will be prepared in manuscript.

Place	Date	Hour	Summary of Events and Information	Remarks and references to Appendices
WORMHOUDT	May 17th		Take O.C. Sanitary Section Guards Division round billets & camps in Wormhoudt.	
	May 18th		Inspect camps R.H.M.N. in morning. Work of building little field to addition huts now finished. Water turned back into ponds & is used over again.	
	May 19th		Inspection lines at ESQUELBEC, ZEGGERS CAPPEL & HERZEELE much improvement shown.	
	20th		Go to POPERINGHE	
POPERINGHE	21st	10:50am	Leave WORMHOUDT to POPERINGHE + arrive at 11:50 am	
	22nd		Send Sanitary Squads for Camps A. B + C + one man to YPRES + one to CANAL BANK. Inspect A. B + C Camps	
	23rd		Visit Camp A. with H.A.Q.M.G + decide to build swimming bath on site close to large pond + then with Sanitarian wrote and Sanitarian on Purita. Start work on alteration of Officers baths at POPERINGHE	

T2134. Wt. W708-776. 500000. 4/15. Sir J. C. & S.

WAR DIARY
or
INTELLIGENCE SUMMARY.
(Erase heading not required.)

Army Form C. 2118.

Place	Date	Hour	Summary of Events and Information	Remarks and references to Appendices
POPERINGHE	May 24th		Start work on Divisional baths at Camp A. Organize squads for the cleaning of latrines & refuse collection in POPERINGHE. 15 men daily for Battalion area supplies & street sweeping. Go to DUNKIRK to purchase engine parts for steam pump at Laundry.	
	25th		Visit "A" Camp in morning. Work at Divisional baths progressing well — This latter as being built between 2 fifth grounds. Visit Various water supplies in area & report thereon.	
	26th		Inspect billets in POPERINGHE. General Sanitation in town very bad indeed. Inspect A & B Camps in afternoon.	
	27th		Go to YPRES & report on water supply at swimming bath near MENIN GATE. Arrange Sanitary matters with Town Major.	

WAR DIARY or INTELLIGENCE SUMMARY

Army Form C. 2118.

Place	Date	Hour	Summary of Events and Information	Remarks and references to Appendices
POPERINGHE	May 28th		Work at Swimming baths preparing tank for trials. Fit water pump to filling the tanks. Inspect Brigade Laundry Lines.	
	May 29th		Alterations to officers baths completed. POPERINGHE. Shelled during afternoon. Fit water pump at Laundry. RUE de BOESCHEPE POPERINGHE	
	May 30th		Visit YPRES & 90 round ration convoy frozen water supplies with R.E. Officer. Inspect A. Camp in afternoon.	
	May 31st		Work at Swimming Baths. A. Camp nearly completed. Tarpaulin and latrine buckets baths & filled to depth of 4'.6". Inspect latrine in POPERINGHE. Improving them in POPERINGHE.	

Ludlow Capt.

O.C. SANITARY SECTION 33.
ATTACHED XXth (LIGHT) DIVISION

CONFIDENTIAL

WAR DIARY

-- of --

Lieut. A. F. GIRVAN, R.A.M.C.(T.F.).

Officer Commanding,

SANITARY SECTION 33,

1st. London (City of London) Sanitary Company,

R.A.M.C. (T.F.).

attached

20th. (LIGHT) DIVISION.

B.E.F. FRANCE.

19th. June, 1916 -to- 30th. June, 1916.

VOLUME 1.

Army Form C. 2118.

WAR DIARY
or
INTELLIGENCE SUMMARY.
(Erase heading not required.)

Instructions regarding War Diaries and Intelligence Summaries are contained in F. S. Regs., Part II. and the Staff Manual respectively. Title pages will be prepared in manuscript.

Place	Date	Hour	Summary of Events and Information	Remarks and references to Appendices
POPERINGE	19/6	Noon	Arrived from England to replace Capt DORE. R.A.M.C.T. Visited with him various staff officers and camps. A.t.y.	
"	20/6		Visited YPRES and various camps w CAPT. DORE. A.t.y.	
"	21/6		Various visits in district. A.t.y.	
"	22/6		" " " " A.t.y.	
"	23/6		" " " " Formally took over from CAPT DORE. Billet inspections A.t.y	
"	24/6		Visited YPRES. Inspected various states of LAITERE. Inspected Div. Baths w CAPT. COWE who's duties I am taking over from tomorrow while he goes on leave to SCOTLAND. A.t.y.	
"	25/6		FORD Ambulance being cleaned + overhauled. office work. Baths. Arrangements for repair of boiler. A.t.y.	
"	26/6		Visited A camp to see to erection of alteration shed. Visited School of Instruction RUE DE BOESCHEPE to advise as to sterilization of water supply. Examined set of sterilizers to be sent to front lines. A.t.y.	
"	27/6		Inspected A camps, Swimming Bath there, and ablution shed under construction. Inspected Divisional Baths. POPERINGE with a view to locating source of re-infection of the men and clothes supposed to be vermin free. At the Divisional Baths LAUNDRY POPERINGE as probably at all others, the problem of the purification of the soapy water is difficult. an attempt has been made to deal with the matter by the construction of a simple plant.	

Army Form C. 2118.

WAR DIARY
or
INTELLIGENCE SUMMARY.
(Erase heading not required.)

Instructions regarding War Diaries and Intelligence Summaries are contained in F. S. Regs., Part II. and the Staff Manual respectively. Title pages will be prepared in manuscript.

Place	Date	Hour	Summary of Events and Information	Remarks and references to Appendices
POPERINGE	June 27		This consists of (a) a settling tank, (b) gauze strainers, (c) a percolation filter with cinders as the filtering material. An attempt is being made to precipitate most of the soap and filth by lime added (in powder) to the soapy water as it leaves the laundry. The plant has only been working a few days but is giving promising results. The obvious defect is the smallness of the settling tank, which ought to be of a capacity equal to 12 hours flow of laundry waste. Space renders this difficult of accomplishment. A.T.G.	see offset 1
"	28		Visited baths & inspected the ironed khaki to see if the destruction of lice was being well carried out. The time allowed (owing to shortage of labour) of about 1 minute per garment permits of hasty treatment only. Started fixing up sterilyzation plant at School of Instruction (for drinking water) A.Y.	
"	29		Visited A camp Irrigated cesspits of "Thresh" disinfector, khaki at baths & found impracticable without greatly reducing no. of baths. Started cinders & Officers Latrines No 1 Mess. Cleansing & rearranging soapy water filter at No 2 Laundry, which was made on a large principle — filtration followed by settlement. Am renewing this procedure. A.T.G.	

T.2134. Wt. W708-776. 500000. 4/15. Sir J. C. & S.

Army Form C. 2118.

WAR DIARY
or
INTELLIGENCE SUMMARY.
(Erase heading not required.)

Instructions regarding War Diaries and Intelligence Summaries are contained in F. S. Regs., Part II. and the Staff Manual respectively. Title pages will be prepared in manuscript.

Place	Date	Hour	Summary of Events and Information	Remarks and references to Appendices
POPERINGE	June 30.		New Filter at Div Baths completed. Great trouble to get clinker or ashes for was filters for Div Laundry, finally got promise of some from railway. Visited Ypres, much inspection work re office work ADF.	

A.F. Gowan
Lieut R.A.M.C.(J.)
O.C. SANITARY SECTION 33,
ATTACHED XXth (LIGHT) DIVISION.

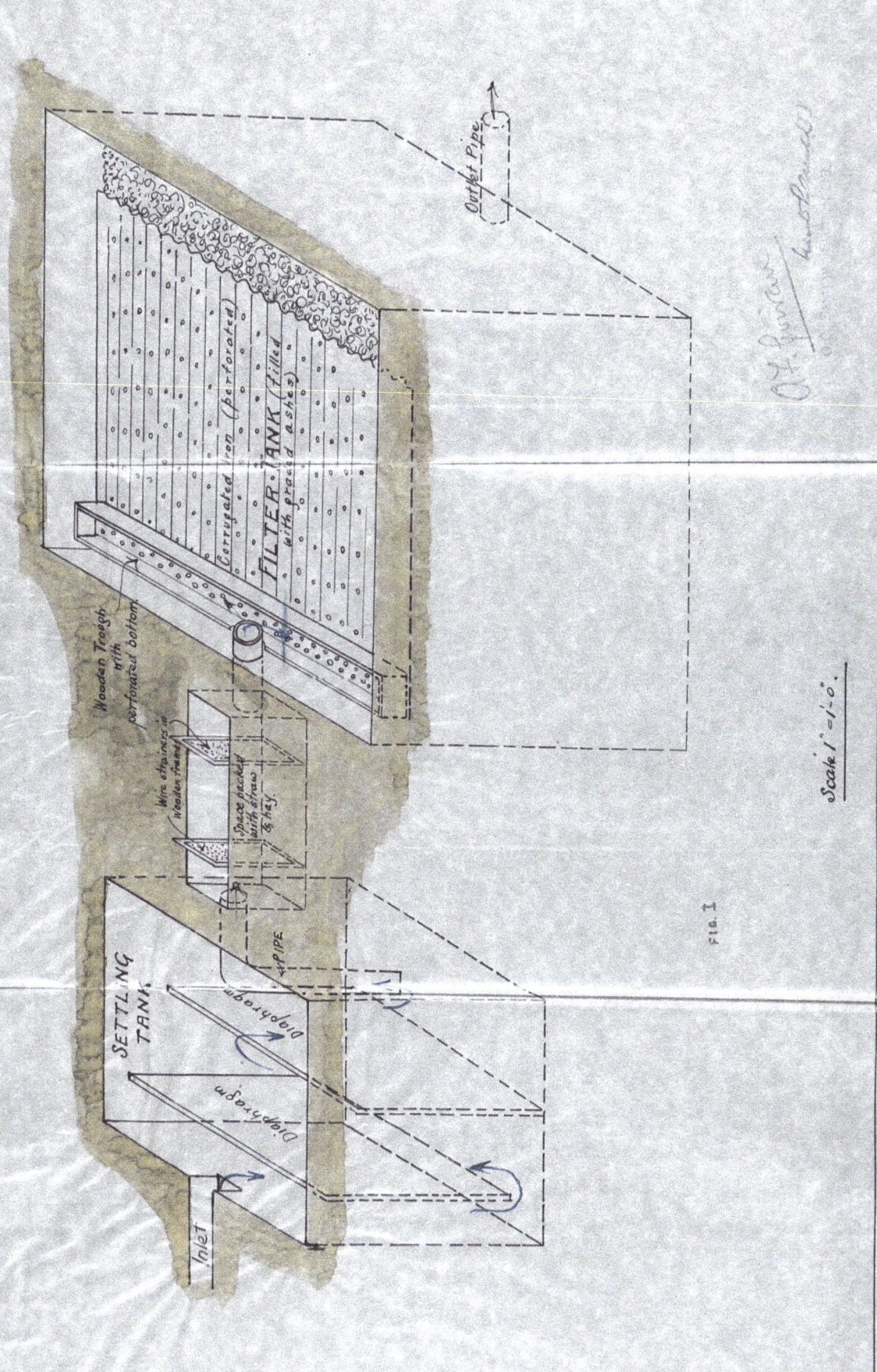

CONFIDENTIAL.

WAR DIARY

---of---

Captain   N.A. DORE,   R.A.M.C. (T.F.).

Officer Commanding;

SANITARY SECTION   33,

1st. London (City of London) Sanitary Coy

R.A.M.C. (T.F.).

attached

20th. (LIGHT) D I V I S I O N.

B. E. F.

FRANCE.

1st. June to 23rd. June 1916.

Volume 8.

WAR DIARY
or
INTELLIGENCE SUMMARY.
(Erase heading not required.)

Army Form C. 2118.

Place	Date	Hour	Summary of Events and Information	Remarks and references to Appendices
POPERINGHE	June 1st		H/c JAMES & Sanitary Section killed by bomb in POPERINGHE. Work continued at swimming baths. "A" Camp.	
	2nd		Go to ELVERDINGE with adjutant. R.E. to inspect new pipeline from the lake to C Camp (A 30). Inspect Arty. Camps & horse picket lines.	
	3rd		Inspect D.A.C. lines & various Vehicles in POPERINGHE	
	4th		Inspect Pioneer Battalion lines at BRANDHOEK Swimming baths at "A" Camp functional with alterations in divisional baths.	
	5th		Commence laundry. POPERINGHE. Swimming baths at "A" Camp open. Report on various water supplies in area.	
	6th		Wet day - Inspect L defences near YPRES. Inspect "C" Camp -	
	7th		Go to YPRES to arrange & arrange for latrine trenches to be erected at the Ramparts	

WAR DIARY
or
INTELLIGENCE SUMMARY.
(Erase heading not required.)

Army Form C. 2118.

Place	Date	Hour	Summary of Events and Information	Remarks and references to Appendices
POPERINGHE	June 7th (Cont)		Support in Prison. Men B had Kitchen duties. Inspected billets in POPERINGHE in afternoon.	
	8th		Inspected AMTB & C Coys in morning. Alterations at Prison finished.	
		9ᵃ	Inspected lines at BRAN D HOEK.	
		10ᵃ	Arrange to construct filled beds in various Camps & here.	
		7ᵃ	Sick return. Hun D.u was loaned to 2nd Army.	
		11ᵃ	Units disposing of manure by burning. Covering with earth. R.F.A. parties already taking on interest in this work. Made alterations at incinerator behind A Camp. Inspected D.A.C. lines & reports on water supplies.	
	12ᵗʰ		hun—	
	13ᵗʰ		Sanitation in POPERINGHE improving. Go up to Canal bank. Find sanitation fairly good—	

Army Form C. 2118.

WAR DIARY
or
INTELLIGENCE SUMMARY.
(Erase heading not required.)

Instructions regarding War Diaries and Intelligence Summaries are contained in F. S. Regs., Part II. and the Staff Manual respectively. Title pages will be prepared in manuscript.

Place	Date	Hour	Summary of Events and Information	Remarks and references to Appendices
POPERINGHE	June 15th		Go to YPRES in morning, inspect artillery line. Afterwards improvements to Town half. Inspect "A" Camp & Transport lines, also O. + C. Camps.	
	16th		Inspect huts in POPERINGHE. Transport lines in bad condition owing to heavy rains. Inspect B.T.C Camp — also Pension Australia. Am also at BRANDHOEK. Am unwell and in Dr Patton's hands.	
	17th		Start work on new filter beds at huts.	
	18th		Inspect huts in POPERINGHE. With attention to battns "A" Camp.	
	19th		Inspect "A" Camp is [unclear]. Lieut GIRVAN arrives to relieve us.	
	20th		Go to YPRES with Lieut GIRVAN. Inspect various Camps in area — also hutto in POPERINGHE.	

Army Form C. 2118.

WAR DIARY
or
INTELLIGENCE SUMMARY.
(Erase heading not required.)

Instructions regarding War Diaries and Intelligence Summaries are contained in F. S. Regs., Part II. and the Staff Manual respectively. Title pages will be prepared in manuscript.

Place	Date	Hour	Summary of Events and Information	Remarks and references to Appendices
POPERINGHE	June 21st		Inspect A.B & C Coups and also Person Battalion Camps. Men to leave for ENGLAND on 23rd inst.	
	22nd		Inspect new filter bed at Iette A. Camp.	
	23rd		Complete arrangements for handing over to Lieut GIRVAN. Leave POPERINGHE Station at 3. P.M. Lieut GIRVAN Continues War Diary.	

Watson Capt RAMC(T)
O.C. SANITARY SECTION 33,
ATTACHED XXth (LIGHT) DIVISION.

CONFIDENTIAL.

WAR DIARY

- of -

Lieut. A. F. GIRVAN. R.A.M.C. (T).
Officer Commanding,

SANITARY SECTION 33,
1st. London (City of London) Sanitary Company,
R.A.M.C. (T.F.)

attached

20th. (Light) D I V I S I O N.
B. E. F.
FRANCE.

JULY 1916.

VOLUME 2.

Army Form C. 2118.

WAR DIARY
or
INTELLIGENCE SUMMARY.
(Erase heading not required.)

Instructions regarding War Diaries and Intelligence Summaries are contained in F. S. Regs., Part II. and the Staff Manual respectively. Title pages will be prepared in manuscript.

Place	Date	Hour	Summary of Events and Information	Remarks and references to Appendices
POPERINGE.	July 1		5000 Blanket hole disinfected in five days. Constructed latrine for Mess for officers.	
"	2		Visited E. camp to arrange for new latrine canvas. Well Road boden, arranged for repairs. Visited A. camp & arranged for extension of existing ablution hut. Various inspections. A.T.F.	
"	3		Searching for barrels for sterile water. Bought 5 dig. wood tops for same. A.T.F.	
"	4		Parade of Bath Laundry staff w Col Dundas to investigate some complaints & identify culprit. A.T.F. Collected 45 Barrels, capacity about 2500 gallons, cleaned & arranged for collection of unit requirements. Visited A camp in connection to talks there etc also camps B & C. with reference to new complaints reported by N.C.O. in charge San. Squads. Also 61st Machine gun Transport. A.T.F.	
"	5		Visited Waganskin Bgd. re complaints of insanitary hut. Visited T.O. 61st Machine gun Transport to persuade to remove manure, friar to reporting ADMS if not speedily done. A.T.F.	
"	6		Visited 59th Bgd. H.Q. Transport much manure & no sanitary devices. Lacked labour in this small camp. Interview with Lut DADMS refresher. Arranged for purchase at a barrel stove for purchase of salad oil barrels house (after steaming) for sterile water. Method of steaming :— A.T.F.	

Army Form C. 2118.

WAR DIARY
or
INTELLIGENCE SUMMARY.
(Erase heading not required.)

Instructions regarding War Diaries and Intelligence Summaries are contained in F. S. Regs., Part II. and the Staff Manual respectively. Title pages will be prepared in manuscript.

Place	Date	Hour	Summary of Events and Information	Remarks and references to Appendices
	July			
POPERINGHE	7		Visitors various Camps & all construction work in hand. Purchased 18. 50 gallon barrels at 10/- each. Discussed use of arsenic in urine pails & ADMS & DADMS. Crude paraffin is preferred Cylla as keeping away flies much better though it has no staying power. aty.	
"	8		Visited Town Major YPRES who has no reported everything as requiring attention. Am changing the H/c on Canal Bank. The present one having had his share in a dangerous neighbourhood. Collected a load of cinders from railway for No2 Laundry filter. aty.	x
"	9		Ablution Shed at A camp now quite finished, except filling of filter w coke. Fatigue of 50 men filling a filter pond at No2 Laundry with lins + earth. 2 G.S. Wagons returned cart in use. 30 men tester. Passed the Section. Collected corrugated iron for filters No2 Laundry. Progress changing position of pumps at baths at A camp. Inspected gas Recruits	aty. aty.
"	10		Drew + delivered various supplies for improvements at camp. Finished job at No2 Laundry, made & planted flower-bed on the site of the previous filthy pond. Fetched lime from Bergues.	aty.
"	11		Inspected & fixing fillets etc at Wormhoult.	aty.
"	12		Met and discussed taking over of rest area with O.C San Sec 6th Div. Inspected ans.	

Army Form C. 2118.

WAR DIARY
or
INTELLIGENCE SUMMARY.
(Erase heading not required.)

Instructions regarding War Diaries and Intelligence Summaries are contained in F. S. Regs., Part II. and the Staff Manual respectively. Title pages will be prepared in manuscript.

Place	Date	Hour	Summary of Events and Information	Remarks and references to Appendices
POPERINGE	July 13		Arrangements for men to rest area. Visits to A camp, inspecting washing trails & latrines	App
"	14		A camp water pumping arrangement proceeding satisfactorily. Vigorous shelling of the town from 10am to about 1pm. 1.30 pm orders received to move all men billeted in town to some place outside at once. Complied by about 4 pm, including officers and about 44	
"	15		Various work connected with moving.	Off
"	16		Moved San Section and attached men to WORMHOUDT with exception of those detailed for KLM & N camps + for inspecting camps B & C after vacation by troops of 20" Div. An original arrangement has been devised & tried out A camp for drawing water from a pond for ablution purposes. In most cases an expensive heavy pump has to be securely fixed with hose etc. or the men dip muddy water from the edge of the pond	

[Sketch showing: WOOD BOX, WOOD CHANNEL 10' to 20' as convenient, 6", Pivot, Water Level]

On tilting the contrivance a supply of water is delivered along the channel to the operator on the bank. | Off |

Army Form C. 2118.

WAR DIARY
or
INTELLIGENCE SUMMARY.
(Erase heading not required.)

Instructions regarding War Diaries and Intelligence Summaries are contained in F. S. Regs., Part II. and the Staff Manual respectively. Title pages will be prepared in manuscript.

Place	Date	Hour	Summary of Events and Information	Remarks and references to Appendices
WORMHOUDT	July 17		Generally inspected area.	Off.
"	18		Inspected KEMM camps & arranged for residence casualties work.	Off.
		midnight	R.d. order to stand by to move an 19". At dawn collected men from	Off.
"	19		BOLEZEELE & KEMM camps. Took surplus stores etc to store in WORMHOUDT at 61st F.Amb. Paid billets etc.	Off.
"	20		Moved to BAILLEUL. Officers, stores & self by Ford Ambulance, 47 men in 2 motor busses, Foden & Truck by road, horse by road. Took over camp from Capt Carruthers + billeted men who cared not to accomodated in tents.	Off.
BAILLEUL	21		Arranged for dispersal of Section at Dranoutre, Neuve Eglise and BAILLEUL. Sent Cpl. & attached men from 59" & 61" Brigades. Also driver of Ford car. The car was taken away to shops as it was in such bad condition.	Off.
"	22		Investigated filters for Goffs & Laundry at DRANOUTRE. Exchanged 1 billrict for men & 1 P.H. button for P.H. Pattern.	Off.
"	23		Sent Cpl. & all remaining attached men, bringing section to mobilization number and equipment. Marched to ST. SYLVESTRE-CAPEL, after being relieved by O.C. San.Sec. 36 Div.	Off.
ST.SYLVESTRE CAPEL			Sent Foden lorry Disinfector by order DMS 2nd Army to CHATEAU COUTHOUVE PROVEN.	Off.

Army Form C. 2118.

WAR DIARY
or
INTELLIGENCE SUMMARY.
(Erase heading not required.)

Instructions regarding War Diaries and Intelligence Summaries are contained in F. S. Regs., Part II. and the Staff Manual respectively. Title pages will be prepared in manuscript.

Place	Date	Hour	Summary of Events and Information	Remarks and references to Appendices
	July			
ST.SYLVESTRE- CAPEL	24		Section resting preparatory to move tomorrow.	Off.
"	25		Marched w section to BAVINCHOVE. arrived about 14.30. Train departed 18.51. Arrived DOULLENS midnight 25-26. Lorry had been despatched by road 9am	Off.
DOULLENS	26	1	Billeted.	AM.
		11	Received orders to assemble at 9.15 o'clock outside town to march to COUIN.	
		1515	Started march to COUIN. Lorry despatched 1345 arr. COUIN. 17 o'clock. Section arrived COUIN about 16 o'clock. Made provision being too filthy to inhabit encamped at about 21-22 o'clock.	Off.
COUIN	27.		Gas Investigated area & discussed taking over from O.C. San Sec 38" (Welsh) Div.	Off.
"	28		" " " " took over from " " "	Off.
	29		The whole area is in a disgustingly dirty state, all ablets full of rubbish, much manure about & the roads at least one inch deep with dust and horse droppings. With difficulty got a fatigue party of 24 men & set sweeping tidying up. Walked to Souly D&LL investigated water supply & condition generally & sent a detachment of six men to erect there — tent —	

Army Form C. 2118.

WAR DIARY
or
INTELLIGENCE SUMMARY.
(Erase heading not required.)

Place	Date	Hour	Summary of Events and Information	Remarks and references to Appendices
	July			
COUIN	30		Road work continued & general cleaning up. Walked to SAILLY DELL, inspected camp & D.H.Hrs. Off.	
"	31		Walked COURCELLES, COUIN CAMP, LA SIGNY FARM. The water here is not chlorinated, nor has been in the past as far as I can discover. There has been a very great demand for disinfectants to-day, as was to be expected. This has clearly revealed the unsatisfactory method which has become the custom in this division namely that the Sanitary Section has become a kind of A.S.C. for many materials such as chloride of lime, cresol, cresol, lime and methylated spirit. At a time of frequent moves, the stores which have to be accumulated to meet the demands have to be left behind or run down to nil (if possible in time) as the transport of the Section is only sufficient to carry it's own antiseptic stores. On reaching a new area, totally foreign refuse disinfectants are urgently needed; valuable time & energy is lost in indentins for new supplies, fetching them (frequently) & redistributing them. It would appear much more sensible for units to indent for themselves direct to the Supply officer. A.F.G.	

A.F.Gorman Lieut Laurence (I)
O.C. SANITARY SECTION 33.
ATTACHED XXth (LIGHT) DIVISION.

CONFIDENTIAL.

W A R D I A R Y

-----of-----

Captain A. F. G I R V A N, R.A.M.C. (T.F.).
Officer Commanding,

SANITARY SECTION 33,
1st. London (City of London) Sanitary Company,
R.A.M.C. (T.F.)

attached
20th. (Light) D I V I S I O N.
B. E. F.
F R A N C E.

A U G U S T   1 9 1 6.

VOLUME----------- 3.

Army Form C. 2118.

WAR DIARY
or
INTELLIGENCE SUMMARY.
(Erase heading not required.)

Instructions regarding War Diaries and Intelligence Summaries are contained in F. S. Regs., Part II. and the Staff Manual respectively. Title pages will be prepared in manuscript.

Place	Date	Hour	Summary of Events and Information	Remarks and references to Appendices
	August			
COUIN	1		Various visits (on foot & bicycle) investigating area. Visited water tanks & dumps HEBUTERNE.	A.Hq.
"	2		Placed Sgnts of men as follows. 5 & 3 at SAILLY – THE DELL – 2 to report to Town Major SAILLY-au-BOIS each morning. & 2 to report to Town Major COURCELLES each morning. 1 at COULINCAMPS. Arranged for road sweeping of COUIN and for dumps for the sweepings. Motored w/ D.A.D.M.S. in morning to SAILLY.	
"	3		Visited 61 F.A. Transport Lines (BOIS DE WARNIMONT) also D.H.Q at SAILLY.	R.T.O. A.Hq.
"	4		Cycled EUSTON, Hence visited various tanks in trenches, OBSERVATION WOOD, LECATEAU.	Lt SIGNY Town Major A.Hq.
"	5		" " " front line trenches of R.S.H.I. on account of large elements for disinfectants. Smell from dead decidedly bad in places. Second line communication trenches very clean. Cycled ST LEGER to arrange for stenting of crater of M Ver Far — a small section without water cent.	
"	6		Ford Ambulance returned, and Rénault car sent to Base from BAILLEUL. The end of this during the last fortnight has been a considerable hindrance.	A.Hq.
"	7		Inspected work of spread at SAILLY-au-BOIS. Endeavored to obtain Morfass districts from R.E. have in stock so construction (some modified ones. Went to Wounhardt to ascertain where certain stores were & in whose possession.	

Army Form C. 2118.

WAR DIARY
or
INTELLIGENCE SUMMARY.
(Erase heading not required.)

Instructions regarding War Diaries and Intelligence Summaries are contained in F. S. Regs., Part II. and the Staff Manual respectively. Title pages will be prepared in manuscript.

Place	Date	Hour	Summary of Events and Information	Remarks and references to Appendices
	Aug			
COUIN	8		Various arrangements made in COUIN in connection with watertrails and water trays.	A.T.G.
"	9		Visited Townshipon SALLY-AU-BOIS and drew up a scheme for him for sanitary arrangement at ". Fixed fences for putting drinking water troughs at SALLY DELL, COURCELLES & COIGNEUX.	A.T.G.
"	10		Visited 12 R.B's in trenches re R.J. demand for disinfectants. Cleaning horse troughs	A.T.G.
"	11		COUIN. Erecting incinerators at various camps. Visited SARTON for cush. St Leger Townmajor. Horse troughs coun. Drawing up plan for refused baths at COUIN-ST LEGER. Visited SALLY DELL re arrange for construction of falling forward water from baths	A.T.G.
"	12		Inspected RSC, DAC, RE etc billets with regard to manure burning	A.T.G.
"	13		Various billet & inspections. Also ASC manure burning	A.T.G.
"	14		Inspected Somerset, DCLI, 12th Kings, 7th KOYLI, all transport lines. All satisfactory in most respects except rather slow burning of manure. Too many flies about	A.T.G.
"	15		Visited SALLY, COURCELLES, PAS etc	A.T.G.
"	16		Got in men from COLINCAMPS & SALLY DELL preparatory to moving to new area	A.T.G.

WAR DIARY
or
INTELLIGENCE SUMMARY.
(Erase heading not required.)

Army Form C. 2118.

Place	Date	Hour	Summary of Events and Information	Remarks and references to Appendices
COUIN	Aug 17th		Moved with section to TERRAMESNIL after handing over sanitary charge of COUIN area to O.C. San. Sec. Guards Division.	App.
TERRAMESNIL	18	11a	Left with section for CANDAS. Including LORRY, FORD & FODEN-THRESH.	App.
CANDAS	19		Standing-bye.	App.
"	20		Section entrained CANDAS to MERRICOURT. Lorry Ford, Foden-Thresh by road.	App.
TREUX	21		TREUX. Section marched MERRICOURT to TREUX. Féis atrocious.	App.
"			Moved to "CITADEL" (F.2.16 Central, Sheet Albert Combined) Section marched. Motor vehicles by road.	App.
"CITADEL"	22		Took on charge of Divisional Laundry at Amiens. A clean clothes depot was started at F.2.1.d. Dirty clothes to be brought to the Foden-Thresh there, these disinfected & taken by Lorry to AMIENS. The Lorry to bring back a load of washed clothing.	App.
"	23		Took over charge of area as regards Sanitation from O.C. San. Sec 24th Div. The area was in a very dirty state. Many divisions being crowded into one valley, overlapping ensues & a dirty area that one wishes to deal with is found to belong to some other division. The number of flies was very great	App.

Army Form C. 2118.

WAR DIARY
or
INTELLIGENCE SUMMARY.
(Erase heading not required.)

Instructions regarding War Diaries and Intelligence Summaries are contained in F. S. Regs., Part II. and the Staff Manual respectively. Title pages will be prepared in manuscript.

Place	Date	Hour	Summary of Events and Information	Remarks and references to Appendices
SOMME	Aug			
CITADEL	23 (cont)		There were a number of open latrines (deep) and large quantities of horse manure. There is said to be a considerable amount of "cholera nostras".	Aff.
"	24.		Erected shelters for clean clothes, changing room etc in connection with clean clothes depôt. Made an office from wood, canvas & carpeted it & also tables, cook house, latrines, ablution bench etc. Took over temporary charge of baths at MÉAULTE from O.C. Day 5th San. Sec (3rd Div). For Ambulance had to be returned for ambulance duties.	Aff.
"	25		Various inspections. Many open latrines, flies and insufficient interested ford. Erecting incinerators. Cleaning up mess left by other previous units. Manifestation of "cholera nostras". Obtained Castor Oil, Chlorodyne and Bismuth Salicylate. This is now going to be very useful. A number of box latrines made & given to small units.	Aff.
"	26		Much spraying of huts & tents with MacKenzie sprays using 10% paraffin & creol. Great temporary improvement in numbers flies in these places. The laundry scheme at Amiens works well.	Aff.
"	27.		Much spraying of huts & messes; experiments with antifly schemes.	Aff.

Army Form C. 2118.

WAR DIARY
or
INTELLIGENCE SUMMARY.
(Erase heading not required.)

Place	Date	Hour	Summary of Events and Information	Remarks and references to Appendices
SOMME	Aug			
CITADEL	28		Suffering from slight attack of diarrhoea. Provft. (Proctor) & castor oil. Office work	A.T.G.
"	29	at 10pm	Went to AMIENS to pay Country charges (3250 francs).	A.T.G.
"	30		Handed over Coaks to O.C. Sam. Sec. Guards. Bn? Work is considerably Reinforced by lack of a car.	A.T.G.
"	31		Inspected Transport lines of 12KRR, 12RB, 7KSLI 6" Ox Bucks. In some of these cases as in many others in this district, it often happens that a site is very dirty on arrival, the unit then stays only one night and is held responsible for the dirty state. Again often a dirty site is vacated and not taken over by anyone. The units adjacent to this site suffer in consequence and are always very unwilling to put the matter right if it is advised their own lines even by a few feet. Copies of my weekly report to ADMS are enclosed as they give a better idea of the work of myself and the section than a diary.	A.T.G. A.T.G.

A.T. Girdwood Captain R.A.M.C.(T.F.)
O.C. SANITARY SECTION 41 DIV.

APPENDIX I

REPORT

for week ending Saturday 12th

Units.	State of Camps and Billets.	Remarks.
Divisional Headquarters.	Good.	
Hd.Qrs. Clerks and Servants Billet.	Good.	
Hd.Qrs. Transport.	Good.	
Camp Commandant.	Good.	
No. 2 Mess.	Good.	
No. 3 Mess.	Good.	The yard and manure heap are very bad.
Div. Signal Coy.	Good.	
Do. Officers' Mess.	Good.	
Do. Sergeants Billet.	Good.	
Do. Transport.	Good.	
C.R.E., Officers Huts.	Good.	
Do. Transport.	Good.	
A.D.M.S.	Good.	
A.D.V.S.	Good.	
D.A.D.O.S.	Good.	
Ordnance Stores.	Good.	
Armourers Workshop.	Good.	
M.M.Police.	Good.	
Do. Horse lines.	Good.	There is a large amount of manure which is being burnt
Traffic Police (2 billets).	Good.	
Hd.Qrs. Post Office.	Good.	
Expeditionary Force Canteen.	Good.	Except for yard which is generally littered with loose paper, etc.
Church Army Hut.	-	Rubbish now removed satisfactorily.

Units.	State of Camps and Billets.	Remarks.
Anti-Gas School.	Good.	
Divisional Baths.	Good.	
Divisional Disinfecting Station.	Good.	
Divisional Band.	Good.	
Salvage Company.	Good.	
Town Major, COUIN.	Fair.	Yard in very untidy condition. Manure very bad.
Mobile Veterinary Section	Good.	

59th. Brigade.

Brigade Headquarters.	Satisfactory.	
Do. Transport.	Satisfactory.	
10th. K.R.R.	Satisfactory.	
Do. Transport.	Satisfactory.	
Do. Q.M.Stores.	Good.	
11th. K.R.R.,Transport.	Satisfactory.	
10th. R.B.	Very good.	
Do. Transport.	Satisfactory.	
11th. R.B., Transport.	Satisfactory.	
Do. Band and Q.M.Stores	Good.	
59th. Machine Gun Coy. Transport.	Satisfactory.	

60th. Brigade.

60th. Bde.Hd.Qrs. Transport.	Satisfactory.	
12th. K.R.R.,Transport.	Satisfactory.	
Do. Transport and Band.	Satisfactory.	
12th. R.B., Transport.	Satisfactory.	
Do. Q.M.Stores.	Satisfactory.	
6th. Oxon and Bucks.L.I.	Good.	
Do. Transport.	Satisfactory.	
6th. Shropshire L.I. Transport.	Satisfactory.	
Do. Q.M.Stores.	Satisfactory.	
Trench Mortar Battery.	Satisfactory.	

Units.	State of Camps and Billets.	Remarks.

61st. Brigade.

Brigade Headquarters.	Good.	
7th. Somerset L.I.	Good.	On vacation of billets in forward area the large amount of rubbish left by previous occupants was either burnt or buried.
Do. Transport.	Satisfactory.	
7th. K.O.Y.L.I.	Good.	
Do. Transport.	Satisfactory.	
12th. King's Liverpools.	Good.	
Do. Transport.	Satisfactory.	
7th. Cornwalls.	Good.	
Do. Transport.	Satisfactory.	
61st. Machine Gun Coy.	Satisfactory.	
Do. Transport.	Satisfactory.	
Trench Mortar Battery.	Fair.	Latrines at COUIN not kept clean. Separate report submitted.

Pioneers.

11th. Durham L.I.	Satisfactory.	
Do. Transport.	Satisfactory.	

Engineers.

83rd. Field Company.	Satisfactory.	
96th. Field Company.	Satisfactory.	
Do. Transport.	Satisfactory.	

A.S.C.

Train Headquarters.	Good.	
159th. Company.	Good.	
160th. Company.	Good.	
161st. Company.	Good.	

ARTILLERY.

Divisional Ammunition Column. S.A.A.Sections.	Satisfactory.	

Units.	State of Camps and Billets.	Remarks.
3rd. Brigade, 8th. Group. 4th. Army. 111th. Battery Wagon Lines. 113th. Do.		Arrangements made for removal of accumulations of manure.

Other Units.

No. 1 Kite Balloon Section.
R.F.C.   Satisfactory.

GENERAL WORK.

   COUIN.

       Collection daily of refuse from Headquarters and Headquarter Troops Billets and offices and Messes.

       Two pits dug for reception of broken glass, etc. at each public incinerator.

       Cellar in billet opposite R.A.Mess cleared out.

       Several shruberies in village cleared of tins and old clothing.

       Supervision of street sweeping from Chateau to foot of COUIN HILL.

       Two stagnant pools in village sprayed.

       Supervision of erection of two excreta incinerators, one at lines of 12th. King's Liverpool Regt. and one at 7th. Somerset's Lines, "A" Camp.

       Plans made for proposed Baths at St. LEGER.

       22 huts in woods COUIN and adjacent thereto sprayed with Formaldehyde.

       Horse troughs at foot of COUIN HILL cleaned.

   St. LEGER.

       Supervision of "P.B." men in charge of incinerator for excreta and refuse.

       Erection of water tank for water bottles.

   COIGNEUX.

       Supervision of "P.B." men in charge of incinerator for excreta and refuse.

   THE DELL.

       Testing of water supplies, tests showing ½ measures per water cart.

   BAILLY.

       Inspection of

SAILLY-au-BOIS.

    Inspection of village billets.

    Supervision of fatigue party cleaning billets and refuse burnt.

    Latrines erected.

COLINCAMPS.

    Inspection of billets in village.

    Approaches to village drinking water tanks cleaned and paved.

    Water supplies visited and tested.

COURCELLES.

    Erection of two ablution benches.

    Latrine for baths erected.

MAILLET MALLET.

    Arrangements made with another Sanitary Section for bathing Cornwalls, Liverpools and Yorkshires.

    Investigation of water supplies.

HEBUTERNE.

    Supervision of and testing water supplies.

GENERALLY.

    Supervision of disinfection of blankets from Field Ambulances and underclothing from Divisional Baths.

    Testing of all water supplies in SAILLY-au-BOIS commenced.

A.H. Goran.

Lieut R.A.M.C. (T).

LIST OF DISINFECTANTS issued for use in
20th. Division during week ending
12th. August 1916.

Chloride of Lime...	7560 lbs.
Creosoli...	445 gals.
Crude Paraffin...	328 gals.
Formalin...	3 gals.
Bleaching Powder...	90 tins.
Clarifying powder...	36 tins.
Soft Soap...	1120 lbs.
Anti-vermin powder...	30 lbs.
Oxford Grease...	70 lbs.

A.T. Girvan

Lieut R.A.M.C. (T.F.).

To.

A.D.M.S.,
20th. Division.

During the week ending 12th. instant 900 blankets from the Field Ambulances and 20,547 articles of underclothing from the Divisional Baths have been passed through the "FODEN" Thresh Steam Disinfector.

R.T. Girvan

Lieut R.A.M.C. (T).

APPENDIX II

R E P O R T

for week ending 26th. August 1916.

Units.	State of Camps and Billets.	Remarks.
Advanced Headquarters.	Good.	
C.R.E.	Good.	(Use common incinerator
C.R.A. (24th. Divn.).	Good.	(New latrines and (ablution bench are (being fixed.
Section – Divn. Signal Company.	Good.	
Headquarters "A" and "Q".	Good.	
Headquarters Transport.	–	Deep trench latrine not covered in. Large amount of manure.
M.M.Police.	–	Open trench latrine.
Salvage Company.	Good.	
Divn. Band.	Good.	
Divn. Signal Company. Transport.	Fair.	Improved during last two days.
2nd. King Edwards Horse. (attached).	–	Open latrines. Large amount of manure. Improving.
6th. Divn. Artillery H.Q.	Good.	
96th. Company R.E. Transport.	Good.	
83rd. Company R.E.	Good.	
Corps Caterpillar Park.	Fairly good.	
Durham L.I., Transport.	Good.	
10th. R.B., Transport.	Good.	
11th. R.B., Transport.	Good.	
10th. K.R.R., Transport.	Good.	
11th. K.R.R., Transport.	Good.	
59th. Hd.Qrs. Transport.	–	Immediate attention to defects promised.
59th. Machine Gun Coy.	–	Old manure to be burnt.

Units.	State of Camps and Billets.	Remarks.

6th. Oxon and Bucks. L.I.
  Transport.   Satisfactory.

12th. R.B., Transport. Satisfactory.

12th. K.R.R., Transport. Satisfactory.

6th. Shropshire.L.I.
  Transport.   Satisfactory.

7th. Yorkshires.)
7th. Cornwalls.)
12th. King's Liverpools)-   Large amount of manure
7th. Somersets.)   and rubbish to be
  Transport lines.)   dealt with in each of
                                        these camps. Big
                                        improvements shewn
                                        already.

GENERAL WORK :

  Disinfections.

    Disinfection carried out following cases of diarrhoea
       and one case of typhilis in the CITADEL area.

    Spraying of Hd.Qrs. Messes and Staff tents, Hd.Qrs.
       Cookhouse, Hd.Qrs. Offices, and various bivouacs
       and cookhouses in area.

  General work :
    Taking over Divisional Baths at MEAULTE.
    Reconstruction of public incinerator for dry refuse.

    Two manure incinerators constructed at lines of King
       Edwards Horse adjoining the Divn Signal Company's
       Transport.

    Various box latrines constructed.

    Construction of newpublicurinaspitx new public urine
       pit.

    Various accumulations of refuse burnt.

    Improvements carried out at No. 2 Post.

    Manure incinerator at lines of 5th. Divn. Artillery
       headquarters Transport.

    Manure incinerator is course of construction at M.P.Police
       Camp.

    Water testing and testing of Divisional water carts carried
       out in area.

    Water instruction given at the Divisional Supply Column.

    Distribution of disinfectants.

    Supervision of Dirty and Clean clothes Depot., disinfection
       of dirty clothing in Thresh Disinfector.

A.F.Goivan Captain. R.A.M.C.

LIST OF DISINFECTANTS

issued for use in the 20th. Division during the week ending 26th. August 1916...

Chloride of Lime...	6660 lbs.
Creosoli...	360 gals.
Paraffin and Crude Paraffin...	265 gals.
Formalin...	16 gals.

A.F. Givans,
Captain R.A.M.C. (S.).

To.

    A.D.M.S.,

        20th. Division.

During the week ending the 26th. August 1916 the following number of articles of dirty clothing have been passed through the Thresh Disinfector...   12,616.

A.F. Gowan
Captain R.A.M.C. (T).
O.C. Sanitary Section
Attached 20th Light Division.

To A.D.M.S.
XX Division.

The following are the particulars and results of water carts in the Division being tested with Zinc Iodide and Starch on the date 24-26 Aug 191, those giving no reaction showing that the water in the carts had not been chlorinated:-

Unit.	Time of Testing Date Hour	Cart Filled Date Hour	No. of water Cart	Results.
20" Divn Signal Company R.E.	24/8/16 10.55	24/8/16 4 pm	E 61444	Oc present
D.H.Q. Staff	25/8/16 3.35	25/8/16 9 am	E 7093	Oc present
12" Kings Liverpool	26/8/16 7.30 am	25/8/16 9 am	E 6416 a	Oc present
12" R.B.	26/8/16 9.50	25/8/16 4 pm	E 7053 a	Oc present Chlorinated badly.
4" Somersets	26/8/16 9.55 am	25/8/16 7.30 pm	E 7069 l	Oc present
		4 pm	E 7308	Oc present
4" Cornwalls	26/8/16 10 am	25/8/16 4 pm	E 71332	Oc present
4" K.O.Y.L.I.	26/8/16 10.5 am	25/8/16 9 am	E 71915	Oc present
12" Kings Liverpools	26/8/16 11.20 am	25/8/16 11 am	E 71345	Oc present
11" R.B.	24/8/16 2.50 pm	24/8/16 10 am	E 71494	Oc present
			E 13657	Oc present
10" K.R.R.	24/8/16 3.20 pm	24/8/16 9 am	E 6422	Oc present
		4 pm	E 85658	Oc present

On work
24/8/16 - Truck at FRICOURT ROAD ....
26/8/16 - Inspected Canadian Eng'r Camp transferring to SUZANNE-sur-SOMME

P.H. Girvan
Captain R.A.M.C.
O.C. Sanitary Section 33
XX Division.

Date 30th August 1916

Confidential.

WAR DIARY

of

Captain A. F. TIRVAN. R.A.M.C. (T.F.)

Officer Commanding

<u>SANITARY SECTION 33,</u>
1st London (City of London) Sanitary Company
R.A.M.C. (T.F.)

attached

<u>20th (LIGHT) DIVISION.</u>
B. E. F.
FRANCE.

SEPTEMBER 1916.

Volume 4.

WAR DIARY
or
INTELLIGENCE SUMMARY.

Army Form C. 2118.

Place	Date	Hour	Summary of Events and Information	Remarks and references to Appendices
	Sep		Copies of weekly report to ADMS are attached as they give a better idea of the work done than a mere diary.	Appendices A.B.C&D.
CITADEL (F.21 Central)	1		Various inspections & work connected with clothes exchange. A.Y.	F.21. A.I.C.A ALBERT Contour Sheet 1/40000
Albert Contour 3. Sheet 1/40000	2		Ditto + experiments with fly killing solutions A.Y.	
	3		Most of my section volunteered to work at Stretcher work etc at CARNOY A.D.S. all who could be taken away from other work (11) were sent there at about 10 am and remained there working continuously till 7am. I recalled some of the men and left 10 men to continue in relays till the work was dealt with. The Section Lorry plied between CARNOY and BRONFAY FARM from 3pm till 10.30pm carrying 9189 "walking wounded" in this period. Acting under G.O.C's instructions via ADMS I detailed 3 men (4 Corporals Spurgery, Hunting & Ede) to proceed to the BRIQETERIE and thence to GUILLEMONT as soon as it should be in our hands, to chlorinate the water supply. These men duly reached their objective, found that all trace of water supply had been destroyed by shell fire, reported to the Staff Capt. at BRIQETERIE and returned safely from this very dangerous mission. A.Y.	F.21.6.4 BRIQETERIE A.4.C.3.3. GUILLEMONT T.19.C ALBERT Contour Sheet 1/40000
	4		10 men still working at CARNOY A.D.S. Inspected Transport Lines. A.Y.	A.Y.
	5		Moved to Faked FORKED TREE (L.2 & 0.9) after handing over at CITADEL to O.C. San Sec 16th Div (Capt Montley) A.Y.	FORKED TREE Co-ord ALBERT F.2.S.E.9.6 Contour Sheet 1/40000

T2134. Wt. W708—776. 500000. 4/15. Sir J. C. & S.

Army Form C. 2118.

WAR DIARY
or
INTELLIGENCE SUMMARY.
(Erase heading not required.)

Instructions regarding War Diaries and Intelligence Summaries are contained in F. S. Regs., Part II. and the Staff Manual respectively. Title pages will be prepared in manuscript.

Place	Date	Hour	Summary of Events and Information	Remarks and references to Appendices
	Sep			
FORKED TREE	5		The Foden Thresh disinfector stuck in the soft ground & the united efforts of 3, 3 ton lorries failed to move it. After great trouble a "caterpillar" was procured & moved it out at once. Sam. See Lorry to D.S.C. for refinish, springs etc.	
"	6		Moved to CORBIE as follows. Men marched. Sam See Lorry 1st Journey — Sanitary Stores, Men's Kits & packs. 2nd Journey. Remainder of Sam Stores & my Kit. Bath's Lorry. 1st Journey clean clothes to CORBIE & my office equipment also dirty (but Threshed) clothes taken to Laundry at AMIENS. 2nd Journey. Dirty unthreshed clothes to CORBIE. Foden-Thresh direct to CORBIE. Move completed by about 5 P.M. O.H.	
CORBIE	7		Various men inoculated. 3 men attached to me "had up" for urinating against wall. 3 days C.B. awarded. Took occupation of Baths. Got Foden installed there. Got baths ready for bathing 100 men per hour to-morrow. Continuing to use laundry at AMIENS. O.H.	
"	8		Inspections of billets in town. Town in very dirty state. Has much work connected with baths & the town. O.H.	
"	9		Fly wires made from resin & castor oil. Collected some disinfectants not removed from CITADEL on Sep 5th. O.H.	

T.2134. Wt. W708—776. 500000. 4/15. Sir J. C. & S.

Army Form C. 2118.

WAR DIARY
or
INTELLIGENCE SUMMARY.
(Erase heading not required.)

Instructions regarding War Diaries and Intelligence Summaries are contained in F. S. Regs., Part II. and the Staff Manual respectively. Title pages will be prepared in manuscript.

Place	Date	Hour	Summary of Events and Information	Remarks and references to Appendices
CORBIE	Sep 9		Sent in following report to ADMS. (Extracted & condensed):— The Sanitary Arrangements of CORBIE are in a very unsatisfactory state & require immediate attention. Troops are billeted mostly in attics & yards which were in a very dirty state when taken into use. The Public Latrines which exist are in a deplorable state of disrepair & neglect, though very few are fly-proof. The stench is bad, & the pails appear to be regularly emptied. The number of one existing latrines is inadequate & there are no signboards to direct troops to the existing ones. Water. Derived from wells and there are scarcely any notices to indicate that the water should be chlorinated. Ablution facilities practically non-existent. from Corps orders. Extracts quoted showing that Town Major is responsible for much of this. Qy. Baths working full pressure — 1000 men per day — various infections Qy.	
"	10		Marto FORKED TREE as follows:— MEN — Marched. San. Sec. Lorry. 1 Journey. Mobile Bath Stores. 2nd Journey. Disinfectants. 30 cwt Lorry from column " Kits, Packs, stores Baths Lorry " Clean clothes to Forked Tree. Subsequently got order to move them to MEAULTE	
"	11		Move to FORKED TREE thence to MEAULTE Duty to AMIENS. Qy.	MEAULTE E.M. ALBERT

WAR DIARY
or
INTELLIGENCE SUMMARY.

Army Form C. 2118.

Place	Date	Hour	Summary of Events and Information	Remarks and references to Appendices
FORKEDTREE	Sep 11	4p	At Tour by Col Dundas to take in Baths at Meaulte	
"		7p	Halted 90'Div.	
"			Baths staff get to MEAULTE & most of the clothing. Also Foden-Tender. A&Q.	
"	12	8a	Baths ready for work 8 am. Many huts & messes sprayed & paraffin	
"			at Forked Tree. Inspected Transport Lines	A.Q.
"	13		Baths working fairly hard. Laundry at AMIENS being used still. Inspected transport lines A.Q.	
"	14		In order to improve the efficiency of the Section & Bar to day attached 1 Sgt & 3 other NCO's to each F. Amb. For making billets & transport only. It would have been better to have attached them to Bge Hq. little this could not be arranged. The object is to obtain closer touch at all times with the brigades especially on the move and when vacating camps. It appears to me that it would really add to the usefulness of a Sanitary Section to a great degree if it were attached to Brigades and not to Divisions. The latter is hardly much pleasanter for the individuals & particularly the Officer, who gets to know & be known by the Division, to take a pride in improving its sanitary efficiency and to learn the best & quickest way of getting things done. But in times of frequent moves, with many divisions concentrated it is not possible to help the whole area clean. The slackness of a neighbouring division may nullify most of the good work of one's own. A&Q.	

Army Form C. 2118.

WAR DIARY
or
INTELLIGENCE SUMMARY.
(Erase heading not required.)

Place	Date	Hour	Summary of Events and Information	Remarks and references to Appendices
	Sep			
FORKED TREE	15		The field ambulances do not appear to be the best places for attaching my Sanitary Squads. For instance to-day they have gone forward in battle order when sanitary matters before can have little attention. As soon as possible I will see the Staff Capts of Brigades & persuade them to settle squads be attached to their Fiel qrs. Standing-Bye. Withdrew some of my attached men & from baths at MEAULTE to my Hqrs at FORKED TREE. A.Y.G.	
"	16		Standing-Bye. Visited Baths at Meaulte. A.Y.G.	
"	17		Moved to CITADEL EAST. Camp at F.21.d.9.8. (Albert Combined Sheet 1/40,000) Office at F.21.6.8.3. Div. H.Q. at Minden Post where I sent 8 men for water-work. Arranged for chlorination of water at MINDEN POST. Post Baths staff at ___. A.Y.G.	
CITADEL	18		Went to TRONES WOOD to see conditions there. Sanitary work very difficult indeed as ground is a mass of mud, shell holes & dead. Withdrew two men from each	
CITADEL	19		of the squads rationed by Field Ambulances. A.Y.G.	
"	20		Bathing arrangements made for 6" Div. Finally cancelled by Q. r 20" Bathing instead. A.Y.G.	
"	21		Moved to FORKED TREE. Arranged Billets at MEAULTE A.Y.G.	
FORKED TREE	22		Moved to MEAULTE. Sent 2 men to H.Q. at TREUX. A.Y.G.	TREUX J.S.B. and T.S.a. ALBERT Combined Sheet 1/40000

Army Form C. 2118.

WAR DIARY
or
INTELLIGENCE SUMMARY.
(Erase heading not required.)

Instructions regarding War Diaries and Intelligence Summaries are contained in F. S. Regs., Part II. and the Staff Manual respectively. Title pages will be prepared in manuscript.

Place	Date	Hour	Summary of Events and Information	Remarks and references to Appendices
	SEP			
MEAULTE	23		Paid Laundry at AMIENS. Shirts are being mended at '65f each. Very reasonable.	A/4.
"	24		AADMS instructed Salvage Coy to return all underclothing to me. Some units have been returning dirty clothes to Salvage instead of to me, especially at time of moving. Inspected Artillery in Bas des TAILLES. Most gone away. The Battery rDAC visited.	A/4.
"	25		Inspected Billets in Méaulte of 61st Bde. Satisfactory with few small exceptions. Drew some samples of water which is used at various "Efficient" to mix with "Grenadine" etc as a drink. Analysed with aid of Thresh Cabinet. The results show a serious source of danger to troops in towns.	Appendix E.
"	26		Various inspections. Méaulte + TREUX.	A/4
"	27		Inspection at TREUX and 2 visits to HQ. Visited O.C. San Sec 5th Div at Forked Tree (Lt Col Spicer)	A/4. 7.30. A.16. A/4
"	28		Inspected horse watering discs. Visited BILLON FARM. Awaiting orders. Look at Baths etc. Met Forked Tree	A/4
"	29		Inspecting office methods. Walk for Tom major " " ". Arranged to Collie trofs of 6th Div and also 2nd Cavalry Division. Visited Corps Water Column.	Appendix F A/4
"	30		Pay Laundry Amiens. Left from I attend a new inspection form for use by my Section in future.	A/4.

A.T. Gurney Capt R.A.M.C.(T)
O.C. SANITARY SECTION 33,
ATTACHED XXIII (LIGHT) DIVISION,

Appendix A.

R E P O R T

for week ending Sunday 3rd. September 1916.

Units.	State of Camps and Billets.	Remarks.
Advanced Divisional Headquarters, MINDEN POST.	Satisfactory.	
Divisional Headquarters	Good.	
No. 2 Mess.	Good.	
No. 3 Mess.	Good.	
Headquarters Transport.	Fair.	Latrine not boxed in. Subsequently this defect was remedied.
M.M. Police	Fair.	Cookhouse floor and surroundings not always clean.
Divisional Signal Coy.	Fair.	Unburnts tins behind divouacs and also food.
6th. Division R.R., H.Q.	Good.	
Salvage Company.	Good.	
2nd. King Edwards Horse.	Fair.	Too much manure. An improvement has subsequently taken place.

CRATERS, CARNOY.

12th. K.R.R.) 12th. R.B.) 6th. Shropshires) 96th. Field Coy. R.E.)	Satisfactory.	A great amount of refuse found on these sites. Reported and on vacations Batts. left parties to clean up.
7th. Cornwalls.) 10th. K.R.R.) 12th. King's (Liverpools).) 7th. Somersets.) 7th. Yorkshires.) 10th. R.B.) 11th. R.B.) 11th. K.R.R.)		This area was left in a very dirty condition by the Batts. of the previ--ous Division. Attention drawn to this and sites have since been cleaned.
59th. Brigade Hd. Qrs. Transport.	Good.	
10th. R.B.,Transport,	Good.	
11th. R.B.,Transport	Good.	
10th. K.R.R. Trans	Good.	

Units.	State of Camps and Billets.	Remarks.
11th. K.R.R., Transport.	Good.	
59th. Machine Gun Coy.	Good.	
11th. Durham, Transport.	Good.	
6th. Oxon. & Bucks. L.I. Transport.	Satisfactory.	
12th. K.R.R , Transport.	Satisfactory.	
12th. R.B., Transport.	Fair.	
6th. Shropshire.	Satisfactory.	
7th. Yorkshires, Transport.	Satisfactory.	
12th. King's (Liverpools). Transport.	Satisfactory.	
7th. Somerset, Transport.	Satisfactory.	
7th. Cornwalls, Transport.	Satisfactory.	

DISINFECTIONS.

Headquarters and Messes sprayed.

Officers Mess and two cookhouses at Divisional Cage sprayed.

Billets, kitchens, etc of C.R.E. and C.R.A. sprayed.

Billets of French Graves Registration Commission, Salvage Company and 11th. R.B. Transport sprayed.

All cases of diarrhoea - disinfection subsequently carried out.

GENERAL WORK.

Hut constructed for Clean Clothes Depot.

Arrangements made to chlorinate water supply tanks at CARNOY.

Supervision of Clean and Dirty Clothes Depot, and disinfection of blankets.

Testing of water carts in Divisional area.

Various constructional work at No 2 Mess.

Box latrines constructed for various units.

Supervision of fatigue party working on incinerators and clearing up and burning refuse and manure in CITADEL area.

Two new manure incinerators constructed.

Capt. R.A.M.C.(T).

O.C. Sanitary Section
Attached XXth (Light) Division.

On Sept. 3rd. all of my Section who could be spared (about 11) worked at stretcher bearing etc. at A.D.S.CARNOY from 12noon to 7am. and subsequently in relays for another 24 hours. Over 1000 cases were dealt with.
The lorry carried 194 "walking wounded" from CARNOY to BROMHAY FARM.

A.F. Girvan

Captain R.A.M.C.(T).

O.C. SANITARY SECTION 33.
ATTACHED XXth (LIGHT) DIVISION.

To.
   A.D.M.S.,
      20th. Division.

During the week ending Sunday 3rd. September the following was done:

    Blankets disinfected....   199.
    Underclothing disinfected...   18,068 articles.

                    Capt. R.A.M.C. (T).
                    O.C. SANITARY SECTION 33,
                    ATTACHED XXth DIVISION.

To:
A.D.M.S.
XX Division.

The following are the particulars and results of water carts in the Division being tested with Zinc Iodide and Starch on the date 29th August 1916, Nose giving no reaction to 3rd Sept showing that the water in the carts had not been chlorinated:-

Unit.	Time of Testing Date Hour	Last Filled Date Hour	No. of Water Cart	Results.
20th Signal Coy. R.E	29/8/16 8.50 am	29/8/16 3 P.M	E68421	Chl present.
6th Shropshire L.I.	29/8/16 10 am	28/8/16 4 P.M.	E 70393	Chl present.
			E69615	Chl present.
Divn. Headquarters	29/8/16 2.35 P.M.	29/8/16 10 am	E 70293	Chl present.
11 Rifle Brigade	31/8/16 2.50 P.M.	31/8/16 noon	E 73607	Chl present.
			E 70294	Chl present.
10th Kings Royal Rifles	1/9/16 3.5 PM	30/8/16 1.30 P.M.	E 64162	Chl present.
160th Coy. A.S.C.	1/9/16 3.15 PM	1/9/16 8 am	E 70323	Chl present.
161st Coy. A.S.C.	1/9/16 3.30 PM	1/9/16 10.30 am	E 70335	Chl present.
7th Cornwalls	2/9/16 10.10 am	1/9/16 3 PM	E 68349	Chl present.
7th Somerset	2/9/16 10.25 am	2/9/16 7 am	E 70308	Chl present.
12th Kings (Liverpools)	2/9/16 10.45 am	2/9/16 11 am	E 70342	Chl present.
			E 66164	Chl present.
59th Machine Gun Coy.	2/9/16 11.15 am	2/9/16 10.15 am	E 85275	Chl present.
12th Rifle Brigade.	3/9/16 11.15 am	3/9/16 10.40 am	E 70836	Chl present.

Other Work

28/8/16 Sterilising plant of the 4th Army Water supply bodies at ETINEHEM inspected.
Tanks at FRICOURT, FRICOURT-BRAY ROAD and SAPPER CORNER visited.

A.F. Govan
Capt. R.A.M.C.(T)
O.C. Sanitary Section 33
XX Division.

Date 10th Sept 1916

Appendix B.

R E P O R T

On Sanitary Condition, etc, for week ending 9th. September 1916.

Units.	State of Camps and Billets.	Remarks.
Divisional Headquarters.	Good.	
No. 1 Mess.	Good.	Special report has already
No. 2 Mess.	Good.	been sent in on the bad
No. 3 Mess.	Good.	condition of the TOWN of
Hd. Qrs. Servants.	Good.	CORBIE.
Hd. Qrs. Transport.	Good.	
Divisional Signal Coy.	Good.	
Do. Transport.	Good.	
M.M.Police.	Good.	
Traffic Police.	Good.	
Salvage Company.	Good.	
C.R.E.	Good.	
60th. Brigade Transport.	Good.	

DISINFECTIONS.

Latrine area at G.O.C's billet at CORBIE disinfected.

GENERAL WORK.

Supervision of fatigue party at the CRATERS, CARNOY.

SUpervision of fatigue party at the CITADEL clearing and burning refuse and manure.

Construction of manure incinerator at the CITADEL.

Construction of clean clothes shed at the CITADEL.

Construction of latrines at Baths, CORBIE.

REpair of latrines at billet of G.O.C. CORBIE.

WATER.

Tanks at FRICOURT and wells at CORBIE visited and tested.

Capt. R.A.M.C.

LIST OF DISINFECTANTS ISSUED

for use in the 20th. DIVISION during the week ending 9th. September 1916.........

Chloride of Lime.........	1140 lbs.
Creosoli.........	100 gallons.
Paraffin.......	50 gallons.
Formalin.......	1 gallon.

A.F. Girvan

Captain R.A.M.C. (T).

O.C. SANITARY SECTION 33,
ATTACHED XXth (LIGHT) DIVISION.

To.

    A.D.M.S.,

       20th. Division,

The following work was done during the week eding the 9th. instant:

Blankets disinfected.	100.
Articles of clothing etc. from 61st. Field Ambulance.	511.
Articles of underclothing passed through "Thresh" Disinfector	7210.
Articles of clothing issued:	
Shirts.........	3148.
Pants..........	2662.
Socks........	2816 pairs.
Towels.....	1120.

A.F. Girvan

Captain R.A.M.C. (T).

O.C. SANITARY SECTION 33.
ATTACHED XXth (LIGHT) DIVISION.

Appendix C

R E P O R T

on Sanitary conditions etc. of Units of 20th. Division during the week ending 9th. September 1916.

Units.	State of Camps and Billets.	Remarks.
Divisional Headquarters.	Good.	
Do. Transport.	Good.	
C.R.E., Transport.	Good.	
Signals Transport.	Good.	
Salvage Company.	Good.	
Divisional Band.	Good.	
Traffic Police;	Good.	
M.M.Police.	Good.	
21st. Lancers. (attached).	Fair.	Too much manure not burnt.
59th. Brigade Hd. Qrs.	Good.	
10th. K.R.R.	Good.	
11th. K.R.R.	Good.	
11th. R.B.	Satisfactory.	
59th. Machine Gun Coy. and Transport.	Satisfactory.	
12th. K.R.R.	Satisfactory.	
12th. R.B.	Satisfactory.	
60th. Machine Gun Coy.	Satisfactory.	
6th. K.S.L.I. and Transport.	Good.	
6th. Oxon. and Bucks.L.I. and Transport.	Good.	
160th. Coy. A.S.C.	Good.	
11th. Durham L.I.	Satisfactory.	

GENERAL WORK.

Headquarters Cookhouses, Messes and Offices Sprayed.

Numerous fly wires made.

Rubbish from headquarters removed.

LIST OF DISINFECTANTS issued:

Chloride of Lime.	2640 lbs.
Creosoli.	210 gallons.
Paraffin.	175 gallons.

LIST OF DISINFECTING:-

Blankets.	100.
Underclothing from Laundry.	13098.

LIST OF CLEAN CLOTHING issued:

Shirts.	3130.
Pants.	2509.
Socks.	2809.
Towels.	266.
Number of men bathed.	2460.

A.F. Givan

Captain R.A.M.C.(T).

O.C. SANITARY SECTION 33,
ATTACHED XXth (LIGHT) DIVISION.

Appendix 5

REPORT
for week ending September 23rd, 1916

FORWARD AREA.

Divisional Headquarters, MINDEN POST.

The Sanitary conditions were good.

A fatigue party cleansing and filling petrol cans with Chlorinated water for Divisional Reserve was supervised.

Various Messing Huts and Latrines were sprayed.

59th. BRIGADE.

With reference to the Sanitary Conditions, the brigade was in the line under such conditions that sanitary supervision was practically impossible.

The supervision of the water supply to the trenches from the advanced dump at GUILLEMONT carried out.

60th. BRIGADE.

With reference to the Sanitary Conditions:

The Transport lines of the Bde. were daily inspected and sanitary conditions were satisfactory. Much refuse & manures had been left by previous Units.

On the Bde. coming out of the trenches, the Camps at the CITADEL, taken over by the 12th. R.B. & 6th. Shropshires were not found to be in a very satisfactory condition. Food and remains of meals had been left exposed and tins of excreta & urine were about the camps. These conditions were remedied. On vacation these sites were left in a satisfactory condition. The water carts left at the Transport lines have been tested & water stations at MONTAUBAN, FRICOURT and THE CITADEL visited.

61st. BRIGADE.

The sanitary conditions were generally speaking in a satisfactory state.

The Headquarters of the Brigade and the Transport lines were daily inspected and found to be in a satisfactory condition.

ARTILLERY AND D.A.C., BOIS DES TAILLES.

These lines were daily inspected.

The predecessors in occupation had littered the Camp site with piles of unburnt tins. Despite the bad weather all these were dealt with by incineration. Fly-proofed latrines were made and manure dealt with satisfactorily at a spot outside the Camps. The general sanitary conditions were good.

The lines were vacated early in the week with the exception of the Headquarters and No. 4 Section D.A.C. and were left in a satisfactory condition. The sanitary conditions of the remaining lines were poor but improvements are in progress.

BACK AREA.

DIVISIONAL HEADQUARTERS, TREUX.

On entering billets a number were found to be in a filthy state and duly reported the next day. These have been cleaned up and all billets are now in a very good state of cleanliness.

59th. BRIGADE.

The sanitary conditions of the Headquarters, Battalions and Transport lines in and around MORLANCOURT are quite satisfactory

The water tanks at MOREUIL have been inspected and tests from water carts carried out.

60th. BRIGADE.

The same applies in regard to sanitation to the 60th. Brigade and fly-proofed latrines are in general use.

61st. BRIGADE.

The sanitary conditions of billets occupied by Headquarters and Battalions in MEAULTE are satisfactory.

Tests have been carried out from the water carts and the

The water supply at the various "Epiceries" requires careful consideration. Drinks are sold composed of "Citron" and "Grenadine" etc. mixed with water from the pumps. Three chance samples have been taken and analysed with the following results :-

Epicerie at Billets Nos.	6.	19.	31.
Ammonia.	Trace.	Trace.	Very Excessive
Salt (expressed as Chlorine per 100,000)	20.	3.	16.
Nitrates(N per 100,000)	Considerable.	Nil.	Considerable.
Nitrates(N per 100,000)	1 to 2.	Nil.	1 to 2.

These results, as far as they go, indicate that the water at Billets Nos. 6 and 31 (especially the latter) is almost certainly polluted. Possibly similar results would be found on investigating the wells at other sources in the village.

Notices are being affixed statating that the water is unfit for drinking, and improvements to various well heads are contemplated.

In the transport lines of the Brigade fly-proofed latrines are being erected by the 9th. Somersets, 7th. Cornwalls and 7th. K.O.Y.L.I. At the lines of the Somersets a large amount of manure had been left to be disposed of and the Camp was in a dirty condition, but improvements are being effected. At the Cornwalls lines there is manure to be disposed of and the King's (Liverpool) lines were left dirty by previous occupants, but improvements are being carried out. The lines of the 7th. K.O.Y.L.I. are in good condition.

GENERAL WORK.

The Town Major of MEAULTE had been advised and assisted with reference to the construction of fly-proofed latrines in the village.

BATHS.

The Baths at MEAULTE have been in active operation.

A list of Units and numbers bathed is appended:

10th and 11th. Rifle Brigade.	100.
83rd. Field Coy., R.E.	120.
10th. King's Royal Rifles.	80.
59th. Machine Gun Coy.	110.
Cavalry Division.	890.
11th. Durhams.	120.
7th. Cornwalls.	500.
7th. K.O.Y.L.I.	400.
7th. Cornwalls.	280.
Total −	2400.

All men have exchanged their dirty underclothing for clean. The dirty has been passed through the "Thresh" Disinfector and conveyed to the Laundry at AMIENS.

Clean clothing issued during the week:

Shirts.	6924.
Pants.	4640.
Socks.	7948.
Towels.	1217.

Dirty clothing received during the week :−

Shirts.	6355.
Pants.	3422.
Socks.	5391.
Towels.	1208.

Dirty clothing passed through the "Thresh" Disinfector during the week − 11,000 articles.

DISINFECTANTS;

The following Disinfectants have been issued during the week :−

Chloride of Lime.	1950 lbs.
Creosoll.	155 gallons.
Paraffin.	230 gallons.
Formalin.	1 gallon.
Bleaching powder for water carts	12 tins.
Bisulphate of Soda tables.	640 bottles.
Anti-frost Bite Grease.	100 lbs.

Captain R.A.M.C. (T.F.).
O.C. SANITARY SECTION 38,
ATTACHED XXII LIGHT DIVISION.

Appendix E.

To:

Town Major, MEAULTE.

I beg to make the following suggestions and remarks to you:-

1. I feel that it would be better if you were to arrange for the burning of all excreta. The density of the population is considerable and the units are frequently shifting. Large accumulations of excreta in deep latrines are sure to have an effect on the wells in the town. A few incinerators made on the Horsfall pattern (I can give you details) would do the work with aid of a half a dozen P.B. men. The excreta would be received in buckets placed in fly-proof latrines & would be conveyed to the nearest incinerator daily by a few more P.B. men.

2. It would also appear to be a good thing if a cart were to go round daily and collect dry refuse and burn it at central incinerators. When units leave in a hurry the incinerators at the billets are generally choked with too much material & an undesirable legacy remains for the newcomers.

3. The water supply at the various "Epiceries" requires careful consideration. Drinks are sold composed of "Citron" and "Grenadine" etc. mixed with water from the pump. I took three chance samples to-day at such places and analysed them as far as I could with the means at my disposal, with the following results:-

Epicerie at Billets Nos.	6.	19.	31.
Ammonia	Trace	Trace	Very excessive.
Salt (expressed as Chlorine per 100,000)	20.	3.	16.
Nitrites (N per 100,000)	Considerable.	Nil	Considerable.
Nitrates (N per 100,000)	1 to 2	Nil.	1 to 2.

These results, as far as they go, indicate that the water at billets No. 6 and 31 (especially the latter) is al--most certainly polluted. Possibly similar results would be found on in vestigating the wells at other sources of refresh--ment for the thirsty soldier.

A wandering O.C. Sanitary Section with a few days here and a few days there has no chance of tackling this pro--blem, which I consider quite important, and within the cap--abilities of an energetic Town Major.

R.F. Gavan

Captain R.A.M.C. (T).
O.C. SANITARY SECTION 33,
ATTACHED XIII (LIGHT) DIVISION.

Appendix F.

REPORT

for Week ending ______ 191_

Signed ______

KEY

1. Latrines.
2. Incinerator.
3. Cookhouse.
4. Grease Trap.
5. Manure disposal.
6. Ablution arrangements.
7. Waste Pit.
8. Camp or Billet.
9. Ventilation or crowding.

Place a X where a defect found and an S where satisfactory.
No mark indicates that no inspection was made.

	Sunday			Monday			Tuesday			Wednesday			Thursday			Friday			Saturday			Entered / Vacated
UNIT:	1	4	7	1	4	7	1	4	7	1	4	7	1	4	7	1	4	7	1	4	7	
	2	5	8	2	5	8	2	5	8	2	5	8	2	5	8	2	5	8	2	5	8	
	3	6	9	3	6	9	3	6	9	3	6	9	3	6	9	3	6	9	3	6	9	

REMARKS:

UNIT:	1	4	7	1	4	7	1	4	7	1	4	7	1	4	7	1	4	7	1	4	7	
	2	5	8	2	5	8	2	5	8	2	5	8	2	5	8	2	5	8	2	5	8	
	3	6	9	3	6	9	3	6	9	3	6	9	3	6	9	3	6	9	3	6	9	

REMARKS:

UNIT:	1	4	7	1	4	7	1	4	7	1	4	7	1	4	7	1	4	7	1	4	7	
	2	5	8	2	5	8	2	5	8	2	5	8	2	5	8	2	5	8	2	5	8	
	3	6	9	3	6	9	3	6	9	3	6	9	3	6	9	3	6	9	3	6	9	

REMARKS:

UNIT:	1	4	7	1	4	7	1	4	7	1	4	7	1	4	7	1	4	7	1	4	7	
	2	5	8	2	5	8	2	5	8	2	5	8	2	5	8	2	5	8	2	5	8	
	3	6	9	3	6	9	3	6	9	3	6	9	3	6	9	3	6	9	3	6	9	

REMARKS:

	1	4	7	1	4	7	1	4	7	1	4	7	1	4	7	1	4	7	1	4	7	
	2	5	8	2	5	8	2	5	8	2	5	8	2	5	8	2	5	8	2	5	8	
	3	6	9	3	6	9	3	6	9	3	6	9	3	6	9	3	6	9	3	6	9	

REMARKS:

	1	4	7	1	4	7	1	4	7	1	4	7	1	4	7	1	4	7	1	4	7	
	2	5	8	2	5	8	2	5	8	2	5	8	2	5	8	2	5	8	2	5	8	
	3	6	9	3	6	9	3	6	9	3	6	9	3	6	9	3	6	9	3	6	9	

REMARKS:

Special Work [illegible]

[illegible signature]

O.C. Sanitary Section [illegible]

[illegible]

Confidential.

WAR DIARY

— of —

Captain A. F. GIRVAN, R.A.M.C (T.F.)

Officer Commanding

33rd SANITARY SECTION

1st London (City of London) Sanitary Company

R.A.M.C. (T.F.)

attached

20th (LIGHT) DIVISION

B.E.F.

FRANCE.

October 1916.

Volume 5.

Army Form C. 2118.

WAR DIARY
or
INTELLIGENCE SUMMARY.
(Erase heading not required.)

Instructions regarding War Diaries and Intelligence Summaries are contained in F. S. Regs., Part II. and the Staff Manual respectively. Title pages will be prepared in manuscript.

Place	Date	Hour	Summary of Events and Information	Remarks and references to Appendices
	Oct			
MÉAULTE	1		Bathing 6th Division all day. Paid section & baths. Visited S/& Ricketts at Bernafay Wood.	A.F.g.
"	2		Sent subsection of 11 men to MINDEN POST	A.F.g.
"	3		Inspected "File factory junction R.O.D camp" by order of D.D.M.S. 14 Corps. Visited MINDEN POST	A.F.g
"	4		Water policed all sources possible to ensure chlorination of carts at MONTAUBAN, CARNOY & TALLUS BOISE	
			Tested & rejected a number of the cans forming a reserve supply of drinking water at BERNAFAY WOOD QY.	
"	5		Constructed very satisfactory filter at baths.	
			[diagram showing filter with Scum boards, Ground level, effluent, River Luce, 2ft 2"]	
			Capacity about 3000 gals (1 day's flow)	
			Treated with chloride of lime solution at rate of 10 ells per hour during working hours.	
			Quite a clear effluent produced.	A.F.g.
"	6		Constructed shelter for bathers at baths. Investigated the method used for cleaning petrol cans prior to use for holding drinking water. Many hours of watching to discover this method found to be most inefficient.	A.F.g.
	7		Visited CARNOY & BERNAFAY WOOD MINDEN POST on various duties	Weekly Report Copy Appendix A. A.F.g

Army Form C. 2118.

WAR DIARY
or
INTELLIGENCE SUMMARY.
(Erase heading not required.)

Instructions regarding War Diaries and Intelligence Summaries are contained in F. S. Regs., Part II. and the Staff Manual respectively. Title pages will be prepared in manuscript.

Place	Date	Hour	Summary of Events and Information	Remarks and references to Appendices
MEAULTE	Oct 8		MINDEN POST to see A.D.M.S. Various inspections.	A.Y.
"	9		Visit AMIENS to buy Laundry. Moved all subsection from MINDEN POST to MEAULTE.	A.Y.g.
"	10		Visited DHQ at TREUX and CORPS HQ at MEAULTE and various water points.	A.Y.g.
"	11		Finishing water points.	A.Y.
"	12		Inspected units of 60th Bge with S. Manchester + the m.o.s of units. Sent out an officer m.c.o to liaise with each ambulance to inspect corresponding Brigade	A.Y.g.
"	13		Visited XIV Corps Chemist and went over all the Water Column present at MEAULTE. Went with him to D.D.M.S XIV Corps re various water matters. Saw A.Y.g.	A.Y.g.
"	14		Rode to MINDEN POST and inspected a number of artillery wagon lines in CARNOY + DEATH VALLEYS	Weekly Report Appendix B.
"	15		Moved to CORBIE as follows:— "Balls" 3 ton Lorry 1. Take at office MEAULTE + take office stores + clean clothing to CORBIE 2. Return take more clothes to CORBIE 3. Return take dirty clothes to AMIENS 4. Return to MEAULTE for night. SANSEC. 1½ Ton " 1. 6am call for rations ready filled proceed to CORBIE 2. Return take more stores to CORBIE 3. Return + do a journey for Field Ambulance. Men. March — light order.	A.Y.g.
"	16		Foden Thresh proceeded to CORBIE after finishing dirty clothes at MEAULTE Baths Lorry " " " with remainder of clothes etc. Handed over Baths MEAULTE to Town Major.	A.Y.g.

Army Form C. 2118.

Instructions regarding War Diaries and Intelligence Summaries are contained in F. S. Regs., Part II. and the Staff Manual respectively. Title pages will be prepared in manuscript.

WAR DIARY
or
INTELLIGENCE SUMMARY.
(Erase heading not required.)

Place	Date	Hour	Summary of Events and Information	Remarks and references to Appendices
	Oct			
CORBIE	17		Took over baths at CORBIE & started working at 2pm. ATF. Visited DAEOURS re sanitation system in use etc. Aff.	
"			Prepared to disinfect 1000 blankets a day by spraying with 2% "Formalin" Went round town with Town Major enquiring sites for latrines. Aff.	
"	18		Blanket disinfection cancelled as we are to move and the blanket possessors move today. ATF	
"	19		Handed over to Town Major CORBIE all disinfectants on hand as they could not well be moved about the country. They comprised 2 cwt soft soap, many boxes of bleaching powder, drums of cresol, paraffin, timber. Moved to VIGNACOURT as follows. (1) Saw See Lorry with mobilization stores + several men myself. (2) Baths Lorry completely full of mens + clean clothing, several men on tail board, (3) Loaned 3 ton Lorry, clothes, stores, men. (4) Foden Thresh with men wherever they could sit, on the cylinders etc. 3 Bicyclists on bicycles, batman on horse. Another 3 ton lorry was required as about 15 men got conveyed by Salvage Coy Lorry + even then all my M.T. was overloaded. ATF.	
VIGNACOURT	20		Arranged billet at BELLOY-SUR-SOMME took over from acting O.C. 56th Dis. Moved advance party of section to BELLOY-S-SOMME. Aff.	

T2134. Wt. W708—776. 50000. 4/15. Sir J. C. & S.

Army Form C. 2118.

WAR DIARY
or
INTELLIGENCE SUMMARY.
(Erase heading not required.)

Instructions regarding War Diaries and Intelligence Summaries are contained in F. S. Regs., Part II. and the Staff Manual respectively. Title pages will be prepared in manuscript.

Place	Date	Hour	Summary of Events and Information	Remarks and references to Appendices
VIGNACOURT	OCT 21 1916		Moved to BELLOY-SUR SOMME doing several journeys with each lorry	A.Q.
BELLOY-SUR SOMME	22		Investigating area.	A.Q.
	23		Started baths at VIGNACOURT and at FLESSELLES. Arrangements very primitive as all water has to be drawn up in bucket from a deep well. 1 Le Blanc Spray at each place. Capacity 40 per hour at each place. Arranged for collection of excreta by cart at PICQUIGNY to a factory chimney which 9 Rfd can be made into a fine incinerator for excreta. Investigated area for site for better baths.	A.Q.
"	24		Went VIGNACOURT, FLESSELLES, VAUX, PICQUIGNY w Col Dundas who expressed himself as satisfied with bath arrangements + prepared to construction of baths at PICQUIGNY if good site found — Found a good site close to river + Rfd to set baths in good order in 4 days after getting material. All efforts to get material have failed so far.	A.Q.
"	25		Incinerator working well but will not be able to deal with excreta from 2000 troops. Got out detailed estimate for material for baths. Went AMIENS for noses missing from baths at VIGNACOURT, none obtainable but some Rose sprays are being altered to fit.	A.Q.
"	26		Indents for material for baths being hastened by A.D.M.S. applied to A.D.M.S. furposts of S. Sanitary Officer now vacant.	A.Q.

Army Form C. 2118.

WAR DIARY
or
INTELLIGENCE SUMMARY.
(Erase heading not required.)

Place	Date	Hour	Summary of Events and Information	Remarks and references to Appendices
BILLON SUR SOMME	Oct 27		Timber for baths fetched from MERICOURT a distance of about 30 miles. A.F. Arranging details of construction of baths at PICQUIGNY. A.F.	
"	28		Inspection of billets. Football match between 61st F.A. & Sanitary Section at YBOX. A.F. & Sanitary Section in morning after visit to baths in construction at [illegible]	
"	29		Bicycled FIESSELLES & VIGNACOURT. A.F. Gaol section. Ball construction proceeding well at PICQUIGNY. A.F.	
"	30		Paid Laundry at AMIENS on visit to A.D.M.S. Inspections at PICQUIGNY and baths there. A.F.	
"	31		Details of bath construction will be given next month. Visit to CAVILLON to take over from outgoing Division. (2nd Indian Cavalry) A.F.	

A.F. Gorman
Captain Comm. (T)
O.C. SANITARY SECTION 33,
ATTACHED XX(th) (LIGHT) DIVISION.

33rd SANITARY SECTION
AND
BATHS & LAUNDRIES,
20th (LIGHT) DIVISION.
No. 3/10/16

Appendix A.

SANITARY REPORT — weekly

Up to and including Saturday 7th. October 1916.

DISPOSITION.

The disposition of Sanitary Section (27 N.C.Os. & men) and attached personnel (31 N.C.O. & men):

Headquarters Sanitary Section, MEAULTE.
14 N.C.Os. & men allotted duties as follows:
S/Sergt. supervising work of section in forward area.
Clerical & personal staff.
Water duties at Reserve supply, MONTAUBAN-BERNAFAY.
Sanitary constructional work in MEAULTE.
Lorry drivers.

BATHS, MEAULTE.
20 N.C.O. & men allotted duties as follows:
Q.M.S. i/c of Baths.
Baths personnel.
Lorry drivers.
Steam THRESH DISINFECTOR drivers.

MINDEN POST.
18 N.C.Os. & men allotted duties as follows:
Sanitary Inspection & duties at Divisional Headquarters.
Water duties.
Sanitary Inspection Artillery D.A.C. & A.S.C.
Supervision of fatigue parties at Advanced & Rear Divn. HQrs.
Distribution of disinfectants & Anti-Frost Bite preparations.

59th BRIGADE.
60th BRIGADE.
61st BRIGADE.
(1 Sergt. i/c Sanitary Inspection
(& 1 N.C.O. i/c Water attached
(to each Brigade.

This disposition varied during the week.

SANITATION.

Inspections have been daily of Units in the Division by Inspectors detailed for this work. The Sanitary Condition found are as follows:

Unit.	State of Camps and Billets.	Remarks.
Divn. Hd. Qrs. (FORKED TREE & MINDEN POST).	Satisfactory	Moved to Minden Post 1/10/16. There are not a sufficient number of latrines at Minden Post. There were 5 only & about 200 men are using them (including the 3rd. London Regt.) (Many of these 200 are not Hd.Qrs. units.)
Divn. Hd. Qrs. "G".	Satisafctory.	Incinerator impossible; some rubbish is burnt daily in a trench, remainder buried. Latrines improved. Two grease traps made.
C.R.A. (Minden Post)	Satisafctory.	Hd.Qrs. Sanitary Arrangements used by this Section. Manure is being slowly burnt
C.R.A. (Advanced).	Satisfactory.	
C.R.E. (Minden Post).	Satisfactory.	Only one latrine for the whole of this section (about 20 men). Hd.Qrs. Incinerator & ablution used.
M.M.P. (8 men only)	Satisfactory.	Hd.Qrs. latrine, incinerator & ablution arrangements used.
Divn. Signal Coy. Transport.	Satisfactory.	Open latrines in use Manure is carted away daily. (Friday-Latrines have been covered in.)
Traffic Control. (about 40 men)	Satisfactory.	Hd. Qrs. latrines incinerator & ablution arrangements used.

59th. BRIGADE.

Unit	State	Remarks
Brigade Headquarters. and Transport.	Satisfactory	
10th. R.B. and Transport.	Satisfactory.	
11th. R.B. and Transport	Satisafctory.	
10th. K.R.R. and Transport.	Satisafctory.	
11th. K.R.R. and Transport.	Satisfactory.	
50th. Machine Gun Coy. & Transport	Satisfactory.	

Units.	State of Camps and Billets.	Remarks.
96th. Field Coy. R.E. and Transport.	Satisfactory.	

60th. BRIGADE.

Units.	State of Camps and Billets.	Remarks.
12th. R.B. and Transport.	Fairly Satisfactory.	Improvements in latrines shown but not at all fly proof. At Transport lines latrines are not fly-proof but otherwise they are satisfactory.
12th. K.R.R. and Transport.	Fairly Satisfactory.	No incinerator. At Transport lines latrines are not fly-proof as it is stated that boxes are difficult to get for this purpose. Where possible they erected. On entering the site it was dirty and a lot of cleaning work has been done.
6th. Oxon. & Bucks. and Transport.	Satisfactory.	Not all latrines are fly proof.
6th. K.S.L.I. and Transport.	Satisfactory.	Not all latrines are fly proof.
60th. Machine Gun Coy. and Transport.	Fairly Satisfactory.	At Transport lines latrines are not fly proof as it is stated that boxes are not obtainable.
83rd. Field Coy. R.E. and Transport.	Satisfactory.	

Note:- The Camp Site which the 60th. Brigade Transport took over was in a very dirty condition & has necessitated a good deal of work. It is now satisfactory.

61st. BRIGADE.

Units.	State of Camps and Billets.	Remarks.
Brigade Hd. Qrs. & Transport.	Satisafctory.	
7th. K.O.Y.L.I. & Transport.	Fairly Satisafctory.	No ablution arrangements. Otherwise satisafctory.
6th. D.C.L.I. and Transport.	Fairly Satisfactory.	No ablution arrangements. Otherwise Satisfactory.

Unit.	State of Camps and Billets.	Remarks.
12th. King's(Liverpool) Regt. & Transport.	Fairly Satisafctory.	No ablution arrangements. Too much manure.
7th. Somerset L.I. and Transport.	Fairly Satisfactory.	No ablution arrangements. Too much manure.
84th. Field Coy. R.E. and Transport.	~~Fairly~~ Satisafctory.	

During the week the Brigade has only been out of action for 48 hours. The Camps were inspected & very few Sanitary arrangements were found and owing to the shortness of the stay no improvements could be made.
On vacation they were inspected and the Camp of the 7th. D.C.L.I. was left in a very unsatisfactory state, but this has since been cleaned up by them.

ARTILLERY. *Wagon lines.*

Unit	State	Remarks
B/91st. R.F.A.	Fair. *Not satisfactory 10/10/16*	Latrines not fly-proof and no ablution arrangements. Manure is buried.
D/91st.R.F.A.	Fair only. *Now greatly improved 10/10/16*	No box latrines, grease trap or ablution arrangements. Have promised to rectify.
92nd. Brigade R.F.A. Headquarters.	Fair. *Wheelwright Nr available attending F.P. latrine. 10/10/16*	Latrines not fly-proof & no ablution arrangements.
A/92nd. R.F.A.	Fair. *Now quite satisfactory 10/10/16*	Latrines not fly-proof & no ablution arrangements.
~~B/8~~ B/92nd R.F.A.	Satisfactory.	
C/92nd. R.F.A.	Fair. *Now vacated in clean condition 10/10/16*	Latrines not fly-proof & no ablution arrangements.
D/92nd R.F.A.	Fair. *Now vacated in clean condition*	Box latrines without ends. No incinerator. No ablution arrangements. Units have promised to rectify these deficiencies.

Unit.	State of Camps and Billets.	Remarks.
A/93rd. R.F.A.	Fair.	No box latrines. No incinerator. No ablution arrangements. Unit has promised to rectify.
B/93rd. R.F.A.	Fair.	No box latrines. No incinerators. Unit has promised to rectify these things.
D/93rd. R.F.A.	Fair only.	No box latrines. No incinerator. No grease pit. Unit has promised to rectify these things.
Divn. Ammunition Column. Sections 1,2,3,&4. S.A.Sections 2&3.	Satisfactory	A number of unburnt tins were left on manure heaps & incinerator. Since vacated.
S.A.Section 4.	Fair only.	No ablution arrangements. No incinerator. Waste pit full of unburnt tins but effort made to burn these.

In the case of units which have been frequently moving and fighting the provision of satisfactory ablution arrangements and disposal of manure could scarcely be expected at once under the conditions obtaining.

WATER.

During the week an investigation was carried out of the various water supplies used by the Division.
Surprise tests for free chlorine have been carried from the water in the carts of the Brigade & the water has been found to be efficiently chlorinated.
The N.C.O. i/c water attached to each Brigade has paid visits to the Brigade sources of supply & has supervised the filling of the petrol cans.

TALUS BOISE.

An examination of this supply was made on 30th. ult.
1. Water carts are filled from a large shallow reservoir. This is uncovered & a lot of dust is blown into it from the track, used very largely by horse traffic. The R.E. Corporal i/c states that reservoir cannot be cleaned until he can obtain a working party. This is filled at times by water pumped from a similar reservoir (also dirty and uncovered) on the opposite side of the road.
2. Nine tanks serve to fill water bottles, petrol cans & dixies. These tanks were dirty but are being cleaned out. They are uncovered. The water is of good quality and comes from a deep chalk well at SUZANNE.

MONTAUBAN.

The Chlorination of water at this refilling point has been carefully supervised and an N.C.O. has been on duty for this purpose.

The water is drawn from a chalk well at CARNOY about 150 feet deep.

The bleaching powder on the carts of the following Units was found to need replenishing & instructions have been given for this to be attended to:

D/92nd. R.F.A.
60th. Machine Gun Coy.
D/93rd. R.F.A.
7th. K.O.Y.L.I.
11th. D.L.I.
81st. Machine Gun Coy.
94th. Field Coy. R.E.
82nd. Field Ambulance.

143 Fillings of Divisional carts were supervised. All were satisfactory with the foregoing exceptions.

CARNOY.

The same applies to this water refilling point.

RESERVE STORE AT MONTAUBAN-BERNAFAY.

I personally made tests of the water in the cans of the reserve store and I was not at all satisfied. The water varied greatly and whereas some cans seemed to be washed properly and a dose of bleaching powder equi--valent to 1.2 parts of chlorine per million was ample, others required 2.4 parts per million. Some cans con--tained obviously dirty water with a smell of petrol and an oily flavour. These tests we continued for two days & ½ of the store was condemned. The source of the supply was subsequently visited and also the cleaning process was investigated and the latter is certainly inefficiently & very unsatisfactorily carried out. I made a suggestion to the A.D.M.S. that the cans con--taining drinking water be plainly marked as such & that they should be properly cleaned under skilled supervision and later I have suggested an arrangement which has been approved, whereby the cans can be steamed on my FODEN-THRESH Disinfector under the super--vision of my N.C.Os. A sample of the water from the store has been taken and submitted for bacteriological analysis.

FRICOURT.

On one day the supplies at MONTAUBAN and CARNOY broke down and many carts refilled at FRICOURT,

GENERAL WORK

Divn. Hd. Qrs. (Rear).

Messes & Mess Kitchens sprayed out daily.
Dug-outs disinfected.
New waste pit, ablution pit & grease pit dug.
Manure incinerator cleaned out & refuse buried.
2 old grease pits filled in.

Divn. Hd.Qrs. (Advanced).

Supervision of erection of latrine.

MEAULTE.

Filter at Divn. Baths cleaned out reconstructed
A skeleton filter had been started but was giving no purification and a great deal of crude soapy water was running into the river. I have completely re-designed the plant which is now in working order & delivering a clear effluent without any soapiness at all.

Latrine erected for bathers at the Baths.

New pump fitted at baths.

Shed erected at Baths for shelter for waiting bathing parties.

Public Latrine constructed.

On orders of D.D.M.S. 14th. Corps. R.O.D. Detachment inspected & certain Sanitary improvements suggested and supervision of erection of excreta incinerator.

Forward Area.

Supervision of burial of 2 horses.

Exposed refuse & excreta in various holes, trenches etc. covered

DISINFECTANTS ISSUED

Chloride of Lime..........	1830 lbs.
Cresoli........	125 galls.
Paraffin........	45 galls.
Bleaching Powder........	6 tins.
Latrine Paper........	16 bundles.
Whale Oil.....	55 galls.
Anti-Frost Grease........	378 lbs.

The difficulty of procuring fly-proof latrines is increasing as ammunition boxes have no lids obtained & other boxes are often needed for firewood.

List of Units Bathed during the week

    6th. Division. .... 4864 men

    2nd. Cavalry Divn............ 270 men

                            Total... 5534 men.

List of Clean Clothing issued
- Shirts...... 5516.
- Pants........ 3243.
- Socks........ 5254.
- Towels...... 1316.

List of Dirty Clothing Received
- Shirts........ 4694.
- Pants.......... 2655.
- Socks........ 3266.
- Towels........ 1115.

No. of Articles passed through THRESH Steam disinfector for Laundry............11,731.

[signature]

Captain R.A.M.C.(T).
O.C. SANITARY SECTION 83,
ATTACHED XXth (LIGHT) DIVISION.

Appendix B.

WEEKLY REPORT.

up to and including Saturday 14th. October 1916.

Disposition.

The disposition of Sanitary Section personnel (27 N.C.Os & men) and attached personnel (22 N.C.Os & men) on Saturday 14th. October 1916 was as follows:-

Headquarters, Sanitary Section MEAULTE.	) 27 N.C.Os & men allotted) duties as follows:) S/Sergt. supervising) work of Section.) Clerical & personal staff) Sanitary inspection of) Artillery & D.A.C. & A.SC) Water duties to Units) other than Brigades.) Supervision of fatigue) parties.) Sanitary constructional) work at MEAULTE.) Lorry drivers.) Fatigues.) Distribution of disinfect) -ants, anti-frost bite) preparation etc.) Disinfection of Blankets.
Baths. MEAULTE.	) N.C.Os & men allotted) duties as follows:) O.R.T. i/c Baths.) Baths personnel.) Lorry drivers.) Steam THRESH disinfect-) -or drivers.
Divisional Headquarters.	) N.C.Os for Sanitary) inspection & duties at) Divisional Headquarters.
59th. Brigade. 60th. Brigade. 61st. Brigade.	) 1 Sergt. i/c & 1 N.C.O.) for Sanitary inspection) & water duties were) attached to each Brigade

This disposition varied during the week.

SANITATION.

Inspections have been made daily of Units in the Division by inspectors detailed for work. The sanitary conditions found were as follows:-

Unit.	State of Camps and Billets.	Remarks.
Divisional Hd.Qrs, (Chateau).	Satisfactory.	New latrines & urine pits constructed.
Divisional Hd. Qrs. (Mens' Billet).	Satisfactory.	Incinerator, grease & waste pits left in very bad state by previous occupants.
No. 2 Mess.	Satisfactory.	
No. 3 Mess.	Satisfactory.	
Divn. Signal Coy.	Fair.	Cookhouse & Billet left in dirty condition by previous unit. The yard of the Billet is always in a dirty condition; food thrown on to midden etc.
Divn. Signal Coy. Transport.	Fairly Satisfactory.	Manure being burned very slowly & a considerable amount left behind.
Traffic Control.	Satisfactory.	
M.M.Police and French Police.	Satisfactory.	Billet & yard left in dirty condition by previous unit. Manure removed weekly by farmer.
Divn. Hd. Qrs. Transport.	Satisfactory.	Manure being slowly burned. Also removed weekly by farmers.
C.R.E.	Satisfactory.	
Divn. Band.	Satisfactory.	New fly-proof latrine constructed & great amount of rubbish cleaned away.

59th. BRIGADE.

Unit	State	Remarks
Brigade Hd.Qrs.	Satisfactory.	
Brigade Hd. Qrs. Transport.	Satisfactory.	
10th.R.B. and Transport.	Satisfactory.	
10th.K.R.R. and Transport.	Satisfactory.	
11th. R.B. and Transport.	Satisfactory.	
11th. K.R.R. and Transport.	Satisfactory.	

Unit.	State of Camps and Billets.	Remarks.
59th. Machine Gun Coy.	Satisfactory.	New latrines constructed. Incinerator cleared out & a large amount of old rubbish buried.
98th. Field Coy. R.E.	Satisfactory.	
159th. Coy. A.S.C.	Satisfactory.	
60th. BRIGADE.		
Brigade Hd.Qrs.	Satisfactory.	Incinerator & grease trap of 6th. K.S.L.I. used by arrangement.
Brigade Hd. Qrs. Transport.	Satisfactory.	
Brigade Signals & Transport,	Satisfactory.	
12th. R.B. and Transport.	Satisfactory.	Box latrines constructed.
12th. K.R.R. and Transport.	Satisfactory	Box latrines constructed.
6th. Oxon. & Bucks. & Transport.	Satisfactory.	New box latrine constructed and urine dug.
6th. K.S.L.I. and Transport.	Particularly Good.	
60th. Machine Gun Coy. & Transport.	Satisfactory.	
Trench Mortar Battery.	Satisfactory.	
84th. Field Coy. R.E.	Satisfactory.	
160th. Coy. A.S.C.	Satisfactory.	
61st. Field Ambulance. (Stretcher Bearers Section).	Satisfactory.	Manure burning.
61st. BRIGADE.		
Brigade Hd.Qrs.	Satisfactory.	
Brigade Hd.Qrs. Transport.	Satisfactory.	
7th. K.O.Y.L.I. & Transport.	Satisfactory.	
8th. D.C.L.I. and Transport.	Satisfactory.	

Unit.	State of Camps and Billets.	Remarks.
12th. King's (Liverpool) Regt. & Transport.	Satisfactory.	
7th. Somerset L.I.	Satisfactory	
81st. Machine Gun Coy. & Transport.	Satisfactory.	
161st. Coy. A.S.C.	Satisfactory.	

ARTILLERY.

Unit	State	Remarks
B/91st. R.F.A.	Satisfactory.	New grease pit required
D/91st. R.F.A.	Satisfactory.	
92nd Brigade Hd.Qrs.	Satisfactory	
A/92nd. R.F.A.	Good.	
B/92nd. R.F.A.	Good.	Manure Buried.
C/92nd. R.F.A.	Poor.	Improvements pro--mised; since when we have left area.
A/93rd. R.F.A.	Satisfactory.	
B/93rd. R.F.A.	Satisfactory.	
D/93rd. R.F.A.	Satisfactory.	
158th. Coy.A.S.C.	Satisfactory.	

OTHER UNITS.

Unit	State	Remarks
Mobile Veterinary Section	Satisfactory.	
Salvage Coy.	Fairly Satisfactory.	No fly-Proof Latrine.
11D.L.I.	Fairly Satisfactory.	Not entirely satisfactory but marked improvement in progress.

WATER.

The Sources at MONTAUBAN & CARNOY were supervised up to the time the Divn. vacated the forward area.

Surprise tests for free chlorine have been carried out on the water carts of the Division with the following results;

(4).

Unit.	Result.
Divn. Signal Coy.	Free Chlorine present.
10th. K.R.R.	" " "
16th. K.R.R.	" " "
10th. R.B.	" " "
11th. R.B.	" " "
59th. Machine Gun Coy.	" " "
159th. Coy. A.S.C.	" " "
95th. Field Coy. R.E.	" " "
60th. Field Ambulance.	" " "
12th. K.R.R.	" " "
12th. R.B.	" " "
6th. Oxon. & Bucks.	" " "
6th. K.S.L.I.	" " "
60th. Machine Gun Coy.	" " "
160th. Coy A.S.C.	" " "
84th. Field Coy R.E.	" " "
61st. Field Ambulance.	" " "
7th. Somerset L.I.	" " "
12th. King's (Liverpool) Regt.	" " "
9th. D.C.L.I.	" " "
85rd. Field Coy. R.E.	" " "
62nd. Field Ambulance.	" " "
Hd. Qrs. D.A.C.	" " "
No. 1 Section D.A.C.	" " "
D/91st. R.F.A.	" " "
Hd. Qrs. 92nd. R.F.A.	" " "
B/92nd. R.F.A.	" " "
D/92nd. R.F.A.	" " "

The sources from which the Division has been drawing water are as follows:-

FRICOURT.
CARNOY.
MINDEN POST.
MONTAUBAN.
VILLE.- Tanks near village supplied from a deep well. R.A.M.C. men under the 4th. Army Water Column test the water daily & chlorinate each cart accordingly.

Well in Y.M.C.A. yard used for cooking purposes.

Several wells in Billets used for cooking pur--poses.

All drinking water has to be drawn from the Battalion Carts.

BUIRE.- Supply Chlorinated by R.A.M.C. men.

MERICOURT. - Deep well in court yard off the square.

DECORDEL.
ALBERT.
MEAULTE. - River water supplied after purification by Water Column.

I feel sure that a number of water bottles get filled at village wells, which must always be regarded as dangerous and those wells are used by the Owners of Billets it is not possible to put them out of action. The only way to make this action less frequent would be by the issue of stringent orders by O.C. Units.

The following deficiencies have been noted in water carts. These deficiencies have been brought to the notice of the various Quartermasters concerned.

Unit.	No. of Cart.	Equipment wanted.	Repairs.
7th. K.O.Y.L.I.	E 70288.	3 cloths. 1 cylinder. 1 Curved brush.	
7th. K.O.Y.L.I.	E 70305.	3 cloths. 1 cylinder. 1 Float.	
7th. Somerset L.I.	E 70308.	1 Cylinder. 1 Hose pipe. 1 Curved brush. 1 Cage & Ball. 1 Float.	
7th. Somerset L.I.	E 70691.	1 Gauze. 1 Curved brush.	Gauze holder wants re-soldering.
12th. King's (Liverpool) Regt.	E70343.	3 cloths. 2 Curved brush.	Part of tap pipe missing. Only 2 taps working.
12th. King's (Liverpool) Regt.	E68164.	1 Curved brush. 1 Cylinder. 2 cloths.	Small leak at centre joint of tap pipe wants stopping
7th. D.C.L.I.	E68349.	1 Spanner. 1 Float.	Pump broken & screw missing. Joint from barrel to tap pipe leaks badly. Washer missing from one tap.
7th. D.C.L.I.	E70332.	1 Hose pipe. 1 Spanner. 1 Float. 1 Curved brush 2 Guazes.	Leaky tap. Tap pipe wants ¼" cut off to allow of tighter screw-ing of this tap;
6gst. M.O.C.	M10030?.	1 curved brush. 3 cloths. 1 float. 1 tank for boiling cloths.	
84th. Field Coy R.E.	E6843	2 Gauzes.	Small leak at central joint of tap pipe.
62nd. Field Ambulance	E70340.	1 Curved brush.	
62nd Field Ambulance.	E64586.	1 Curved brush.	
do do do Hospital.	E70315	2 Gauzes 1 Curved brush.	

Unit.	No. of Cart.	Repairs.
13th. R.B.	E70836.	Leaks slightly left side bottom of tank.
13th. R.B.	E63973.	India rubber pipe from cylinder to tank perishing. Tap out of order.
84th. R.E.	M34282.	Only one cloth, this in bad condition. No spares. Pump out of order.
12th. K.R.R.	E63977.	Crack (about 10 to 12 inches long) by rivets down left side of tank. Pipe feeding taps badly leaking. Also leaks under iron band that holds tank in position and one band broken.
12th. K.R.R.	E62817.	Leaks in body of tank.

GENERAL WORK.

Meaulte.

Fly proof latrine fixed to billets of 7th.K.O.Y.L.I. 7th.D.C.L.I. and 62nd Field Ambulance.

Various well-head repaired.

Troux.

Supervision of fatigue parties cleaning out and burning refuse near large incinerator and digging new latrines & urine pits at Divn. Hd. Qrs.

Sandpits.

About 500 yards disused trench containing old clothing, tins & refuse covered.

2 old disused incinerators & uncovered waste pits filled in.

3 old latrines demolished & 2 refuse pits & about 100 yards of trench cleared.

DISINFECTIONS.

Headquarters Messes & Mess kitchens sprayed daily.

Manure heaps at Transport lines sprayed frequently.

All billets occupied by 7th. D.C.L.I. sprayed.

Messes, Mess kitchens & Latrines at 61st Brigade Hd. Qrs. sprayed.

Some blankets were disinfected for Camp Commandant Sandpits. Some of these blankets were very lousy and arrangements had been made to continue this work, when the Section had to proceed to CORBIE. The blankets will therefore remain lousy. This state of affairs is bound to be chronic until some other arrangements are made with regard to blankets.

If sanitary sections undertake the work they will usually be moving just at the time when the blankets can be most easily spared. If they do not undertake the work there will probably be an increase of lousiness and also of skin diseases.

Everyone concerned is anxious for some other arrangement and I think a strong letter from you on the subject to "Q" would give them the authority they desire to back up the efforts they have already made to get this matter put on a sounder footing

---

List of parties bathed during the week:

7th. Somerset L.I.	628.
7th. K.O.Y.L.I.	436.
7th. D.C.L.I.	431.
6th. K.S.L.I.	526.
11th. Durham L.I.	155.
12th. King's (Liverpool) Regt.	350.
10th. K.R.R.	470.
12th. K.R.R.	438.
6th. Oxon. & Bucks.	385.
12th. R.B.	355.
61st. M.G.C.	122.
60th. M.G.C.	134.
83rd. Field Coy. R.E.	100.
84th. Field Coy. R.E.	135.
60th. Field Ambulance	30.
62nd. Field Ambulance	144.
91st. Brigade R.F.A.	20.
92nd. Brigade R.F.A.	25.
20th Divn. Salvage Coy.	40.
20th. Divn. Trench Mor. Battery	30.
160th. Coy. A.S.C.	50.
14th. Corps Water Supply Col. A.S.C.(M.T.)	60.
Prisoners of War Camp Guard	30.
R.G.A.	20.
Total.	5024.

List of Clean Clothing issued.

Shirts	6772.
Pants	5799.
Socks	5508.
Towels	1568.

List of Dirty Clothing Received.

Shirts	6781.
Pants	5401.
Socks	5961.
Towels	1457.

No. of Articles passed through "THRESH" Steam Disinfector for Laundry............ 18,400.

No. of Blankets passed through "THRESH" Steam Disinfector for Indian Hospital, MEAULTE............ 100.

List of Disinfectants issued.

Chloride of Lime..........	2790 lbs.
Cresoli...............	156 galls.
Paraffin........	180 galls.
Formaldehyde.........	2 galls.
Bleaching Powder........	72 tins.
Clarifying Powder......	8 tins.
Latrine Paper.......	18 bundles.
Anti-Vermin Powder.......	40 lbs.
Whale Oil........	5 galls.
Anti-Frost Bite Grease.......	60 tins.

[signature]

Captain R.A.M.C.(T.F.).
O.C. SANITARY SECTION 33,
ATTACHED XXth (LIGHT) DIVISION.

Appendix C

To.

A.D.M.S.
20th. Division.

Owing to frequent moves by most units and short periods of rest in any one place, no detailed report is submitted this week.

Many inspections of water carts have been made and all were found to be chlorinated satisfactorily.

The following carts have been found to be defective.

7th. K.O.Y.L.I., Cart No. 0705 V/1915, new left side wheel wanted. Barrel leaks at several places from loose rivet holes.

7th. K.O.Y.L.I., Cart No. 70288 V/1914, barrel leaks at rivet holes.

Many billet inspections have made and conditions were as satisfactory as could be expected with the following exception.

M.M.P. and French Police billet at CORBIE was vacated on October 1-th. leaving a number of unburnt tins and refuse.

List of Disinfectants issued:

Chloride of Lime.........	1500 lbs.
Creosoli........	60 galls.
Paraffin.....	35 galls.
Formaldehyde.........	3 galls.
Bleaching Powder........	24 tins.
Latrine Paper..........	3 bundles.

List of Parties Bathed:

12th. King's (Liverpool) Regt...	24.
7th. Somerset L.I......	140.
7th. D.C.L.I.......	58.
R.F.A. T.M. Battery........	42.
M.G.C..60th. Brigade.......	24.
20th. Divn. Hd. Qrs.....	30.
12th. K.R.R......	70.
12th. R.B...........	148.
20th. Divn. Salvage Coy.......	34.
R.F.A. Hd. Qrs............	42.
62nd. Field Ambulance......	120.
German Prisoners......	400.
Total.....	1112.

List of Clean Clothing issued :

Shirts.....	608.
Pants...	481.
Socks....	501.
Towels....	55.

List of Dirty Clothing Received:

Shirts......	608.
Pants......	481.
Socks......	501.
Towels.........	55.

No. of Articles passed through "THRESH" Steam Disinfector for Laundry........ 3645.

[signature]

Captain R.A.M.C.(T).

O.C. SANITARY SECTION 33,
ATTACHED XXth (LIGHT) DIVISION.

Appendix D.

REPORT

для week ending 28th. October 1916.

Disposition.

The disposition of Sanitary Section personnel (27 N.C.Os and men), and attached personnel (32 N.C.Os & men) on Saturday 28th. October 1916 was as follows:

Headquarters, Sanitary Section BELLOY-Sur-SOMME.	29 N.C.Os & men allotted duties as follows: S/Sergt. supervising work of Section. Clerical & personal staff. Sanitary of inspection of Headquarters, Divisional Troops, A.S.C. & 7th. D.C.L.I Water duties to Divn. Troops. Supervision of fatigue parties. Sanitary constructional work at BELLOY-Sur-SOMME. Lorry Drivers. Fatigues. Distribution of Disinfectants.
Baths, FLESSELLES.	13 N.C.O.s & men allotted duties as follows Q.M.S. i/c Baths. Baths personnel. Lorry drivers. Steam "THRESH" Disinfector Drivers.
Baths, VIGNACOURT.	7 N.C.O.s & men allotted duties as follows: L/Corporal i/c Baths. Baths personnel.
PICQUIGNY.	1 Sergt. i/c & 2 N.C.Os for Sanitary inspection & 1 N.C.O. i/c Water, attached 59th. Brigade. 1 Corporal i/c Constructional work for new Baths.
VAUX, 60th. Brigade. St.SAUVEUR, 61st Brigade.	1 Sergt. i/c & 1 N.C.O. for Sanitary inspection & 1 N.C.O. i/c Water, attached to each Bde.

SANITATION.

Inspections have been made daily of Units in the Division, by inspectors detailed for the work. The Sanitary Conditions found were as follows:

Unit.	State of Camps and Billets.	Remarks.
G.O.C/s. Billet & No.1 Mess.	Good.	New latrine made for servants. All rubbish etc. removed daily by Hd. Qrs. fatigues.
No.2 Mess & "O" & "A" & "Q".	Good.	New latrine made. New incinerator, waste pit & ablution pit made.
No.3 Mess	Good.	New latrine made.
Hd. Qrs. Transport.	Good.	Manure deposited in large manure pit at Chateau.
D.A.D.O.S.	Satisfactory.	Billet was in a very dirty state when taken over. New latrines made & grease pit, waste pit & urine pit dug.
Salvage Coy.	Satisfactory.	New latrine made incinerator built, & waste pit, grease pit & urine pit dug.
Divn. Signal Coy.	Satisfactory.	Billet was in a very dirty state when taken over. New latrine made & urine & grease pits dug. Manure is now removed daily & is taken away by farmer.
Divn. Signal Coy. Transport.	Satisfactory.	Manure is being burnt.
M.M.Police	Satisfactory.	Billet was in a very dirty state when taken over. Manure has been moved to bottom of garden 50 yards from billet, and is being burnt.

Unit.	State of Camps and Billets.	Remarks.
Traffic Control.	Satisfactory.	Sanitary arrangements are/shared with M.M.P. as there is no room for latrines in this billet.
Divn. School of Instruction.	Satisfactory.	New latrine dug. Several loads of old tins & rubbish removed.
32nd. Mobile Veterinary Section.	Satisfactory.	Trench latrine used. Refuse buried. Manure removed to an adjoining orchard for a civilian.
59th. Bde. Hd. Qrs. & Transport.	Satisfactory.	
59th. Bde. Signals.	Satisfactory.	
10th. K.R.R. & Transport.	Satisfactory	Except no fly-proofed latrines. Excreta & rubb-ish collected daily & burnt.
11th. K.R.R. & Transport.	Satisfactory.	
10th R.B. & Transport.	Satisfactory.	Except no fly-proofed latrines.
11th. R.B. & Transport.	Satisfactory.	
59th. Machine Gun Coy. & Trench.	Satisfactory.	
60th. Brigade Hd.Qrs. & Signals.	Satisfactory.	
12th. K.R.R.	Satisfactory.	
12th. R.B.	Satisfactory.	
6th. Oxon. & Bucks.L.I. & Transport.	Satisfactory.	
6th. Shropsshire L.I.	Excellent.	
60th. Machine Gun Coy.	Satisfactory.	Arrangements made with Mayor for removal of manure.

Unit.	State of Camps and Billets.	Remarks.
Trench Mortar Batt.	Satisfactory.	Incinerator shared with Machine Gun Coy.
150th. Coy A.S.C.	Satisfactory.	
61st Bde. Hd. Qrs.	Satisfactory.	
7th. K.O.Y.L.I. & Transport.	Satisfactory.	
12th. King's (Liverpool) Regt. & Transport.	Satisfactory.	
7th. Somerset L.I. & Transport.	Satisfactory.	Unit being unable to get boxes or timber deep trench latrines have been used and are satisfactory.
7th. Cornwalls.	Satisfactory.	Shallow trench latrines used. Public latrines in course of construction. Urine pits dug. Ablution benches to be built.
61st. Machine Gun Coy. & Transport.	Satisfactory	
Trench Mortar Batt.	Satisfactory.	

The Sanitary Conditions of the Divn. are in a very satisfactory state & a lot of work has been put in on construction of fly-proofed latrines and the digging of waste pits and urine pits during the week. Difficulty in procuring timber has been experienced & this delayed work which otherwise would have been done earlier in the week. Some units still find difficulty in obtaining boxes for making fly-proofed latrines.

The principal defect is lack of ablution benches and waste pits for soapy water in many units, but this relatively unimportant matter is receiving attention.

WATER.

Tests have been made from the water carts in the divn. and in each case the water has been found to be satisfactorily chlorinated.

The 59th. Brigade draws its water from the pump in the Square at PICQUIGNY.

An examination of the water carts of the 59th. Bde. has been carried out with the following results:

Unit.	Cart No.	Remarks.
10th. K.R.R.	E64162.	Barrel, and pipe feeding taps, leak slightly
10th. K.R.R.	E85658	Good condition. Deficient in long handled brushes for cleaning.
11th. K.R.R.	E69621	Leaks slightly; one tap not usable. Cart to be re-paired shortly.
11TH. K.R.R.	E85003	Leaks slightly. Equipment either complete or indented for.
10th. R.B.	E70307	Barrel leaks slightly.
10th. R.B.	E131272	Good condition. Equipment Complete.
11th. R.B.	E73657) E70294)	Good condition.
59th. M.G.C.		Cart has been condemned by I.O.M. and new one is indented for. Leaks badly and taps are defective; pumps out of order. (These facts have been reported previously.) Pending the arrival of the new cart, water is boiled for drinking. The well from which it is drawn is 50 feet deep, well bricked in and covered. No obvious source of contamination is near.
159th. Coy A.S.C.	E70295	Cart in good condition and equipment is complete. Cart was repaired 6 weeks ago.

Unit.	Cart No.	Remarks.
60th. Field Ambulance	E70313	Leaks slightly; some equipment lost up the line, but deficiencies have been indented for.
60th. Field Ambulance.	E85618	New cart.
60th. Field Ambulance.	E70336.	Leaks slightly; equipment complete.

A further examination of the water carts of the 61st. Brigade has been carried out with the following results and a list of equipment and repairs required handed to the M.O. i/c or Quartermaster concerned :

Unit.	Cart No.	Remarks.
7th. K.O.Y.L.I.	E70288.	Barrel leaks at rivet holes.
161st. Coy.A.S.C.	E70335.	Equipment wanted : 1 Curved brush. 2 Cloths. 1 Cylinder.

The water carts of the Machine Gun Company and the A.S.C. have been cleaned thoroughly inside and instructions given to all men in charge of the carts to keep them scrupulously clean.

GENERAL WORK :-

BELLOY-sur-SOMME.

Supervising rebuilding of incinerator and digging of refuse pits at Salvage Company's Billet.

Supervising burning of a collection of tins and other rubbish dumped in the village.

Supervising construction of urine pits in the village.

Supervising digging of waste pits and burial of burnt tins at Divisional Headquarters, Transport.

Building incinerator at Divisional Headquarters.

Public latrine erected in the village.

Supervision of erection of new latrines, and digging of waste pits, grease pits and ablution pits at G.O.C's Billet, Divisional Headquarters, No. 3 Mess, D.A.D.O.S. Divisional Signal Company's Billet, Divisional School of Instruction and Billets of 7th. Cornwalls.

Preparing signboards in French for marking latrines on evacuation of area.

PICQUIGNY.

Superintending collection and disposal of refuse and excreta from Billets and town and incineration of it.

Construction of Baths. A good site has been selected on an island on the Somme in a decayed mill. After much trouble timber has been secured and a great deal of construction work put in. It is hoped to have the work sufficiently advanced by the 1st. November to start bathing.

MONTONVILLERS.

Superintendence of fatigue party opening and cleansing drain from Chateau occupied by the 61st. Field Ambulance.

VIGNACOURT.

Baths were put into operation at the rate of 40 men per hour two days after entering present area.

FLESSELLES.

Baths were put into operation at the rate of 40 men per hour two days after entering present area.

DISINFECTION.

Disinfection of room and bedclothing following case of German Measles in 11th. Rifle Brigade at PICQUIGNY.

Disinfection following case of German Measles in 7th. Somerset L.I. and 7th. K.O.Y.L.I. at VAUX and St. VAST respectively.

Disinfection following case of German measles at Billet No. 102 Rue d'Amiens, FLESSELLES, occupied by 12th. K.R.R. Clothing of contacts and the billet thoroughly sprayed.

About 100 blankets were disinfected for Field Ambulances by passing through the Thresh.

DISINFECTANTS ISSUED.

Chloride of Lime.	2900 lbs.
Creosoli.	205 gals.
Paraffin.	150 gals.
Formalin.	3 gals.
Bleaching powder.	48 tins.
Anti-vermin powder.	60 lbs.
Oxford Grease.	60 lbs.

Captain R.A.M.C. (T).
O.C. Sanitary Section 33,
Attached XXth (Light) Division.

P.S. The supervision and checking of my inspectors and work generally has been rendered very difficult by lack of a car, particularly as there has been so much to be done in the construction of baths.

33rd Sanitary Section

COMMITTEE FOR THE
MEDICAL HISTORY OF THE WAR
Date -3 JAN.1917

ORIGINAL

Vol 13

Confidential

WAR DIARY

— of —

Captain A. F. GIRVAN. R.A.M.C. (T.F.)

Officer Commanding

33rd SANITARY SECTION

1st London (City of London) Sanitary Coy.
R.A.M.C. (T.F.)

ATTACHED

20th (LIGHT) DIVISION

B.E.F.

FRANCE.

November 1916

Volume 6.

Army Form C. 2118.

WAR DIARY
or
INTELLIGENCE SUMMARY.
(Erase heading not required.)

Instructions regarding War Diaries and Intelligence Summaries are contained in F. S. Regs., Part II. and the Staff Manual respectively. Title pages will be prepared in manuscript.

Place	Date	Hour	Summary of Events and Information	Remarks and references to Appendices
BELLOY SUR SOMME	Nov 1		Moved Section to RIENCOURT except for 1 man and 3 fatigues to guard stores which could not be moved in three lorry journeys. These stores consist of disinfectants and a Blanc Bains Douches à 12 Pommes. Moved Bath Plan personnel and clothes from Vignacourt and Flesselles to PICQUIGNY in time to open baths there at 11 am The floor plan of these Baths is indicated below	Appendix A.

R. SOMME.

WAR DIARY
or
INTELLIGENCE SUMMARY.
(Erase heading not required.)

Army Form C. 2118.

Place	Date	Hour	Summary of Events and Information	Remarks and references to Appendices
BELLOY SUR SOMME	Nov 1		These Baths involved a great deal of work, as dangerous masonry had to be pulled down, concrete floors put in, windows cemented to doors, doors made in walls, all benches etc had to be made and all materials brought from MEAULTE over 30 miles away by the 30 cwt Sun Sea Lorry. A BLANC BAINS-DOUCHES à 12 POMMES was installed. Upstairs accommodation provides for the whole of the Baths staff etc for billets. The Baths were ready for use in 5 days from the start. A.F.G.	
RIENCOURT	2		Various arrangements in connection with new area. Finding own 1 mile now converted to baths AMy	
"	3		A Bath House, minus water arrangements or heating, was in existence at RIENCOURT. Ante spray Blanc apparatus was installed and clothes boyler and baths were ready for use at full rate of 50 per hour on Nov 5. A.F.G.	
"	4		Visited MOLLIENS-VIDAME to search for site for baths. One found in square, has been used before. Building there, but nothing else except benches. Water has to be carried there. Installed for Blanc apparatus, tanks to hold the water & pumps. When these are received 2 days will see them quite ready. A.F.G.	Appendix R.
"	5		Visited HANGEST & BOURDON re Baths. Wrote a report answering complaint from N. 12 Mobile Lab. that water carts were not being cleaned properly. In my opinion the division was completely cleared. A.F.G.	

WAR DIARY
or
INTELLIGENCE SUMMARY.
(Erase heading not required.)

Army Form C. 2118.

Place	Date	Hour	Summary of Events and Information	Remarks and references to Appendices
RIENCOURT	NOV 6		Visit to Laundry at AMIENS today and to inspect caretaker's house damaged by Lorry	O/F
"	7		Various inspections + office work	O/F
"	8		Agreement for lease of mill at PICQUIGNY signed by owner. Passed to AA&QMG for retention	O/F
"	9		Lorry fetching tanks from MERICOURT	O/F
"	10		Meeting at ADMS' office to discuss winter plan arrived for XIV Corps	O/F
"	11		Instructed water duty men of 10 RB Saisseval in duties	O/F Appendix C.
"	12		Coy day of section. Various inspections. Tested various well & rain water reservoirs for chlorides with Truck Cabinet	O/F
"	13		SSO informed that requirements of whole Div while at approx. 20 gals per day and that of anti-frostbite grease 200 lbs per day. Bulk lorry taking all special establishments of water & oil tanks at PICQUIGNY and at RIENCOURT to respective town majors	O/F
"	14		Handed over billets to Capt MATHEWS 34 San Sec 17th Div.	O/F
"	15		Move to CORBIE. Got up at 5 am. San Sec CODY left at 6 am with self, last officer & General Staff	O/F Appendix D
			All men except staff + a few fatigues marched to CAVILLON (3 miles) + there entrussed for CORBIE. Baths lorry took remainder of stores to CORBIE. Batman + cyclists by road. Then CorPS G.T. Tech 1	
			Took over billets CORBIE from Capt Crawford O.C. San Sec 29th Div.	O/F

Army Form C. 2118.

WAR DIARY
or
INTELLIGENCE SUMMARY.
(Erase heading not required.)

Instructions regarding War Diaries and Intelligence Summaries are contained in F. S. Regs., Part II. and the Staff Manual respectively. Title pages will be prepared in manuscript.

Place	Date	Hour	Summary of Events and Information	Remarks and references to Appendices
	Nov			
CORBIE	16		Cadres arrived from Amiens and bathing started at Corbie 3 pm.	
			Arranged for 59. Bde to be relieved by Genel's Div. at Ville sur Ancre.	
			Sent in report on vacation of area including 20 maps made by one (or 2 Cox.) re indicating sites of latrines etc. Saw DAQMG XIV Corps re starting of Laundry at Corbie CORBIE. OSF.	
"	17		Investigating site for sand laundry machine from + list of machinery.	
			Various Confiners. OSF. 5 Salvage Coy. later men reported to OF	
"	18		Laundry preparations & plans. Inspections. OSF.	Appendix E.
"	19			Appendix F.
			A nursery sand site has been found & plans are made for washing machine.	
			I certify to carry out + drying Engine. Also a copper drying room to be heated from an existing boiler by steam pipes. OSF.	
"	20		Laundry plans further referred. Work started by RE. Said Laundry Coy at Amiens and examined washing done. OSF. Various inspections of billets OSF	
"	21		Going over normal work with Capt. Sabin who is carrying on for me during my charge to K.R. OSF	
"	22		Various inspections + visit with Gen. Commanding Div. to proposed laundry OSF	

T2134. Wt. W708—776. 500000. 4/15. Sir J. C. & S.

Army Form C. 2118.

WAR DIARY
or
INTELLIGENCE SUMMARY.
(Erase heading not required.)

Instructions regarding War Diaries and Intelligence Summaries are contained in F.S. Regs., Part II. and the Staff Manual respectively. Title pages will be prepared in manuscript.

Place	Date	Hour	Summary of Events and Information	Remarks and references to Appendices
CORBIE	Nov 23		Attended conference of O.C. San Secs XIV Corps at MEAULTE Corps HQ at which various subjects were discussed viz (1) Probable provision of train to be attached to each Sanitary Section (2) The question of attaching Sanitary Sections to areas in the Corps Area. (3) Deep versus shallow type of latrines. (4) Whether O's C San Secs should have Blue tab. Various other matters. Hence proceeded on leave to U.K. leaving Capt Sub. DARNIS to carry on from A.L.G.	

(signature)
Captain Renvie (T.F.)
O.C. SANITARY SECTION 38.
ATTACHED XXth (LIGHT) DIVISION.

P.T.O

Army Form C. 2118.

WAR DIARY
or
INTELLIGENCE SUMMARY.
(Erase heading not required.)

Instructions regarding War Diaries and Intelligence Summaries are contained in F. S. Regs., Part II. and the Staff Manual respectively. Title pages will be prepared in manuscript.

Place	Date	Hour	Summary of Events and Information	Remarks and references to Appendices
CORBIE	23/11/16		Learned temporarily from CAPT M.F. GIRVAN RAMC(T.D) on leave. Inspected premises at Divisional Baths CORBIE with reference to proposed alteration for starting Divisional Laundry. Inspection of billets CORBIE.	
	24/11/16		Inspection of billets in and around CORBIE	
	25/11/16		Inspection of billets in other areas of CORBIE	
	26.XI.16		Lecture at 29th Divl School of Instruction DAOURS. Paid detachment. Visited Divisional Baths & Laundry at VILLE-SUR-ANCRE.	
	27.XI.16		Inspected at VILLE, TREUX, MÉRICOURT. Visited R.E. Storeyard CITADEL reference possibility of utilising spare material for purposes of new Divisional Laundry.	
	28.XI.16		Went to AMIENS to pay Laundry Bill. Owners away - unable to settle account or discuss Coal Contract	
	29.XI.16		Went to baths CORBIE met representative of CRE & Works Officer with reference to various structural alterations to premises and adaptation of same to erection of Laundry. New part	

Army Form C. 2118.

WAR DIARY
or
INTELLIGENCE SUMMARY.
(Erase heading not required.)

Instructions regarding War Diaries and Intelligence Summaries are contained in F. S. Regs., Part II. and the Staff Manual respectively. Title pages will be prepared in manuscript.

Place	Date	Hour	Summary of Events and Information	Remarks and references to Appendices
	29.xi.16		of bath previous utilised for additional rooms required for dealing with disinfection of blankets (vermin)	
	30.xi.16		Visited AMIENS laundry — payment of account, discussion of coal contract.	

END OF VOLUME VI

A.D.M.S.
"CAPHERMC"
"Datoms" XX b.Div.
for [illegible] 38.
ATTACHED XXth (Light) DIVISION.

Appendix A.

R E P O R T

on Sanitary Conditions, Water Supplies and
Sanitary improvements carried out in area
occupied by the 20th. (Light) DIVISION
21st. October to 1st. November 1916.

BELLOY-sur-SOMME (Headquarters).

The sanitary conditions of this village have been considerably improved. The village has been occupied by Divisional Headquarters, Divisional Troops and one Battalion. One suspected case of diphtheria has occurred and disinfection was carried out.

Improvements effected :

    Erection of 4 Public Latrines with a seating accommodation of 18 seats.

    Digging of 5 public urine pits.

    Erection of one public Incinerator.

    Erection of one incinerator at Divisional Headquarters.

    Burning of collection of tins and other refuse dumped in village.

    Digging of waste pits and burial of burnt tins at Divisional Headquarters Transport and digging ablution pits at various billets.

Water :

    Wells Nos. 1, 5, 6 and 7. The water is of excellent quality - ½ measure of bleaching powder per cart being sufficient.

    Wells Nos. 2, 3 and 9. The drawing apparatus of these is out of order and tests have not been able to be made.

    Wells Nos. 4, 6 and 7. These are on private property.

    Well No. 8. This is also on private property, and is for washing water only.

PICQUIGNY.

The Town has been occupied by a Brigade less Battalions at BREILLY and the Machine Gun Company and Trench Mortar Battery at YZEUX.

Considerable improvements in the sanitary conditions of the Town have been carried out. Refuse and excreta have been collected by means of a locally hired cart and a horse from a local Unit, and partly burnt at the Horsfall Incinerator marked B and the public Incinerator marked A.

Baths have been constructed. A good site (Rue de MOULIN) on an island on the SOMME in a decayed Mill was selected on the 24th. October. After much trouble timber was obtained from MEAULTE, 30 miles distant, and work was commenced on the 26th. Work was sufficiently far advanced to be able to commence bathing on the 1st. November at the rate of 100 men per hour. A 12 Rose Le Blanc Spray is installed and bathing will be at the rate of 120 men per hour. Clean and dirty clothes Depots and dressing, undressing and ironing room are provided. The water is drawn from the SOMME and owing to the large flow and consequently big dilution of the soapy water, it is not proposed to construct a filter. The Baths personnel can be billeted above some of the rooms, so that the place is self-contained. A rough plan of the Baths is annexed.

9 Latrines have been constructed by this Division, two of which are temporary, with a seating accommodation of 34 seats and one is a trench latrine.

3 Incinerators have been built and one re-constructed.

The wells from which the Brigade has drawn water are marked on the annexed plan of the Town, and the quality is good, requiring one measure of bleaching powder to cart. Notice boards have been fixed to the Pumps showing the amount of bleaching powder necessary.

BREILLY.

6 latrines have been constructed with a seating accommodation of 20 seats and of which one is a Trench Latrine.

2 Incinerators have been built.

YZEUX.

This village has been in occupation by a Machine Gun Company and a Trench Mortar Battery.

6 Latrines and 3 incinerators are already in existence and no more have been constructed.

FLESSELLES.

This village was in occupation by Brigade Headquarters and two Battalions. The men were billeted in barns and to prevent nuisance from the adjacent middens, the men drained them and used liberal quantities of disinfectants.

8 new Latrines were constructed but owing to the difficulty of obtaining wood, they are mostly of the trench type.

6 temporary incinerators were built and again the difficulty of obtaining the necessary material prevented their being made into permanent ones.

Soakage and urine pits were dug.

Existing latrines have a seating accommodation of 32 seats.

There are three wells in the village as follows :

    Rue de VILLERS BOCAGE - about 100 metres deep, the water being good.

    Rue de L'EGLISE - water good and well about 100 metres deep.

    Rue NEUVE - water good.

The water carts, however, did not draw from these sources but refilled at NAOURS.

VIGNACOURT.

Half of a Brigade was billeted in this village. The billets were almost all barns, affording good shelter, but the adjoining middens in the farmyards are all in bad condition, owing to lack of civilian labour.

3 new latrines, with a seating accommodation of 5 seats, 1 turf incinerator and 1 soakage pit were constructed by this Division.

There is exisitng latrine accommodation of 55 seats.

As regards water, there is a deep well, being about 100 metres deep, in the Cotton Factory near to the Church, and this was selected for use. The water is good, requiring 1 measure of bleaching powder per water cart.

MONTONVILLERS.

This village was in occupation by a Machine Gun Company and a Trench Mortar Battery.

The drain at the Chateau, which was found stopped, was opened, flushed and got into working order again.

Tins round the incinerator, which was re-built, were burned. One 5 seated latrine was erected and urine and soakage pits dug.

TIRANCOURT.

This village has been in occupation by Brigade Hd.Qrs. and an A.S.C.Company.

No new latrines or incinerators have been constructed, there already being a sufficiently.

The well selected for use is in the yard of the Estaminet opposite to the Chalet and at an appreciably greater elevation It passes through the clay to the chalk. The peat band is thus avoided by crossing the main road for water.

Urine and grease pits have been dug as needed.

LA CHAUSSEE.

This village has been occupied by a Machine Gun Coy. and a Trench Mortar Battery.

Now new latrines or incinerators have been constructed there already being a sufficiency. The existing latrines are fly-proofed and the incinerators are in good condition.

Urine and grease pits have been dug as needed.

Water : The peat band runs just below the triangular island site in the GRANDE RUE. In the Rue NEUVE is a well (Well No. 1.) through the clay to the chalk with brick lining to the chalk. The water is of excellent quality and the entrance to the well is protected to a height of about 3 feet above the surface. The depth of the well is about 13 metres. This well was selected for use by the troops in occupation. The water from the well in the Rue de la TERRIER is not quite of such good quality. The abruptness of the descent from the chalk to the peat causes great variations within short distances in the depth and width of the clay band.

One case of diphtheria occurred in this village and disinfection was duly carried out.

ST. VAST.

This was in occupation by one Battalion. The men were billeted in barns.

Two new latrines have been constructed by this Division with a seating accommodation of 10 seats and existing ones have a seating accommodation of 20 seats.

Grease and urine pits have been dug as needed.

Water :

  Well No. 1. Stable within 6 yards.
       Dunghill within 10 yards.

  Well No. 2. Dunghill within 12 yards.

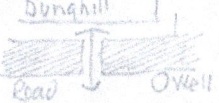

  Wells Nos. 3 and 4. Well No. 4 was selected for use
        and is considered by the Mairie to be
        certainly the best in the village. Water
        is reached at a depth of about 33 metres
        through ½ metre of surface soil, the

remainder being chalk. The brick lining extends to a depth of 1 metre only, i.e. until the compact chalk is reached.

Well No. 5. Stable, cesspool and dunghill within 12 yards

FREMONT.

This village has been occupied by Headquarters and three Companies of a Battalion. The men were billeted in barns.

No new latrines or incinerators have been constructed. Existing latrines have a seating accommodation of 12 seats. The existing incinerators are rather dilapidated and new ones are needed, but it has been impossible to effect any improvements.

Grease and urine pits have been dug as needed.

Water : The water is at a depth of about 80 metres and the cost of constructing wells is therefore prohibitive. There is only one well in the village and this adjoins a foul pond. The brickwork lining at one part extends only to a depth of three feet and the water is quite unfit for drinking. The water carts of the Battalion arefil at VAUX. There are pumps which tap reserviors of rain water in many houses. This water is used by the civilians for drinking when derived from slate roofs. The gutters at the bottom of the slate roofs run into pipes which convey the water into well bricked and cemented reservoirs. The water inthese is of good quality. There are similar reservoirs receiving water from tile roofs. These roofs are covered with moss, etc. and the water is of bad quality and is not used by the civilians for drinking. As troops were not likely to make distinctions between slate and tile roofs, the use of all these pumps were forbidden.

VAUX.

This village was occupied by a Battalion, one company of another Battalion and a Field Ambulance.

One new latrine with 6 seats and one permanent incinerator and one urinal have been constructed.

Grease and urine pits have been dug as needed.

The Chateau taken over by the Field Ambulance was in a very foul state and various sanitary improvements were effected.

Water : The wells in Grieff Street (wells No. 7,8 9 & 10½ near the centre of the village are near crowded billets & consequently the water has suffered in quality from dirty pails etc. but it is still good in most cases. Nos. 5 & 6 were selected for use of the troops. No. 5 is in an open space & No. 6 is away from the main street. Water is reached through & in the chalk at about 22 metres In some cases (as in No. 3) there is no lining whatever and in others only a few courses of brick-work.

11 cases of German Measles occurred from one Battalion and disinfection was carried out, the straw from some of the billets being burnt. After the Battalion had vacated disinfection was again carried out.

St. SAUVEUR.

This village was in occupation by a Field Ambulance.

One latrine (6 seats) has been erected by this Division.

Water : There are only two supplies, easily accessible to carts; one a well in the chalk about 20 metres deep at the top of the main road, and here the quality of the water has suffered from the dirty pails lowered into it, and the other supply a pump at the side of a Cafe on the road to the right at the bottom of the main street. Here the gravel is tapped through a boring running through 2 metres of peat, 1 of clay and 5 or 6 of gravel. There are good wells in the clay band, half way down the main street. They are generally about 12 metres deep and bricked down to the chalk, but they are not accessible to water carts. The low lying part of the village is on peat soil and good water is derived from the gravel by borings, but almost all the pumps have been put out of action by careless handling.

GENERAL REMARKS.

The first difficulty which presented itself on arrival in the area was that of rpocuring timber and the material for sanitary improvements, and several days passed without any improvements by constructional work being done. At last timber and other material was procured bu it had to be fetched from a dump 20 miles away and then directly work was progressing the Division moved into a new area.

In most of the villages no ablution benches exist with the result that troops wash around pumps and the ground becomes fouled, there not being sufficient brickwork at the well heads. Many wells, too, possess no permanent pails with the result that all kinds of dirtypails get lowered into the wells and the quality of the water suffers.

In some cases billets were found to be in a dirty state and a good deal of cleaning up work has been done.

With regard to latrines there are few with shelters and in wet weather the surrounding ground becomes deplorable. There has been no attempt made to remedy this state of affairs, time having to be devoted to other things.

Captain R.A.M.C. (T).

BATHS, PICQUIGNY
Rough Plan

River Somme

Bath House | Drying Room | Khaki | Clean Clothes Depot
Covered way | Undressing Room | Dirty Clothes
Old Water Mill | Bridge | Rue de MOULIN

SANITARY SECTION 33 ATTACHED XXth (LIGHT) DIVISION

Captain RAND (T.E.)
O.C. Sanitary Section 33,
20th Division.

October 1916.

Appendix B.

R E P O R T

for week ending 4th. November 1916.

DISPOSITION.

The disposition of the Sanitary Section personnel (27 N.C.O's and men) and attached personnel (32 N.C.O's and men) on Saturday, 4th. November 1916 was as follows :-

Headquarters, Sanitary Section, REINCOURT.	20 N.C.O's and men allotted duties as follows : S/Sergt. supervising the work of Section. Clerical and personal staff. Sanitary inspection of Headquarters, Divisional Troops, A.S.C. and 7th. Somerset L.I. Water duties to Divisional Troops. Supervision of fatigue parties. Construction work at Divn. Baths. Lorry drivers. Fatigues. Distribution of disinfectants
Baths, PICQUIGNY.	20 N.C.O's and men allotted duties as follows : Q.M.S. i/c Baths. Baths personnel. Lorry drivers. Steam "Thresh" Disinfector drivers.
59th. Brigade.	1 Sergt. i/c and 2 N.C.O's for Sanitary inspection and 1 N.C.O. for water duties attached to the Brigade.
60th. Brigade. 61st. Brigade.	1 Sergt. i/c, 1 N.C.O. for Sanitary inspection and 1 N.C.O. for water duties attached to each Brigade.

SANITATION.

Inspections have been made daily of Units in the Division, by Inspectors detailed for the work. The sanitary conditions were found as follows:

Unit.	State of Camps and Billets.	Remarks.
Divisional Headquarters.	Satisfactory.	
No. 1 Mess.	Satisfactory.	
No. 2 Mess.	Satisfactory.	No latrines at this billet. Public latri- for officers have

Units.	State of Camps and Billets.	Remarks.
No. 5 Mess.	Satisfactory.	No fatigues are available at OISSY for sanitary work.
Headquarters Servants and Headquarters Transport.	Satisfactory.	Hd.Qrs. Transport already reported on state of leaving BELLOY.
D.A.D.O.S.	Satisfactory.	
M.M.Police and Signal Company (Joint Billet)	Satisfactory.	On leaving BELLOY the M.M.P. left a Trench Latrine uncovered and manure in the stables.
Traffic Control.	Satisfactory.	Public Latrines and incinerator used.
Salvage Company.	Satisfactory except	on leaving BELLOY several loads of manure left in and about stables.
Divisional Signal Coy. Transport.	Satisfactory.	
Divisional Band.	Satisfactory.	
Mobile Veterinary Section.	Satisfactory.	
Divisional School of Instruction.	Satisfactory.	

59th. Brigade.

Brigade Headquarters.	Satisfactory.	
Headquarters Transport.	Satisfactory.	
Brigade Signals.	Satisfactory.	
10th. K.R.R. and Transport.	Satisfactory.	On vacating billets everything left in a satisfactory. The billets taken over at AILLY were found to be in a bad and dirty condition.
11th. K.R.R. & Transport.	Satisfactory.	Do.
10th. R.B. and Transport.	Satisfactory.	

Units.	State of Camps and Billets.	Remarks.
11th. R.B and Transport.	Satisfactory.	
5½th. Machine Gun Coy. and Transport.	Satisfactory.	
Trench Mortar Battery.	Satisfactory.	
159th. Company A.S.C.	Satisfactory.	

80th. Brigade.

Units.	State of Camps and Billets.	Remarks.
Headquarters and Signals.	Satisfactory.	
12th. K.R.R. and Transport.	Satisfactory.	At Transport Billet at LE MESGE washing is done at present in a brook.
12th. R.B. and Transport.	Satisfactory.	
6th. Oxon and Bucks.L.I. and Transport.	Satisfactory.	
6th. Shropshires and Transport.	Satisfactory.	D. Company and Transport are attending to their ablution arrangements.
Machine Gun Company and Trench Mortar Battery.	Satisfactory.	
61st. Field Ambulance.	Satisfactory.	
160th. Company A.S.C.	Satisfactory.	

61st. Brigade.

Units.	State of Camps and Billets.	Remarks.
Brigade Headquarters and Transport.	Satisfactory.	
12th. King's Liverpool and Transport.	Satisfactory.	
7th. K.O.Y.L.I. and Transport.	Satisfactory.	Deep trench latrines used.
7th. Cornwalls and Transport.	Satisfactory.	Deep trench latrines used.
7th. Somerset L.I. and Transport.	Satisfactory.	
161st. Company A.S.C.	Satisfactory.	

On the Brigade leaving the last area disinfection of the Billets of the 7th. Somerset L.I. and the Machine Gun Company were thoroughly disinfected, infectious disease having occurred in these Units.

WATER.

Divisional Headquarters and Divisional Troops.

Tests for free chlorine have been made from the following carts and the water found to be efficiently chlorinated:
Divisional Headquarters. Cart No. 70293. November 2.
November 5.
Divisional Signal Coy. Cart.No. 68421. November 3.
November 4.

Investigations have been carried out of the water sources at CAVILLON, REINCOURT and OISSY.

Notices stating that quantity of bleaching powder necessary have been affixed to three wells at OISSY and by all pumps liable to be frequented by troops in REINCOURT.

59th. Brigade.

Tests for free chlorine have been made from the following carts and the water found to be efficiently chlorinated:

10th. Kings Royal Rifles.	Cart.No.64168.)	October 31.
	68658.)	November 1.
11th. Kings Royal Rifles.	Cart.No.69681.)	October 31.
	86003.)	November 1.
10th. Rifle Brigade.	Cart No.79337.)	November 1.
	131272.)	November 4.
11th. Rifle Brigade.	Cart.No.73657.)	October 30.
	70554.)	November 1.
		November 3.
159th. Coy. A.S.C.	Cart.No.70245.	October 31.
		November 4.
60th. Field Ambulance.	All carts.	Daily.

The cart of the 59th. Machine Gun Company is out of repair and a note of the arrangements made by this Unit appears in my last weeks report.

60th. Brigade.

Tests for free Chlorine had been made from the following carts and the water found to be efficiently chlorinated:

12th. Kings Royal Rifles.	Cart.No.68617.)	October 31.
	68977.)	November 4.
12th. Rifle Brigade.	Cart.No.80838.)	October 31.
	68973.)	
6th. Oxon and Bucks.L.I.	Cart.No.68316.)	October 30.
	70323.)	
6th. Shropshire L.I.	Cart.No.68615.)	October 30.
	70323.)	
60th. Machine Gun Coy.	Cart.No.100084.	November 3.
160th. Coy. A.S.C.	Cart.No.70322.	October 30.
61st. Field Ambulance.	Cart.No.70306.)	
	70324.)	November 4.
	70356.)	

61st. Brigade.

Tests for free Chlorine have been made from the following carts and the water found to be efficiently chlorinated :-

Unit	Cart No.	Date
7th. K.O.Y.L.I.	Cart.No.7028&) 0705.)	October 29.
12th. Kings Liverpools.	Cart.No.70343) 68104.)	Daily from November 2.
7th. Cornwalls.	Cart.No.68349) 70332.)	
61st. Machine Gun Company.	Cart.No.103309.	October 29.
161st. Company A.S.C.	Cart.No.9035E.	October 29.

All the above carts were again tested on arrival in the new area and found to be chlorinated.

Investigations have been carried out of the various water sources in the Brigade area.

GENERAL WORK.

PICQUIGNY.

The Baths have now been completed and 4000 men have been bathed and provided with clean clothes.

Daily collections of excreta and refuse from all billets have been made and since the 1st. November the excreta has been removed twice daily.

REINCOURT.

A good Bath-house was in existence, but there was not heating or water arrangements. A BLANC system has been installed with eight sprays and the Baths have started at the full rate, clean clothing being provided. A filter for purifying the effluent is being constructed.

One Public Incinerator, latrine, urine and grease pit have been constructed.

Three cases of German Measles (?) occurred in the 7th. Somerset L.I. and disinfection was duly carried out.

MOLLIENS VIDAME.

Arrangements are being made to instal a Bath-house to bath at the rate of 50 men per hour.

DISINFECTIONS.

Cookhouse of 60th. Brigade Trench Mortar Battery sprayed.

Cases of German Measles at VAUX, Diphtheria at LA CHAUSSEE, and German Measles at REINCOURT - disinfection was carried out following these cases

GENERAL REMARKS.

A full list of the work done appears in the report submitted on the Division leaving the last area.

List of parties Bathed:

18th. King's (Liverpool) Regt.........	700.
7th. Somerset L.I......	594.
11th. R.B.....	580.
7th. K.O.Y.L.I......	580.
7th. D.C.L.I......	360.
11th. K.R.R.....	674.
10th. R.B.. .	645.
59th. Bde. Trench Mor. Batt......	50.
61st. Bde. Trench Mor. Batt......	55.
Divn. Hd. Qrs. &Signals....	4196.-46
Total....	4150.

List of Clean Clothing issued:

Shirts....	3645.
Pants....	2806.
Socks....	2654.
Towels....	503.

List of Dirty Clothing Received...

Shirts...	3405.
Pants...	2752
Socks...	2595.
Towels...	808.

Articles of Clothing passed through "THRESH" Steam
  Disinfector for Laundry.... 14,772.

List of Disinfectants issued.

Chloride of Lime....	2620 lbs.
Creosoli....	180 galls.
Paraffin....	110 galls.
Formalin...	1 gall.
Bleaching Powder.	12 tins.
Anti-Vermin Powder...	80 tins.
Whale Oil.	5 galls.
Anti-Frost Bite Grease..	50 tins.

Captain R.A.M.C. (T).
O.C. Sanitary Section 33,
Attached XXth (Light) Division.

Appendix C.

REPORT

for week ending 11th. November 1916

DISPOSITION.

The disposition of the Sanitary Section personnel (27 N.C.Os. and men) and attached personnel (32 N.C.Os. and men) on Saturday 11th. Nov. 1916 was as follows:

Headquarters, Sanitary Section REINCOURT.	24 N.C.Os and men are allotted duties as follows: S/Sergt. supervising work of Section; Clerical and personal staff, Sanitary inspection of Headquarters, Divn. Trps. A.S.C., and 7th. Somerset L.I. Water duties to Divn. Troops. Supervision of fatigue parties. Construction work at Divisional Baths. Lorry Drivers. Fatigues. Distribution of disin--fectants.
Baths, REINCOURT.	5 N.C.O. and men allott--ed duties as follows: L/Cpl. i/c Baths. Baths personnel.
Baths, PICQUIGNY.	17 N.C.O.s and men allott-ed duties as follows: Q.M.S. i/c Baths. Baths personnel. Lorry Drivers. Steam "Thresh" Disinfect--or Drivers.
59th. Brigade.	1 Sergt. i/c and 2 N.C.Os for Sanitary inspection & 1 N.C.O. for water duties attached to each Brigade.
60th. Brigade. 61st. Brigade.	1 Sergt. i/c, 1 N.C.O. for Sanitary inspection and 1 N.C.O. for water duties attached to each Brigade.

(1).

SANITATION.

Inspections have been made daily of Units in the Division, by inspectors detailed for this work. The Sanitary conditions found were as follows:

Unit.	State of Camps and Billets.	Remarks.
Divn. Headquarters.	Satisfactory.	
No.1 Mess	Satisfactory.	
No.2 Mess	Satisfactory.	
No. 3 Mess.	Satisfactory.	New latrines for Officers constructed.
Hd. Qrs. Servants & Hd. Qrs. Transport.	Satisfactory.	
D.A.D.O.S.	Satisfactory.	
M.M.Police & Signal Coy.(Joint Billet)	Satisfactory.	Signal's cookhouse generally in rather dirty condition & ground outside billet door dirty.
Traffic Control.	Satisfactory.	New grease & Ablution pits made.
Salvage Coy.	Satisfactory.	New grease & urine pits made.
H.Q.Signal Coy. Transport.	Satisfactory, except:	*Manure accumulating very rapidly in the yard & little being removed. Sanitary arrangements shared with Salvage Coy.
Divn. Band.	Satisfactory.	
Mobile Vet. Sec.	Satisfactory.	
Divisional School of Instruction.	Satisfactory.	

58th. Brigade.

Brigade Headquarters.	Satisfactory.	
Headquarters Transport.	Satisfactory.	Box latrines almost complete.
Brigade Signals.	Satisfactory.	Large amount of rubbish removed from cellar under billet.

(2).

Unit.	State of Camps and Billets.	Remarks.
10th. K.R.R. & Transport.	Satisfactory	
11th. K.R.R. & Transport.	Satisfactory.	This Unit left Ailly for Breilly on 8/11/16. Billets left in good condition.
10th. R.B. & Transport.	Satisfactory.	
11th. R.B. & Transport.	Satisfactory.	Removed to Billets vacated by Australians. Billets were in a dirty condition when taken over.
59th. M.G.C. & Transport.	Satisfactory.	
Trench Mortar Battry.	Satisfactory.	
159th. A.S.C. & Transport.	Satisfactory.	
60th. Field Ambulance & Transport.	Satisfactory	Large amount of manure left at Transport billet by Australians.

60th. Brigade.

Unit.	State of Camps and Billets.	Remarks.
Headquarters & Signals.	Satisfactory.	
12th. K.R.R. & Transport.	Satisfactory.	
12th. R.B. & Transport.	Satisfactory.	
6th. Shropshires & Transport.	Satisfactory.	
Machine Gun Coy. & T.M.Battery.	Satisfactory.	
160th. Coy. A.S.C.	Satisfactory.	One pit at supplies to be renewed.
61st. Field Ambulance & Transport.	Satisafactory.	

61st. Brigade.

Unit.	State of Camps and Billets.	Remarks.
Brigade Hd. Qrs. and Transport.	Satisfactory.	No Sanitary arrange-ments on arrival. New latrines, incinerators grease pits and urine pits made.

Units.	State of Camps and Billets.	Remarks.
18th. King's(L'pool) Regt. & Transport.	Satisfactory.	
7th. K.O.Y.L.I. & Transport.	Satisfactory.	
7th. Cornwalls & Transport.	Satisfactory	No arrangements on arrival. New latrines urine pits etc. made.
7th. Somerset L.I. & Transport.	Satisfactory	
61st. Trench Mor. Battery.	Satisfactory.	New urine pit made.

Other Units.

11th. Durham L.I. & Transport	Satisfactory.	Billets at Picquigny taken over from Australians in a very dirty condition. Manure removed by local farmer.
96th. Coy. R.E.	Satisfactory.	Billets taken-over from Australians in a very dirty condition.

WATER.

Divisional Headquarters and Divisional Troops.

Tests for free chlorine have been made from the following carts and the water found to be efficiently chlorinated:
Divisional Headquarters   Cart No.70295.   Pump not in working order,

Divn. Signal Coy.   Cart No.66421.

Investigations made of the water supply at CAVILLON, REINCOURT and OISSY.
Two 50 gallon tanks placed on village green at OISSY. Contents chlorinated.

59th. Brigade.

Tests for free chlorine have been made from the carts in this Brigade and all were efficiently chlorinated with the following exceptions:

7/11/6   10th. R.B.   Cart No.E131275)   Not sufficiently
                             No.E70307)   chlorinated.
                                                 This has now been remedied.

60th. Brigade.

Tests for free/chlorine have been made from the carts in this Brigade and all were efficiently chlorinated.

61st. Brigade.

Tests for free chlorine have been made from the carts in this Brigade and all were efficiently chlorinated with the following exception:

9/11/16   84th. Coy R.E.   Cart No. E34222.   Not sufficient-
                                              -ly chlorinated.

GENERAL WORK. * See also 2nd Report.

PICQUIGNY

Daily collections of excreta and refuse. About 10 tons of rubbish has been collected and destroyed in the incinerator. The acting Town Major has arranged with the local farmers to plough the excreta into the land.

PEINCOURT.

"Beehive" incinerator cleared out.
Public latrines, urinals etc. constructed in village and at Sports ground.
Latrine and urinal and filter bed constructed at Baths.
Many repairs carried out on the roof etc. at Baths.
Numerous sign boards made and erected in the village.

DISINFECTION.

Disinfection carried out following a cases of German Measles at a billet of 7th. Somerset L.I.
1745 blankets Disinfected.

List of Disinfectants issued:

Chloride of Lime...	2940 lbs.
Creosoli......	185 galls.
Paraffin...	100 galls.
Formalin....	5 galls.
Bleaching Powder...	32 tins.
Oxford Powder....	20 tins.

List of Clean Clothing issued:

Shirts.....	5051.
Pants...	4077.
Socks...	1915.
Towels....	751.

List of Dirty Clothing received:

Shirts...	4813.
Pants...	3825.
Socks...	4181.
Towels....	751.

Articles of Clothing passed through "THRESH"
Disinfector for Laundry...... ..   16,500.

List of Parties Bathed at PICQUIGNY

  10th. K.R.R.....   194.
  11th. K.R.R...   120.
  12th. K.R.R....   687.
  10th. K.R.R...   284.
  10th. R.B.....   46
  11th. RBB....   523.
  6th. K.S.L.I....   464.
  11th. Durham L.I...   700.
  60th. Field Ambulance...   62.
  59th. Brigade M.G.C.   140.
  59th. Brigade T.M.Battery..   50.
  189th. Coy. A.S.C...   40.
  4th. Australian Division..   640.
          Total... 5750.

List of Parties Bathed at REINCOURT.

  Divn. Signal Company...   12.
  Divn. School of Instruction...   8.
  Traffic Control...   15.
  60th. Machine Gun Company...   140.
  60th. Trench Mortar Battery...   44.
  7th. Cornwalls.   346.
  7th. K.O.Y.L.I...   372.
  12th. Rifle Brigade.   412.
  6th. Oxon and Bucks. L.I.   470.
  Salvage Company.   12.
  7th. Somerset L.I.   557.
  12th. King's Liverpool Regt.   340.
              2478.

  A filter has been constructed for purifying the soapy effluent from the Baths at REINCOURT. The method of precipitation by Chloride of Lime was adopted.

  A public fly-proofed latrine etc. was erected on the Polo Ground for spectators at Football Matches, etc.

  Maps of all villages in the Divisional Area have been prepared (ab initio) showing :
  1. Sanitary conveniences in existence.
  2. Those constructed by the 20th. Division.
  3. Wells.

              Captain R.A.M.C. (T).
         O.C. SANITARY SECTION 38,
          ATTACHED XXth (LIGHT) DIVISION.

R E P O R T

on Sanitary Conditions and Water Supplies of, and Improvements carried out in area occupied by the 20th. (Light) Division during the period 1/11/16 and 14/11/16.

CAVILLON.

This village was in occupation by Divisional Headquarters.

There is one public Incinerator in the centre of the village where all the refuse from the Billets is burnt. The burnt refuse is buried in a field on the N. side of the CAVILLON-FOURDRINOY Road about 300 yards from the centre of the village.

No new latrines or incinerators have been constructed, there being already a sufficienty. There are two Officers Latrines with a seating accommodation of 5 seats, one Sergeants Latrine and two Public Latrines with a seating accommodation of 13 seats.

All refuse is collected daily from all billets by Hd.Qrs. fatigues, one of whom is in constant attendance at the Incinerator.

There are two deep wells in the village, but both seem to be unavailable. One is in the Chateau grounds and water can be pumped by means of an oil engine, but this has not been used for some time, and the other is a village well, the drawing apparatus of it being out of order. The part broken was sent to M. Lepartre, 11 Rue de COTTENCHY, AMIENS, over a year ago, but owing to this firm being a munitions firm permission has to be obtained from the French Authorities to proceed with civil work. I communicated with the French Mission who replied that such permission would not be granted and advised that the Divisional Engineers be asked to repair it. By this time this Division's Engineers had departed so that nothing could be done. The only available other sources for drinking are to be found as rain-water stored in underground cisterns by the inhabitants. These cisterns are to be found in any house of any size. Its apparent purity varies according to the care exercised in keeping these cisterns clean. In some, animalculae are plentiful, but wherever the Horrock's Test was applied the result showed that one measure of bleaching powder per cart was sufficient. The testing of water from carts so treated always verified this. The Corporal in charge of the Headquarters water cart was informed of the presence of good wells at REINCOURT.

OISSY.

This village was occupied by various Units of Divisional Troops.

There are three public incinerators and each Unit is responsible for the disposal of its own refuse.

One permanent latrine for Officers with a seating accommodation of two seats has been constructed by this Division. There are four existing latrines with a seating accommodation of 17 seats.

There is a public ablution bench in the farmyard of the Chateau.

Among other village water supplies there are two which should be noted. There is a supply of good water at the FERME CHATELIN. There is a similar supply at the FERME DACHEUX but there is no pump. This well is in the higher part of the village and the well is 22 metres deep. All the wells in the village are private property. All the water is good, giving a permanent blue in the first cup of the Horrocks Test. In order to meet the needs of the village two fifty gallon tanks have been erected in the lower part of the village.. These are filled at 4 p.m. daily by two men from the Divisional Salvage Company and my N.C.O. in charge of the water duties to Divisional Headquarters chlorinates them. They then remain untouched until 6.a.m. the next morning when they are available for use.

REINCOURT.

This village was in occupation by one Battalion and the Headquarters of the Divisional Sanitary Section.

The report of the previous Sanitary Section said that owing to the uncertainty of the length of their stay in the area (about one month) no Baths had been possible. It was found, however, that there was a good Bath-house in existence at REINCOURT, but there was no heating or water arrangements. A BLANC system was installed with eight sprays and the Baths were started at the full rate, clean clothes being provided, within four days after arriving in the area. 60 men per hour can be bathed. It was found that the Battalion occupying the village made a practice of using the small pond from which the water supply for the Baths is derived for watering their horses and washing their vehicles. A strand of barbed wire has therefore being placed in such a way so as to permit the former but to prevent the latter taking place. A filter has been constructed for purifying the soapy effluent. The method of precipitation by Chloride of Lime was adopted.

Six public and private latrines have been constructed by this Division with a seating accommodation of 16 seats. One permanent set of four seats, for public use, with roof and shelter has been provided, and the others are deep trench latrines. Existing latrines have a seating accommodation of five seats.

Five public incinerators have been constructed by this Division, three of angle iron pickets, expanded metal and corrugated iron and two of bricks. These last two are small, being sufficient to cope with refuse from small billets. Three public incinerators are already existing.

Three cases of German Measles have occurred during the occupation of the villages by the 20th. Division. Disinfection has duly been carried out following the removal of the patients.

There are two public wells in the village marked on the map, the rest being private. Pump No. 1 is temporarily out of order. The water is good, needing one measure of bleaching powder per cart.

PICQUIGNY.

No plan of this town is submitted, one having been submitted on this Division vacating the last area. Except for the Headquarters and Signals of the Brigade, this Town was temporarily out of this Division's area, during the occupation of the Town by the Australians. Since their departure this Division has been in occupation there, and on taking over the billets again much clearing up work had to be done following the departure of the Australians. During all this time the Baths there, which were constructed by this Division, have been run by me and the full number of 100 men per hour bathed.

The system of collecting excreta and refuse as detailed in my previous report has been in operation during the whole time.

BREILLY.

No plan of this village is submitted, one having been sent with my last report. The remarks concerning the clearing up work done following the re-occupation of the village after the Australians departure made in the case of PICQUIGNY equally apply here.

AILLY.

This village was in occupation by the Battalion.

Four new latrines were constructed by this Division with a seating accommodation of 14 seats and one trench latrine. Five new incinerators have been constructed.

The water supply is a municipal one and is obtained from taps along the main street. The water is of good quality, requiring one measure of bleaching powder per cart.

One case of German measles occurred and disinfection was carried out.

SAISSEVAL.

This village was in occupation by one Battalion.

9 Latrines have been constructed by this Division with a seating accommodation of 14 seats, one Officers latrine and four trench latrines. Also five incinerators

The water supply of this village is not satisfactory. There are four wells. No. 2 marked on the map is 150 feet deep and requires two measures of bleaching powder AFTER filtering through the clothes. No. 3 and No. 4 are 120 feet and 240 feet deep respectively. It saves time if all the cart draw water from PICQUIGNY.

FOURDRINOY.

This village was in occupation by the Divisional School of Instruction and an A.S.C. Company.

One new latrine has been constructed of three seats and one trench latrine and there are four latrines of 16 seats and one open latrine existing.

There are three existing incinerators.

The water supply here is very bad indeed and it is advisable for water carts to either draw at PICQUIGNY or CAVILLON. There are two wells in the village but both are dis-used by the civil inhabitants and apparently, according to the civilians, are used more or less as receptacles for dead pigs and all refuse. Nearly all houses have rain-water cisterns, but according to the inhabitants none of this is used locally for drinking. That at the Divisional School of Instruction requires one measure of bleaching powder.

SOUES.

This village was occupied by an Infantry Brigade Headquarters, a Machine Gun Company and a Trench Mortar Battery.

One fly-proofed latrine, one seat, and one trench latrine have been made and three incinerators. Existing latrines have a seating accommodation of 12 seats.

Wells Nos. 1 and 2 marked on the map require each one measure of bleaching powder per cart.

CROUY.

This village was only occupied by one Company of a Battalion.

Several trench latrines and two box ones were made, and two incinerators.

One pump, No. 2, requires one measure of bleaching powder per water cart and Nos. 1 and 3 are in farmyards.

LE MESGE.

This village was only occupied by one Company of a Battalion.

Six fly-proofed latrines have been constructed with a seating accommodation of 18 seats, one with 8 tins, and two trench latrines.

HANGEST.

This village was in occupation by one Battalion.

One fly-proof latrine, two bucket latrine with 11 buckets, one pole latrine and 7 trench latrines have been constructed by this Divn. 4 Incinerators, one of which is a temporary structure, have been built.

St. PIERRE.

This village was in occupation by Headquarters and two companies of one battalion.

Four trench latrines have been constructed and Three incinerators.

The only well marked on the map requires one measure of bleaching powder per water cart.

RICHECOURT FARM.

This farm situated on the SOUES-HANGEST Road, was in occupation by a Field Ambulance.

One latrine of ten seats and one stone incinerator were constructed by the 20th. Divn.

There are two wells, one, requiring one measure of bleaching powder per water cart available for drinking purposes, and one for washing water only.

The Field Ambulance in occupation arranged a temporary bath house for personnel, clean clothes being supplied by me.

BOURDON.

This village was in occupation by the Divisional Pioneer battalion

One fly-proof of two seats, four latrines of 12 tins and five trench latrines, and two incinerators, one of which is a temporary, structure have been made. *The M.O. is has made an arrangement for bathing his men, clean clothing being supplied by us*

MOLLIENS-VIDAME.

This village was in occupation by a Bde. Hd. Qrs., a Field Ambulance, an A.S.C. Coy., and one Battalion.

One latrine and one incinerator were in existence and a latrine of ten seats and one incinerator were constructed by this Division.

Baths were in existence in the triangular island facing the Hotel de Ville. It was proposed to start these and 3 "SOYERS" Stoves were placed in the care of the Town Major for water heating and tubs were to be purchased by D.A.D.O.S. No water supply was available & a cart was to bring water, and thus a small bath-house could be put into working order *to fast 50 men per hour*. At the last minute, however, it was found that troops in occupation had removed some of the canvas/screening of the baths and some of the forms and generally necessitating constructional work before the place could be used. Owing to the Division moving there was not time for this to be done.

Water.

The village stands in a valley from the S. end of which a considerable stream formerly ran, its site being marked by a ditch at the back of the houses on the E. side of the Rue de Camps. Much soil was carried down by storms and the river gradually silted up. It now rises at OISSY but still runs from DREUIL from Feb-July. There is now an alluvial band (terre rapportee) deposited on the chalk. This band stretches at the Place, approx. from the Cfe du Centre to the Poste and has a maximum depth of about 2 metres. Otherwise the town stands on chalk. The water is near the surface. There is a well at almost every house, but a considerable number of the covers fit very loosely especially near the pump tube or have been badly broken by troops. In the cases of crowded billets, where wholesale washing has frequently taken place in the bucket which often stands on the well cover, the water has suffered badly. In some cases the pumps have been broken by the troops.

Of the good wells remaining some are not accessible to water carts and the use of some has been refused by occupiers. All the wells in this village are within private property.

The best well is that in the yard of the Maire. It stands on the chalk, above the alluvial band, in an isolated position and rather more than half its total depth of 12 to 14 metres is protected by brickwork. Half of the water carts drawing water in and from this village refilled from this source and the other refilled from a pump in the yard of the house opposite.

Another excellent well is that at the Ancienne Brasserie (M.Fontaine) near the Brigade Post Office. It was used before the war for the manufacture of beer and is protected by brickwork to the bottom. Two horses from Bde. Hd. Qrs. had just been billeted in the well room within 10 feet of the open top of the well (hidden by material). These were immediately removed to another billet.

There are two borings in the chalk (15 to 18 metres deep) near the Church. One is at the Epicerie (M.Lefevre). The other which feeds 2 or 3 pumps, is at the side of a house, (near the Church), belonging to M. Emile Magnier.

The pump at the Epicerie provides water very slowly and is therefore unsuitable for water carts. The other house was locked.

DREUIL.

This village was in occupation by a French Mortar Battery.

One latrine was constructed and incinerator

Water.

There are 3 wells, (About 20 metres deep), in the few houses which line the Molliens-Vidame-Riencourt road.

Close to this road, and parallel to it, runs a road with a row of houses containing 7 wells - all artesian - running through 2 or 4 metres of a light coloured sand followed by 3 metres of flint to a calcareous substratum.

On the opposite side of the valley but a little higher runs the road of this hamlet, also parallel to the main road, and containing the School and the Maire's house. There are 7 wells in the chalk along this road.

The best water is obtained from the well on the Maire's premises at the end of this road. It passes through very small chalk for 2 metres, then through big flints to the compact chalk. It is prot--ected inside to the bottom by brickwork. The Trench Mortar Batt, use this well.

CAMP en AMIENOIS

This village was in occupation by one Battalion.

7 fly-proofed latrines were constructed by this Unit with a seating capacity of 16 seats, and one incinerator made of angle iron pickets and expanding metal.

MONTAGNE.

This village was occupied by one Battalion,

3 latrines with 9 seats have been constructed by this Divn. and one incinerator built of angle iron pickets and expanding metal.

Notes on water supply of villages of Camp-en-Amienois, Le Fayel and Montagne.

The water supply of these villages is strikingly similar to that of the villages of St. Vast-en-Amienois and Fremont and the re--marks and conclusions which follow would probably apply to most of the villages which stand at a high elevation within a considerable area.

Wells. Water is only obtained at a considerable depth. The cost of excavating such wells is considerable and in consequence the number of wells is small

Village.	No. of Wells.	Depth(metres)	Strata traversed
Montagne	2	95-100.	Chalk only.
Le Fayel	1	95.	do.
Camp-en-Amienois.	2	85)Clay	8metre
		)Siliceous*	2 do
		)Chalk.	75 do

*This siliceous stratum outcrops in patches between Camp-en--Amienois and Le Fayel.

The wells usually stand in a prominent position on the roadside The water is of excellent quality but one measure of bleaching pow--der should be added owing to the uncertainty introduced by certain factors.

A danger in times of peace arises from the fact that where the well passes entirely through the chalk, the brickwork lining inside the well extends to a depth of 1 metre only i.e. until the compact is reached. Those passing through a super-stratum of clay are better protected, a lining of large flints succeeding a few courses of brickwork until the chalk is reached

Since the war the water has suffered in quality, though far less than the wells in the yards of crowded billets, from

1. Washing near the well.
2. The lowering of different receptacles into the well

A clean large receptacle should be provided and the guard should see that it is the only receptacle used by soldiers for drawing the water. It cannot be permanently fixed to the windlass in the villages with deepest wells, (e.g. Camp-en-Amienois, Montagne, and Le Fayel) as the civilians use special barrels (contents about 9 galls) for themselves. (These barrels are very clean inside and outside.)

Where no such arrangement is in force among the civilians e.g. St Vast-en-Amienois, the receptacle should be permanently fixed fitted to the chain of the windlass. A large receptacle is necessary to save time in drawing water from such deep wells.

The framework of the well suffered badly in some cases from the chain being almost invariably allowed by troops to unwind by itself instead of by hand. It soon acquires a great momentum with injury to the bearings. One well at Camp-en-Amienois (that on the Place) has been put out of action in this way. These wells are few in number, in isolated villages standing high, and of very great value for military purposes. The only alternatives to their use the influence of foul rain-water or journeying to another village. Those injured by the troops should be immediately repaired.

<u>Rain-water Reservoirs</u>.

The reservoirs have usually the appearance of ordinary wells, being generally circular chambers sunk about 5 metres below ground and tapped by a pump or by windlass or pulley. They are often mistaken by cooks and other troops for ordinary wells.

Tile roofs - the water from tile roofs in these villages is never used by the civilians except as drinking water for cattle or for washing.

Slate roofs - These are little affected by moss. The great danger arises from the dust and from bird droppings, mainly pigeons, passing usually without any filtration into the reservoir and remaining there for many years gradually accumulating to a varying depth up to about 1 foot. The chain supplied to lower the pail into one class of these reservoirs is of such a length as to prevent the bottom of the pail reaching too near to the bottom of the well.

Filter chambers - In the case of a few of these reservoirs the water passes through a filter chamber before entering the reservoir. The chambers is sometimes very small and contains a few pieces of charcoal resting on stones supported by a perforated grating. The best filters consist of a chamber about 3 feet deep containing a layer of charcoal resting on small stones. The entrance pipe passes through the stones and charcoal within about 2 inches of the bottom of the chamber and the water is thus forced through the filtering medium to an exit pipe at the top of the filter chamber. In the case of the smaller chambers mentioned, the position of the pipes is reversed. The best filter chambers are cleaned out about 2 or 3 times a year if the proprietor has time. New charcoal is added at less frequent intervals, this being somewhat difficult to obtain.

Cover of Reservoir - This is often covered partly or wholly by a trough of drinking water for cattle, for which purpose the water is largely used. The cover is often partly broken, allowing the overflow of the troughs and washing pails to return to the reservoir. Those reservoirs which open at the top and have a chain and pulley are mostly well protected.

The quality of the water after a heavy rainfall is much improved.

    Particulars of reservoirs -
      At house of M. Echille Pruvost, CAMP-LEZ-AMIENOIS.
      Filter - none.
      Reservoir - 5 metres deep. Not cleaned out since M. Pruvost
        entered into occupation 16 years ago. The depth of the
        mud at the bottom is about 12 inches. Two courses of
        the circular protective brickwork over the well have

VIDAME elicited the information that no further cases of dysentry have occured since those mentioned in the Sanitary Report of the 2nd. Indian Cavalry Division.

There is noticable lack of ablution arrangements in the area, but again the great difficulty of procuring timber prevented appreciable work being done in remedying this state of affairs

A public latrine (4 seats) and a urine pit have been provided at the sports ground - SOUES-PICQUIGNY road.

The disposal of excreta at Picquigny is a difficult pro-blem. There is very little space available for deep trench latrines so that the excreta has to be collected daily. It can either be buried and the ground marked "foul" (as indeed it will be in course of time) or it can be spread on a field and ploughed into the ground. Both of these methods have been adopted but the latter would be dangerous in the fly season.

Another alternative is to burn the excreta. A tall fact-ory chimney and improvised incinerator is in existence. This could be made to deal with a great deal of it if the incinerator portion of it were entirely reconstructed. Sawdust can be obtained at DREUIL near AMIENS. This would be by far the best and most satisfactory plan

CONSTRUCTED BY THE 20th. DIVISION.

Village.	F.P.Latrines. Seats.	Incinerators.
1. Cavillon	-	-
2. Cissy.	2	-
3. Rioncourt.	16	5.
4. Picquigny.	See previous report.	
5. Breilly.	do do do	
6. Ailly.	14.	5.
7. Saisseval.	14.	5.
8. Fourdrinoy.	5.	-
9. Soues.	4.	3.
10. Crouy.	1.	2.
11. Le Mesge.	5.	-
12. Hangest.	-	4.
13. St. Pierre.	2.	3.
14. Richecourt Farm.	10.	1.
15. Bourdon.	2.	2.
16. Molliens-Vidame.	10.	1.
17. Dreuil.	-	1.
18. Camps-en-Amienois.	1.	1.
19. Montagne.	2.	1.

The above list is approximated only. There are certainly F.P. latrines in existence which are not given on the above list or on the maps of the some of the towns. The details would have been completed in a few days.

[signature]

Captain. R.A.M.C.(T.F.)
O.C. Sanitary Section 33,
Attached XXth (Light) Division.

Appendix E.

R E P O R T

for week ending 18th. November 1916.

DISPOSITION.

The disposition of the Sanitary Section personnel (27 N.C.O's and men) and attached personnel (37 N.C.O's and men) on Saturday 18th. Nov.1916 was as follows:-

Headquarters, Sanitary Section, CORBIE.	(26 N.C.O's and men allotted duties as follows: S/Sergt. supervising work of Section. Clerical & personal staff. Sanitary inspection of Hd. Qrs., Divn. Troops and 11th. D.L.I. Water duties to Divn. Troops Supervision of Fatigue parties. Constructional work. Lorry Drivers. Attached personnel. Distribution of Disinfectants.
Baths, CORBIE.	(28 N.C.O's and men allotted duties as follows: Q.M.S. i/c Baths. Baths personnel. Laundry personnel. Lorry drivers. Steam "Thresh" Disinfector Drivers.
59th. Brigade. 60th. Brigade.	(1Sergt. i/c, 1 N.C.O. for Sanitary Inspection and 1 N.C.O. for water duties attached to each Brigade
61st. Brigade.	(1 Sergt. i/c, 1 N.C.O. for Sanitary Inspection and 2 N.C.O's for water duties.

Some slight alteration in the personnel of the Brigade Squads has been made in the week.

SANITATION.

Inspections have been made daily of Units in the Division by Inspectors detailed for this work.

The Sanitary conditions found were as follows:

The Division vacated the Reserve area, Area 3, on the 15/11/16 and conditions were left satisfactory except where stated in the Remarks column below:

Units.	State of Camps and Billets.	Remarks.
Divn. Hd. Qrs.	Satisfactory.	New urine pit constructed at CORBIE.
G.O.C. and No.1 Mess.	Satisfactory.	
No. 2 Mess.	Satisfactory.	
No. 3 Mess.	Satisfactory.	
Hd.Qrs. Transport.	Satisfactory.	At CORBIE the manure is being slowly burnt. A large amount was left on the site by the last unit in occupation. Public latrines are used.
Hd.Qrs.Mess, Servants Cookhouse & billet.	Satisfactory.	New grease pit provided.
D.A.D.O.S.	Satisfactory.	Sanitary arrangements left in a dirty condition by previous unit in occupation.
M.M.Police.	Satisfactory.	
C.R.E. Mess.	Satisfactory.	
C.R.E. Transport.	Satisfactory.	A large amount of manure left by units previously occupying ground. Manure is being slowly burnt. Public latrines are used.
Divn. Signal Coy.	Satisfactory.	New urine pit & grease pit constructed.
Divn. Signal Coy. Transport.	Satisfactory.	At CISSY 4 or 5 loads of manure were left but it was being removed by a farmer at the time of the Inspectors visit and it was promised to be removed in 2 days. At CORBIE a large amount of manure was left by the last occupants and the waste pit was left in a filthy condition. Public latrines and incinerators are used.
Traffic Control.	Satisfactory.	

Unit.	State of Camps and billets.	Remarks.
Salvage Coy. and Band.	Satisfactory.	The Divn. Band billet at OISSY was left in Fair condition, a small amount of old clothing being left in billet. At CORBIE public latrines are used.
Mobile Vet. Section.	Satisfactory.	
Divn. Baths.	Satisfactory.	

At CORBIE all rubbish and waste is collected and all latrines emptied daily by the Town Sanitary Squad. A special report on the state of the sanitary conditions at CORBIE has already been submitted.

59th. Brigade.

Brigade Hd.qrs.	Satisfactory.	
10th. K.R.R. and Transport.	Satisfactory.	
10th. R.B. and Transport.	Satisfactory.	
11th. K.R.R. and Transport.	Satisfactory.	
11th. R.B. and Transport.	Satisfactory.	
59th. Machine Gun Coy. & Transport.	Satisfactory.	
159th. Coy. A.S.C.	Satisfactory.	
96th. Field Coy.R.E.	Satisfactory.	
Trench Mortar Batt.	Satisfactory.	

At VILLE there is daily collection of rubbish from billets. Permanent latrines are built by Town Major's squad. The excreta from one large latrine is buried in an adjoining filed. All other latrines are built over deep trenches

60th. Brigade.

Bde. Hd.Qrs. Signals & Transport.	Satisfactory.	
12th. K.R.R. and Transport.	Satisfactory.	At Corbie there were many tins and much rubbish left by previous occupants. This has been dealt with by incinerators.

Unit.	State of Camps and Billets.	Remarks.
12th. R.B. and Transport.	Satisfactory.	
6th. K.S.L.I. & Transport.	Satisfactory.	This unit vacated CORBIE on the 18/11/16 & left billets etc. clean.
6th. Oxon. & Bucks. L.I. and Transport.	Satisfactory.	
60th. Machine Gun Coy. & Transport.	Satisfactory.	
T.M. Battery.	Satisfactory.	
160th. Coy. A.S.C.	Satisfactory.	
61st. Field Ambulance and Transport.	Satisfactory.	On taking over this billet (an old Corps Rest Station) was found to be in a very unsatisfactory condition.

This Brigade has been in occupation of CORBIE and the remarks reference the collection of excreta and refuse above equally apply here.

61st. Brigade.

During the past week this Brigade has been constantly moving and supervision has therefore become somewhat difficult. Added to this the Sergt. i/c became a casualty which left only 1 man i/c Sanitation of the Brigade for some days. Further the distance between Divn. Hd. Qrs. and Brigade rendered difficult my personal supervision or the sending rapidly of any further personnel.

7th. Somerset L.I. and Transport.	Satisfactory.	
7th. K.O.Y.L.I.	Satisfactory.	
61st Machine Gun Coy.	Satisfactory.	
Trench Mortar Batt.	Satisfactory.	
161st. Coy. A.S.C.	Satisfactory.	

Other Units.

Divn. School of Instruction. (FOURDRINOY).	Satisfactory.	

Unit.	State of Camps, and Billets.	Remarks.
84th. Field Coy.R.E.	Satisfactory.	
11th. Durham L.I.	Satisfactory.	

WATER.

CORBIE.

The following pumps and supplies have been tested and it was found that one measure of bleaching powder per cart was sufficient.

      Pump in Rue August Gindre
       "   " Rue 14th. Juillet.
       "   " Rue Bullot.
       "   " yard next No.12 Place de la Republique.
      Supply at Factory Rondeau.
      Spring in Rue du Moulin.

The supply from the pump in the yard of the Girls' Primary School (next Billet No.29 Rue Hersent) is an unsatisfactory one. The pump is 8 yards from a cesspool draining a series of latrines and urinals. During the recent prolonged occupation of the School by the No.5 C.C.S. these were used by patients, including infectious cases. They are not now in use and the surroundings are clean. On testing by the "Horrocks" Test it was found that ½ measure per cart was sufficient. No apparent source of contamination can be seen but on testing by the "Thresh" it was found that the water was markedly contaminated with urine. Up to that time the supply had been used by the Salvage Coy. for cooking but the pump was immediate-ly labelled, "Unfit for drinking or cooking". It is proposed to take a sample of the water for Bacteriological Examination. Boards on the Town Supplies stating that ½ measure Bleaching Powder per cart was sufficient have been changed to 1 measure. A notice has been affixed by the pump in the Rue August Gindre prohibiting washing there. Tests have been made for free chlorine from the following carts and the water found to be efficiently chlorinated.

  Divn.Hd.Qrs.   Cart No.70293   Tested 12/11/16. 14/11/16.
  Divn. Signal Coy.   " " 68421   "   13/11/16. 15/11/16.

60th. Brigade.

12th. K.R.R.	Cart No. 130883.	Tested	1&/11/16 18/11/16.
	" " 97507.		14/11/16.
12th. R.B.	" " 70836.	"	13/11/16 16/11/16.
	" " 63973.	"	18/11/16.
6th. Oxon. & Bucks. L.I.	" " 68318	"	15/11/16.
	" " 70333.	"	17/11/16.
6th. Shropshire L.I.	" " 69415.	"	13/11/16.
	70323-70323.	"	16/11/16.
60th. Machine Gun Company.	" " 100584.	"	14/11/16 17/11/16*
160th. Coy. A.S.C.	" " 70322.	"	13/11/16.
60th. Field Ambulance.	" 70306.) " 70324.) " 70350.)	"	14/11/16.

59th. Brigade.

Tests for free Chlorine have been made from the following carts and the Water found to be efficiently chlorinated.

10th. K.R.R.	Cart. No. 64162	Tested	13/11/16.
	" " 85658.	"	17/11/16.
11th. R.B.	" " 73651	"	13/11/16.
	" " 70294.	"	18/11/16.
11th. K.R.R.	" " 86003.	"	13/11/16.
	" " 69621	"	16/11/16.
59th. Machine Gun Coy.	" " 85275.	"	16/11/16. 18/11/16.
159th. Coy. A.S.C.	" 70295.	"	17/11/16. 18/11/16.
96th. Field Coy. R.E.	No number.	"	18/11/16.
60th. Field Amb.	Two carts, one is at M.D.S.	"	Daily.

61st. Brigade.

The sources of supply in this area are as follows:

<u>The Chateau, TAILLY.</u>

A boring in the chalk, 2 metres deep.

<u>La Fontaine Libertine, Laleu.</u>

A spring, supplied by an underground stream running through fissures in the chalk hills and a very considerable delivery. Emerges at the roadside in a protected reservoir.

Steps have been taken by my Water N.C.O. to have the spring guarded and a guard has been arranged for through Bde.Hd.Qrs. Arrangements have also been made with the 84th. Field Coy. R.E. for a pump to be temporarily fixed to the reservoir, enabling carts to be quickly filled and avoiding the necessity of lowering receptacles into the reservoir.

The surroundings of the spring are satisfactory and 1 measure of bleaching powder per cart was ordered.

Other Sources.

In the area there are some deep wells, mostly inaccessible to water carts and some ran water reservoirs, mostly without filters.

GENERAL WORK.

Plans have been made of the new Divisional Laundry, it is proposed to construct at the present baths CORBIE. The room at present used as a billet by the X M.A.C. and the two rooms (one over the other) immediately to the left of it will be used. The present M.A.C. Billet will be utilised as the wash-house it having a cement floor and here the rotary reversing washer, the centrifugal wringer, the oil engine and the hot and cold tanks will be installed. The top room immediately to the left will be used as the drying room and the room below as an ironing and mending room. It is hoped to construct a filter capable of dealing with the effluent. The Laundry will be able to deal with about 15,000 garments per week.

DISINFECTIONS.

Disinfection was carried out following a case of German Measles in the 10th. K.R.R.

The new Cinema and No.3 Mess CORBIE have been sprayed.

Blankets disinfected during the week - 80.

DISINFECTANTS ISSUED.

Chloride of Lime...	240 lbs.
Cresesoli...	20 galls.
Formalin...	1 gall.
Whale Oil....	10 galls.

LIST OF PARTIES BATHED.

6th. K.S.L.I	200 men.
11th. K.R.R.	450 "
11th. R.B......	350 "
83rd. Field Coy. R.E....	150 "
12th. K.R.R...	290 "
6th. Oxon. & Bucks. L.I....	230 "
60th. M.G.C......	108 "
20th. Divn. & 4th. Divn R.F.A.....	80. "
12th. R.B..	186 "
60th. T.M.Battery.	50. "
11th. Durham L.I....	310 "

LIST OF CLEAN CLOTHING ISSUED.

Shirts.....	2058.
Pants.....	1756.
Socks...	1767.
Towels....	120.
Vests....	74.

LIST OF DIRTY CLOTHING RECEIVED.

Shirts......	2736.
Pants....	2610.
Socks... ..	2460.
Towels....	120.
Vests.....	74.

ARTICLES OF CLOTHING PASSED THROUGH "THRESH" DISINFECTOR FOR
LAUNDRY...... 14,173.

Captain R.A.M.C., D.A.D.M.S.
for. O.C. Sanitary Section 33.
Attached XXth (Light) Division.

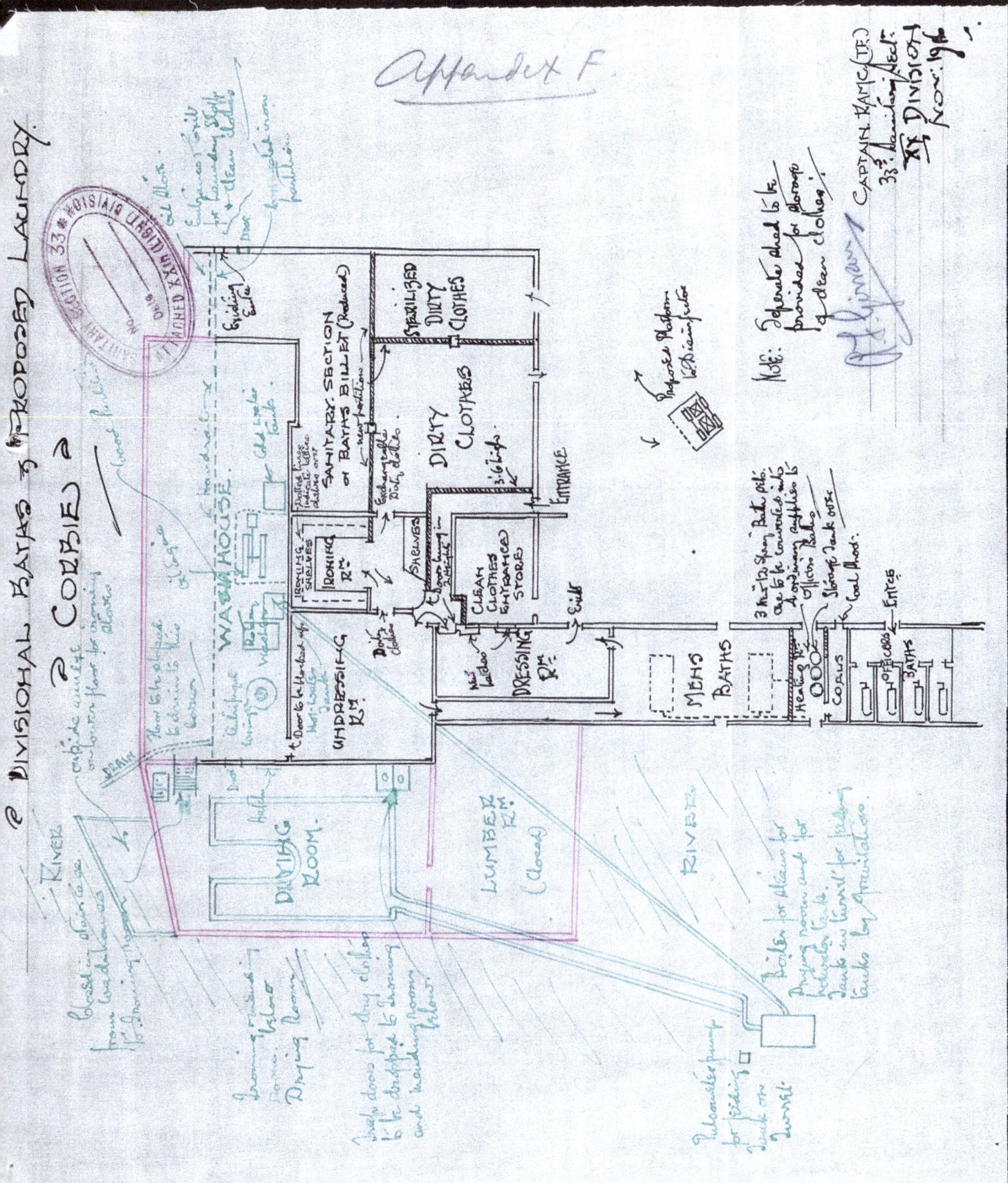

Confidential

WAR DIARY

— of —

Captain A.F. GIRVAN. R.A.M.C. (T.F.)
Officer Commanding

33rd Sanitary Section
1st London (City of London) Sanitary Company
R.A.M.C. (T.F.)

attached
20th (LIGHT) DIVISION
B.E.F.
FRANCE.

December 1916

Volume 7.

COMMITTEE FOR THE MEDICAL HISTORY OF THE WAR
Date 31 JAN. 1917

Army Form C. 2118.

Page 1.

War Diary of Capt.
A.F. Turton. R.A.M.C.
O.C. 33's Sanitary Section.

WAR DIARY
or
INTELLIGENCE SUMMARY.
(Erase heading not required.)

Instructions regarding War Diaries and Intelligence Summaries are contained in F.S. Regs., Part II. and the Staff Manual respectively. Title pages will be prepared in manuscript.

Place	Date	Hour	Summary of Events and Information	Remarks and references to Appendices
			Capt A.C.H. SUMR RAMC D.ADMS 20th Div for O.C. 33 Sanr Sect	Appendix A.
			VOLUME VIII page I	
CORBIE	1.XII.16		Inspections of billets etc at VAUX. Visited Baths at CORBIE - re laundry.	
	2.XII.16		Inspections at CORBIE. Inspection of billets & Sources of water Supply at SAILLY-LE-SEC. Interview with A.A.T.Q.M.G. re Coal Contracts for Laundry at AMIENS. Interview with Town Major CORBIE re Sanitary Policy and improvements in general Sanitation of this Town	Appendix B.
	3.XII.16		Visited Baths & Laundry. Interviewed A.A.T.Q. M.G. re Progress of work. Arranged for disinfection of blankets at the rate of 1000 per day to commence on 5th inst. Blanket Roster to be commenced. Inspections at VAUX	
	4.XII.16		Nothing Special to report.	
	5.XII.16		Paid Laundry Bill at AMIENS. New Coal arrangements made at rate of 70 frs per 1000 kilos. Visited Baths at CORBIE. Inspections	
	6.XII.16		Blanket roster commenced. Units not sending properly. Large increase in Stock of underclothing. Towels ordered by A.A.T.Q.M.G.	
	8.XII.16		Visited forward Area. Interview with O.C. Sanr Sect 29th Div re arrangements dispositions etc. Handed over to Capt A.F. GIRVAN. O.C. 33 Sanr Sect returned fr. leave	

A.C.H. Suhr
Capt. R.A.M.C. DADMS

Army Form C. 2118.
Page 2
Lan Dengfsswan R. Mat
Capt. R.F. SIRVAN. R.M.
O.C. SANITARY SECTION 33.
ATTACHED XXth LIGHT DIV.

WAR DIARY
or
INTELLIGENCE SUMMARY.
(Erase heading not required.)

Place	Date	Hour	Summary of Events and Information	Remarks and references to Appendices
CORBIE	1916 Dec 8	Noon	Returned from leave to U.K. and re-assumed command of 33 Sanitary Section 20 Division	
"	9		Refitting of the threshers again visited. Laundry in process of construction. Little progress has been made in all this respect all has gone been considered with vigour and efficiency during my absence. M.O.	Appendix C.
"	10		Arranging for man into forward area and fortifying near or San Sec 20th Div.	App. Appendix D(1)
"	11		First portion of move completed satisfactorily. M.O.	Appendix D(2) Appendix E.
MONTAUBAN A2 d 97 Allakewlin Sheet.	12		Second portion of move completed satisfactorily. The new site is in an ocean of mud trenches + shell holes, D.H.Q. in Armstrong huts, camps of Nissen huts and some in tents (without boards). My office in tent first night. M.O.	
"	13		Various arrangements necessitated by unusual conditions. E.g. G.S. wagon required daily to draw rations from PLATEAU (MARICOURT), 2 G.S. wagons required to bring clean clothes to clean clothes store A2d central from a lorry which brings them from CORBIE to BRICOURT, and a G.S. wagon conveying clothes from A2d central to baths MONTAUBAN (via MARICOURT on account of traffic routes) Arranged for drying sheds BRIQETERIE + GUILLEMONT to be run entirely by Town Majors of Bernafay + GUILLEMONT (AKOILE). San Sec lorry has permission from IV Army H to move in the prescribed area + flits between CORBIE + A2d 97 MONTAUBAN daily. M.O.	

Army Form C. 2118.

Page 3.
War Diary
Capt. A.F. BRYAN. R.A.M.C.(T)
O.C. SANITARY SECTION 83.
ATTACHED XXth (Light) Division

WAR DIARY
or
INTELLIGENCE SUMMARY.
(Erase heading not required.)

Instructions regarding War Diaries and Intelligence Summaries are contained in F. S. Regs., Part II. and the Staff Manual respectively. Title pages will be prepared in manuscript.

Place	Date	Hour	Summary of Events and Information	Remarks and references to Appendices
MONTAUBAN 1.2d 9.7	Dec 1916 14		Went to drying rooms TRONES WOOD to inspect arrangements and see that all was going well. Also baths MONTAUBAN (with Col. DUNDAS A.A-Q.M.G.). Difficulty in connection with supply of clothes & transport.	
"	15		Blanket disinfection started in hut in Camp a1. Inspected water point at CARNOY.	
"	16		MAIDEN POST and MONTAUBAN (infect.) Drying rooms TRONES WOOD shelled. Off. Baths started MONTAUBAN at 50 for hour with clean clothes. Visited GUILLEMONT water point & various things. Were found defective & all to remedied. G.S. wagon carrying rations from PLATEAU shelled. Driver & horse slightly wounded. Horses bolted before pulled up just as near wheel was coming off. Shelled again at COSY CORNER. Horses again bolted & were pulled up about 50 yards after the near off wheel had come off. Disposition of section as per Appendix II Off.	Appendix F
"	17		Went to drying rooms Trones Wood. Also BRIQUETERIE no water point there. Found leak & no protection against Frost. Paid baths & drying room personnel at those places.	
"	18		Visit to Amiens to pay Laundry (about 5700 francs). Arranged for larger number of garments to be washed daily and for larger coal supply, all drying being now done by artificial means during winter.	

Army Form C. 2118.

War Diary
page 1
Captain A.F.S. RUAN
R.A.M.C. [AF]
O.C. SANITARY SECTION 83.
ATTACHED XXth (LIGHT) DIVISION

WAR DIARY
or
INTELLIGENCE SUMMARY.
(Erase heading not required.)

Instructions regarding War Diaries and Intelligence Summaries are contained in F.S. Regs., Part II. and the Staff Manual respectively. Title pages will be prepared in manuscript.

Place	Date	Hour	Summary of Events and Information	Remarks and references to Appendices
MONTAUBAN AREA	Dec 1916 19		A.F. GARVAN. CAPT. R.A.M.C. T.F. O.C. 23 San. Sec. 20th Div. Drying rooms and Baths working. Camp inspection afternoon.	A.F.G.
"	20		" " " After work all afternoon. Would Capt Mathews O.C. San Sec. Div. to meet me	A.F.G.
"	21		Preparing notes of area, writing report etc. to hand over to 14th Div. Capt Mathews visited me. Movement order drawn up.	A.F.G. Appendix F.
"	22		Awaiting O/C Baths 14th Div. (14th Div Race separate Officer for this job)	A.F.G. Appendix G.
"	23		Handed over Drying Room 7056 (Bernafay-Trônes Wood Road), Baths and their contents to a 14th Div San. Sec. N.C.O. at each place. Also clothes (Service Dress) at my clothes exchange Camp 21. Complete change of staff was effected in each case thus ensuring the means of continuity. O/C Baths 14th Div Capt Woodgatt arrived last night and was taken away ill to F Ambulance this morning. A new O/C Baths 14th Div is to arrive tonight. Visited COMBLES in afternoon to see what arrangements existed for foot drying as this place will presently come in my area. Also visited catacombs there & San. Sec. Lorry broke down in CORBIE.	Appendix H. A.F.G. Appendix I.
CORBIE	24		Completed move to CORBIE after handing over to CAPT MATTHEWS O.C. SanSec 14th Div. San. Sec Lorry repaired overnight. Baths stow lorry and two others used as such also, latter two specially for duty clothes.	A.F.G.
"	25		Arranged for renewal of dirty clothes still remaining at MONTAUBAN. Inspection Corbie	A.F.G.

T2134. Wt. W708—776. 500000. 4/15. Sir J. C. & S.

Army Form C. 2118.

Page 5.
War Diary of
Captain P. SIRVAN
R.A.M.C. (T.F.)

O.C. Sanitary Section 33.
ATTACHED XXIII (LIGHT) DIVISION

WAR DIARY
or
INTELLIGENCE SUMMARY.

(Erase heading not required.)

Instructions regarding War Diaries and Intelligence Summaries are contained in F. S. Regs., Part II. and the Staff Manual respectively. Title pages will be prepared in manuscript.

Place	Date	Hour	Summary of Events and Information	Remarks and references to Appendices
CORBIE	1916 Dec 26		Awaited Requisition officer at all Cabre as per appointment. He did not arrive. Went fully into plans for Redoubt (in process of construction at the tubes) with Capt Muddell R.E.	
		9.30 am	Went over laundry with Divisional Commander	
		9.50	" " A.A.Q.M.G. & D.A.D.M.S. 26 Div.	
		11 a	" " and talks to D.A.D.O.S. 26 Div.	
		2.30	Passed round CORBIE with Town Sanitary officer and Capt. to CRE to get remedy. Latrine in a ½ finished state. complete by an R.E. Found that urinals were all to late river.	A.J.
"	27		Various influenzas. Dinner in evening of San Sec. and Baths Staff attended. I pressed B.S.M.	
"	28		Visit to Laundry attempts to ascertain why Clothes were failing to arrive in proper quantity. Agreement signed by him. Payment freight prices of coal & washing rates	A.J.
"	29		Visited Capt Pearson O.C. San Sec. Guards Div. relative to taking over from that Division. No written matter received relative to sanitary or other matter but shown round Laundry Ville in detail, though it is unlikely that I shall have the opportunity of taking it over.	A.J.
"	30.		Preparing Lecture to 4th Army School of Sanitation	A.J. Appendix I.

Army Form C. 2118.

Page 6
War Diary of
Capt. A.F. Girvan
R.A.M.C.(T.F.)

O.C. Sanitary Section 33,
ATTACHED XXth (LIGHT) DIVISION

WAR DIARY
or
INTELLIGENCE SUMMARY.
(Erase heading not required.)

Instructions regarding War Diaries and Intelligence Summaries are contained in F. S. Regs., Part II. and the Staff Manual respectively. Title pages will be prepared in manuscript.

Place	Date	Hour	Summary of Events and Information	Remarks and references to Appendices
CORBIE	Dec 1916 31		Visited BRONFAY FARM with A.A & Q.M.G. relative to establishment there of a clean clothes store and drying room. A.G.	

A.F. Girvan
Captain R.A.M.C. (T.F.)
O.C. Sanitary Section 33,
Attached XXth (Light) Division.

Appendix A.

REPORT

for week ending 25th. Nov. 1916.

DISPOSITION.

No change has taken place in the disposition of the of the personnel of the Sanitary Section and attached N.C.O's and men during the week and it remains the same as stated in my report for week ending 18/11/16.

SANITATION.

Inspections have been daily of Units in the Divn. by inspectors detailed for this work. The Sanitary con--ditions found were as follows:

Units.	State of Camps and Billets.	Remarks.
CORBIE.		
Divn. Hd. Qrs.	Satisfactory.	
Divn. H.Q. and Transport.	Satisfactory.	Manure at Transport being burned. Public latrines used.
Divn. H.Q. cook--house & Billet.	Satisfactory.	
G.O.C.& No,1 Mess.	Satisfactory.	
No. 2 Mess.	Satisfactory.	
No. 3 Mess.	Satisfactory.	
C.R.E. Mess,Place de la Republique.	Satisfactory.	
C.R.E. Transport. Bray Road.	Satisfactory.	Manure is being burnt on incinerator. Public latrines are used.
Divn. Signal Coy. Rue de College.	Satisfactory.	Public latrines are used.
Divn. Signal Coy. Transport, Bray Road.	Satisfactory.	Manure is being burnt on 2 incinerators. Public latrines are used. No cook--ing is done in these lines.

Units.	State of Camps and Billets.	Remarks.
D.A.D.O.S., Place de la Republique.	Satisfactory.	
Salvage Coy. and Divn. Band.	Satisfactory.	Public latrines are used.
Traffic Control, 27 Place de la Republique.	Satisfactory.	Public latrines are used.
M.M.Police, Rue Victor Hugo.	Satisfactory.	Public latrines are used.
Divn. Baths.	Satisfactory.	
Hd.Qrs. Officers' Chargers, No.8 Rue August Gindre.	Satisfactory.	Manure is now being removed daily by civilians
Hd. Qrs. Sergts' Mess, Rue August Gindre.	Satisfactory.	
11th., Durham L.I.	Satisfactory.	On the 21/11/16 the Battn. moved to another quarter and on 25/11/16 vacated the town leaving billets in a satisfactory state.

DAOURS.

84th. Field Coy. R.E.	(Fairly Satisfactory.	The Hd. Qrs. drivers billet required cleaning up and this was done. At the billet at No.12 Rue de l'Eglise the latrine was too near the cookhouse & billet and the ground around the urinal was sodden with urine. The Sergt-Major was informed of these defects and it was promised that they should be remedied, which has since been done.

59th. Brigade.

Treux, Maricourt, Ville.

Bde.Hd.Qrs., Signals & Transport.	Satisfactory.	
10th. K.R.R. and Transport.	Satisfactory.	
11th. K.R.R. and Transport.	Satisfactory.	

Units.	State of Camps and Billets.	Remarks.
10th. R.B. and Transport.	Satisfactory.	
11th. R.B. and Transport.	Satisfactory.	
Machine Gun Coy. Transport and Trench Mortar Batt.	Satisfactory.	Some billets suffer from accumulations of rubbish left by previous Divisions.
60th. Field Ambulance and Transport.	Satisfactory.	
159th. Coy. A.S.C.	Satisfactory.	
96th. Field Coy. R.E.	Satisfactory.	

60th. BRIGADE, CORBIE.

Units.	State of Camps and Billets.	Remarks.
Bde. H.Q., Signals and Transport.	Satisfactory.	Burnt refuse from [incinerator] is placed in a hole which is being filled in by tenants of property. Manure is heaped by arrangement with owner of premises for removal.
12th. K.R.R. and Transport.	Satisfactory.	Accumulation of manure & refuse left by previous occupants. Public latrines are used and refuse is burnt at public incinerator.
12th. R.B. and Transport.	Satisfactory.	Manure is taken to dump allotted by Town Major. No waste pits; refuse taken by Town Authorities to Public incinerator.
6th. Oxon. & Bucks L.I. and Transport.	Satisfactory.	Some billets left in a filthy condition by previous occupants. Public latrines are used and refuse is collected by Town staff.
60th. Machine Gun Coy. & Transport.	Satisfactory.	Manure is placed on a dump at the bottom of field. The dump outside has been removed & the refuse adjacent to the billet carted to public dump.

Units.	State of Camps and Billets.	Remarks.
61st. Field Ambulance and Transport and T.M.Battery.	Satisfactory.	Manure is placed on Town manure dump. The pile of old tins and refuse from inside the grounds has been taken to the Town dump.
83rd. Field Coy. R.E.& Transport.	Satisfactory.	Public latrines are used. Refuse is burnt at public incinerator.
168th. Coy. A.S.C. and Transport.	Satisfactory.	An accumulaton of manure left by previous occupants. Manure disposed of at dump.

61st. BRIGADE.

This Brigade has been moving during the week and supervision has thus been rendered more difficult than when the Brigade is stationary.

12th. King's (Liverpool) Regt.	Satisfactory.	No incinerators were in existence owing to lack of material. Refuse was there-fore burnt in waste pits. On vacation billets were left in a satisfactory con--dition.
7th. Somerset L.I.	Satisfactory.	
7th. Cornwalls L.I.	Satisfactory.	
61st. Machine Gun Coy.	Satisfactory.	
62nd. Field Ambulance.	Satisfactory.	
161st. Coy. A.S.C.	Satisfactory.	

WATER.

Tests for free chlorine have been made from the following carts and the water found to be efficiently chlorinated:

```
Divn. Signal Coy.
11th. Durham. L.I.      2 carts.
10th. K.R.R.            2 carts.
11th. K.R.R.            2 carts
10th. R.B.              2 carts.
11th. R.B.              2 carts.
58th. Machine Gun Coy.  1 cart.
159th. Coy. A.S.C.
96th. Field Coy. R.E.
60th. Field Ambulance   2 carts.
12th. K.R.R.            2 carts.
12th. R.B.              2 carts.
6th. Oxon.& Bucks L.I.  2 carts.
60th. Machine Gun Coy.  1 cart.
```

160th. Coy. A.S.C.
83rd. Field Coy. R.E.   2 carts.
61st. Field Ambulance. 3 carts.

Pumps at the Rue Detrichoir and Divn. Baths CORBIE and Tanks and various supplies at VILLE tested.

The water cart of the 59th. Machine Gun Coy. is badly in need of repair or replacement.

GENERAL WORK.
Construction of permanent lid to excreta cart of Town Major CORBIE?

General supervision of reconstruction of public latrines and urinals in CORBIE.

LIST OF PARTIES BATHED.

12th. K.R.R.	325.
12th. R.B.	220.
11th. D.L.I.	176.
61st Field Ambulance	120.
R.E. Divn. Hd. Qrs.	42.
83rd. Field Coy. R.E.	74.
84th. Field Coy. R.E.	200.
R.F.A.	196.
R.F.A. C/250 50th. Divn.	50.
29th. Divn. Grenade School	60.
29th. Divn. Band	50.
29th. Division	30.
156th. Coy. A.S.C.	20.
10th. M.A.C.	65.
28th. Siege Battery	60.
5th. Bde. R.H.A.	21.
14th. Corps. A.S.C.	120.
Salvage Company	20.
49th. H.A.G. 14th. Corps.	30.
Total.	1852.

LIST OF CLEAN CLOTHING ISSUED.

Shirts	3960.
Pants	3447.
Socks	3825.
Towels	250.
Vests	213.

LIST OF DIRTY CLOTHING RECEIVED.

Shirts	2526.
Pants	2147.
Socks	2225.
Towels	250.
Vests	213.

No. of Articles passed through "THRESH" Disinfector for Laundry......   7,430.

LIST OF DISINFECTANTS ISSUED.

        Chloride of Lime...   2740 lbs.
        Creosoli..   160 galls.
        Paraffin...   5 galls.
        Bleaching Powder...   66 tins.
        Whale Oil..   50 galls.

[signature]

Capt. R.A.M.C., D.A.D.M.S.
for O.C. SANITARY SECTION 38,
ATTACHED XXIII (LIGHT) DIVISION.

Appendix B.

REPORT

for week ending 2nd. December 1916

DISPOSITION.

No change has taken place in the disposition of the personnel of the Sanitary Section and attached N.C.O's and men during the week and it remains the same as stated in my report for week ending 25/11/16.

SANITATION.

Inspections have been made daily of Units ine the Division by inspectors detailed for this work. The sanitary conditions found were as follows:

Units.	State of Camps and Billets.	Remarks.
Divn. Hd. Qrs.	Satisfactory.	
G.O.C. & No.1 Mess.	Satisfactory.	
No.2 Mess Rue du College.	Satisfactory.	
No.3 Mess 21,Place de la Republique..	Satisfactory.	
H.Q. Transport. Bray Road.	Satisfactory.	Manure is being burned daily.
C.R.E. Mess, 22 Place de la Republique.	Satisfactory.	
C.R.E. Transport. Bray Road.	Satisfactory.	
C.R.E. Men's Billet.	Satisfactory.	Removed on Thursday from Rue du College to No.5 Rue Auguste Gindre. Old billet left in clean condition.
Divn. Signal Coy.	Satisfactory.	
do Transport Bray Road.	Satisfactory.	Manure is beingburned continuously.

(1).

Units.	State of Camps and Billets.	Remarks.
D.A.D.O.S.16, Place de la Republique.	Satisfactory.	
Salvage Coy. & Divn. Band, School-room Rue Hersent.	Satisfactory.	
M.M. Police, Rue Victor Hugo.	Satisfactory.	
M.M. Police, Horse Lines, Route de Vaux.	Satisfactory.	Manure removed daily by farmer.
Traffic Control. 27, Place de la Republique.	Satisfactory.	
Divn. Baths.	Satisfactory	
H.Q. Officers' Chargers, 5 Rue Auguste Gindre.	Satisfactory.	Manure removed daily by civilians.
32nd. Mob. Vet. Sec.	Satisfactory.	A small amount of manure is being removed daily by civilians.
C.R.A. 61a, Rue Faidherbe.	Satisfactory.	
C.R.A., Men's Billet 60, Rue Faidherbe.	Satisfactory.	Waste pit was left in a very dirty condition by previous occupants but it is also used by Civilians & French Troops.
H.Q. Sergts' Mess. Rue Auguste Gindre.	Satisfactory.	Vacated 30/11/16 and billet taken over by 7th. D.C.L.I.
61st. Machine Gun Company.	-	Entered on Thursday Joint billet with Divn. Sig. Coy.

58th. Brigade.

Bde. Hd. Qrs. & Signals.	Satisfactory.	
10th. K.R.R. & Transport.	Satisfactory.	Majority of transport animals are now kept in stables at Mericourt.
11th. K.R.R. & Transport.	Satisfactory.	

Units.	State of Camps and Billets.	Remarks.
10th. R.B. & Transport.	Satisfactory.	Except ablutions arrangements, which is receiving attention. Billets vacated and left in a satisfactory condition on Battn. moving to Carnoy.
11th. R.B. & Transport.	Satisfactory.	Took over Billets vacated by 10th. R.B.
59th. Machine Gun Company, & Trench Mortar Battery.	Satisfactory.	A heap of old rubbish has been buried.
60th. Field Ambulance.	Satisfactory.	Permanent ablution bench constructed by Amb. at Ville.
96th. Field Coy. R.E.	Satisfactory.	The bulk of this Unit is stationed at Corbie and away from the Bde. area.
159th. Coy. A.S.C.	Satisfactory.	
60th. Brigade.		
Bde. H.Q. and Signals.	See "Remarks" Column.	Paper thrown about latrine & earth falling in. Front to build up. Billet not tidy; Food & refuse left by Artillery.
12th. R.B.	Satisfactory.	Vacated on Tuesday and left satisfactory.
12th. K.R.R. & Transport.	Satisfactory.	
6th. Oxon, & Bucks. L.I. & Transport.	See "Remarks" Column.	On vacation on Wed. some billets were left defective, as follows: Machine Gun Sec... Refuse & tins dumped in bags in yard C. Coy... 11 Plat.. Tins left in eaves, B. Coy.... Clothing & refuse.
60th. Machine Gun Company.	Satisfactory.	Except for water and refuse thrown out of Officers Mess kitchen.
60th. Trench Mortar Battery.	Satisfactory.	
60th. Field Ambulance.	Satisfactory.	
160th. Coy. A.S.C.	Satisfactory.	
83rd. Field Coy. R.E.	Satisfactory.	

Units.	State of Camps and Billets.	Remarks.

61st. Brigade.

Bde. H.Q. & Transport.   Satisfactory.   On leaving the billet the horse lines were not properly cleaned up, the proximity of a well rendering cleanliness doubly necessary.

7th. K.O.Y.L.I.   Satisfactory.

13th. King's (L'pool) Regt. & Transport.   Satisfactory.

7th. D.C.L.I.   Satisfactory.

7th. Somerset L.I. & Transport.   Satisfactory.

Trench Mortar Batt.   Satisfactory.

161st. Coy. A.S.C.   Satisfactory.   The last billet taken over by this coy. was left in a dirty and very unsatis-factory state by previous occupants.

This Brigade has again been moving during the week and sanitary supervision rendered somewhat difficult although doubly important.

Other Units.

D.A.C.
No.1 Section.   Satisfactory.   Last billet taken over left in a very unsatisfactory state by previous occupants.

84th. Field Coy. R.E.   Satisfactory.

Water.

Tests for free chlorine have been made from the following carts and the water found to be efficiently chlorinated:

    Divn. Signal Coy.
    7th. K.O.Y.L.I.
    61st. Machine Gun Coy.
    10th. K.R.R.
    11th. K.R.R.
    10th. R.B.
    11th. R.B.
    159th. Coy. A.S.C.
    60th. Field Ambulance
    12th. K.R.R.
    6th. Oxon. & Bucks. L.I.
    60th. Machine Gun Coy.
    160th. Coy. A.S.C.
    61st. Field Ambulance
    7th., D.C.L.I.

Tests and investigations of many sources of supply in CORBIE and in Brigade area have been made by the water N.C.O's to Divn. H.Q. and the Brigades.

The 59th. Machine Gun Coy. has now drawn a new cart from Ordnance (E85693). The cart is sound and in good condition but it has no spare parts. On the water being tested by my water N.C.O. on 28/11/16 the water was found unchlorinated but since then it has been satisfactorily chlorinated.

The water cart of the 10th. K.R.R. (E64162) leaks badly from rivet holes at bottom.

My water N.C.O. with the 61st. Brigade, which has been on the move, has been able to travel ahead and advise on the water supplies of the villages occupied.

Other Work.

CORBIE.

Supervising work of fatigue party assisting the Town Major's staff in repairing public latrines.

VAUX.

Disinfecting billet of 12th. King's (Liverpool) Regt.

Blankets disinfected during the week .... 589.

List of Parties Bathed

20th. Divn Hd. Qrs. Traffic....	20.
12th. K.R.R.	412.
6th. Oxon.& Bucks L.I....	240.
12th. King's (Liverpool) Regt.	240.
do do do do	369.
7th. K.O.Y.L.I.....	20.
7th. Somerset L.I.	305.
6th. K.S.L.I...	208.
61st. Field Ambulance	89;
91st. Brigade R.F.A....	583
155th. Battery R.G.A.....	35.
26th. Battery. R.G.A....	49.
R.G.A.....	70;
H.A.G....	51.
10th. Battery R.F.A. 29th. Divn.	40.
29th. Divn. Grenade School....	60.
163rd. Coy. A.S.C.....	23.
14th. Corps A.S.C....	12.
14th. & 15th. M.A.C....	50
Total...	2870.

List of Clean Clothing Issued

    Shirts.........   3333.
    Pants........   2625.
    Socks..   2975.
    Towels..   556.
    Vests.........   ...

List of Dirty Clothing Received

    Shirts.......   4720.
    Pants....   3810.
    Socks...   4166.
    Towels....   556.
    Vests....   500.

No. of Articles passed through "Thresh" Disinfector
for Laundry.........   16,036.

List of Disinfectants Issued.

    Chloride of Lime....   1560 lbs.
    Cresol.....   150 galls.
    Bleaching Powder...   28 tins.
    Whale Oil.....   135 galls.

                    [signature]

              Capt. R.A.M.C., D.A.D.M.S.
        for O.C. SANITARY SECTION 33.
              ATTACHED XIIIth (LIGHT) DIVISION.

Appendix C.

To.

A.D.M.S.,

20th. Division.

In my opinion the advantages and disadvantages of detaching a Sanitary Section from its Division are summarised below:

ADVANTAGES.

1. A better knowledge of the area will be obtained.
2. The length of stay in the Area being known, plans for the initiation of constructional work, such as Baths, etc., can be made on definite data.

DISADVANTAGES

1. The personal factor will be lost. The A.D.M.S., A.A.& Q.M.G., C.R.E., S.S.O. and D.A.D.O.S. will be much more likely to help a man they know personally and whose work they know and whom has the brotherhood of the Division than a stranger. Such help is vital for efficiency. This applies also, although perhaps to a somewhat lesser degree, to Regimental Medical Officers, where often the personal touch will produce immediate results.

2. No two Sanitary Sections do the same— same work. For instance some do the distribution of disinfectants for their Division, others do not. Some have elaborate systems in operations for the inspection of every unit in the Division as regards sanitation and water supplies These involve the preparation of card indices and duplicated forms and attaching some of the Section to Brigades. All this kind of work would be thrown completely out of gear, after very great trouble, in getting it into operation, and the Division would be without supervision ate times of moving – when super- -vision is particular needed.

3. The knowledge of the past history of units and the best way to secure good work from them would be lost. The knowledge has taken a long time to acquire and plays quite an important part in maintaining efficiency.

4. The suggested period of stay in one area, viz. one month is too short to make the suggested change worth while. Any longer stay would be hard on the Section in the most forward area.

5. One of the chief aims of a Sanitary Section is to see that Units are educated up to the view that Sanitation is a most important factor and that every unit should see that on vacating a billet or transport lines they are left in a better condition than was found on entry. This can only be done by a close touch with units and a vigorous inspection both when in occupation and immediately after vacation, and this close touch can only be maintained when a Section is part of a Division.

Most of the advantages of the Area system can be obtained with the existing Divisional system by arranging for greater uniformity of work in the various Sections and by insisting on the preparation of detailed plans of work done or in progress and the handing over of these plans from O.C. to O.C.

For the above reasons I am strongly in favour of the Sanitary Section remaining Divisional.

Captain R.A.M.C.(T.F.).
Commanding
33rd. Sanitary Section.

Appendix D(1)

AFTER DAILY ORDERS
-by-
Captain A.F.GIRVAN, R.A.M.C. (T.F.),
Commanding 33rd. Sanitary Section.

Sunday 10th. December 1916.

1. **MOVE.**

   (a)(1) The Baths and Laundry Staff will remain at
       CORBIE, except Lce Corporal BEARDSWORTH.H.
       and personnel alreadydespatched to control
       the Spray Baths and Drying Rooms in new Area.
   (2). The THRESH Disinfector will remain at CORBIE
       and will be used for clothes from the Front
       Area.
   (3) The 3 ton Lorry No. 11823 and Sanitary Section
       Lorry will remain at CORBIE.
   (4) Corporal GAUNT. E.L. will remain at CORBIE
       i/c sanitation and water supplies on Divisional
       Headquarters Details, Artillery and such other
       20th. Divisional Units as may remain at CORBIE
       and in the neighbouring villages. He will be
       billeted at the Baths.
   (5) The above personnel and Lorries will be rationed
       with Divisional Headquarters Details remaining
       at CORBIE.

   (b). Staff Sergeant BEAUMONT. A.E. with Lce Corporals
       SPURGEON. T.C., HUNTING.E.A. and MATHER.T.J.
       will proceed at 8.a.m. on Monday 11th. December
       to Headquarters 29th. Divisional Sanitary Section
       at A.2.d.9.7. and take over from 29th. Divisional
       Sanitary Section. They will make their own
       way there.

   (c).(1). The remainder of the Sanitary Section and
       attached personnel (less the Office Staff,
       storekeeper and batman) under the charge of
       Lce Corporal McHUGH. P. will parade at 9.30.
       a.m. on Monday 11th. December 1916 heavy
       marching order and proceed to TREUX by the
       Sanitary Section lorry. The kitchen utensils
       and rations will be taken by this lorry.
   (2). The above party (less Lce Corporal HILL.E.
       and three men) will proceed from TREUX on
       Tuesday 12th. December at 8.a.m., heavy
       marching order and march to the Sanitary
       Section Camp at A.2.d.9.7. (opposite
       Y.M.C.A. hut) on the MONTAUBAN-CARNOY Road).
       The kitchen utensils and staff will remain
       at TREUX and proceed by the Sanitary Section
       Lorry; these to be ready by 8.a.m.
   (3). Lce Corporal HILL.E. and three men will
       proceed from TREUX on Tuesday 12th. December
       to GROVETOWN Coal Dump to arrive there not
       later than 1.30 p.m. The party will there
       load with disinfectants the two G.S.Wagons
       supplied bythe S.S.O. and proceed with them
       to the Sanitary Section Camp at A.2.d.9.7.

(2).

(d). The Sanitary Section Office will close at
CORBIE at 7.a.m. on Tuesday 12th. December and
will open at A.2.d.9.7. at 3.p.m. on the same
day.

(e). The Sanitary stores, men's kits and one blanket
per man will remain at CORBIE i/c Pte.
HARRISON. T.O. until Tuesday 12th. December
and will on that day be removed to the Sanitary
Section Camp at A.2.d.9.7. by the Sanitary
Section Lorry and the "Baths" Lorry.

(f). Certain Mobilization Stores will be left at the
Baths CORBIE. They will be conveyed there by
The Sanitary Section Lorry on its return from
TREUX on the 11th. December.

(g). Pte. BEAGLES. A.W. will proceed mounted on
Tuesday 12th. December direct to the new
Camp.

2. BATHS.

The Baths, CORBIE will remain working according to the
allottment given by the Town Major CORBIE, but no clothing
will be exchanged by the Baths Staff except to 20th.
Division Units.

3. CLEAN AND DIRTY CLOTHING.

(a). Clean clothing will be conveyed to SANDPITS from
Baths CORBIE and dirty clothing from SANDPITS to
CORBIE daily by Sanitary Section Lorry. Clothing
will be carried between the forward area and
SANDPITS by G.S. Wagon.
(b). The "Baths" Lorry will carry disinfected dirty
clothing to AMIENS from CORBIE and clean clothing
from AMIENS to CORBIE daily.
(c). Daily States of clothing will be rendered as
heretofore by Q.M.S. i/c Baths to Sanitary Section
Headquarters by D.R.L.S.

4. CANTEEN.

A Divisional Canteen is established at TRONES WOOD
North of the Divisional Drying Sheds.

5. SPECIAL LEAVE.

Special leave has been granted to the following men
to commence on the 14th. December 1916.
No. M2/103835. Pte. FOSTER. W. A.S.C. (M.T.).

Captain R.A.M.C. (T.F.).
Officer Commanding,
33rd. Sanitary Section.

Appendix D(2)

DAILY ORDERS NO. 40
-by-
Captain A.F.GIRVAN, R.A.M.C.(T.F.).
Commanding 33rd. Sanitary Section.

Monday 11th. December 1916.

1. <u>MOVE</u>.

   (a) Paragraph 1 (e) of After Daily Orders of Sunday 10th. December 1916 is cancelled and the following substituted:
The Sanitary Stores, men's kits and one blanket per man will remain at CORBIE i/c Pte.HARRISON, T.O. until Tuesday 12th. December. On that day part of these stores will be removed to Sanitary Section Camp at A.2.d.9.7. by the "Baths" Lorry to leave CORBIE at 9.30 a.m. and on the following day the remainder by the Sanitary Section lorry. Pte.HARRISON,T.O. will remain at CORBIE until these stores have been removed.

   (b) The Sanitary Section Lorry will be placed at the disposal of Divisional Headquarters on Tuesday 12th. December and the driver will on that day report at the Camp Commandant's Office at 8 a.m.

2. <u>BATHS</u>.

Paragraph 2 of After Daily Orders of Sunday 10th December 1916 is cancelled and the following substituted:
The Baths CORBIE will remain working according to the allotment given by the Town Major of CORBIE, but no clothing will be exchanged by the Baths Staff except to 20th. Division Units and to the parties of Artillery bathing from 9 a.m. to 10 a.m. on every other day.

3. <u>CLEAN AND DIRTY CLOTHING</u>.

Paragraph 3 (a) of After Daily Orders of Sunday 10th December 1916 is cancelled and the following substituted:
(a) Clean clothing will be conveyed to the Forward area from the Baths CORBIE daily by Sanitary Section Lorry. The drivers of this lorry is always to carry with his special pass issued by Fourth Army Headquarters.

4. <u>CENSORSHIP</u>.

It is useless to present for censoring postcards pictues of Towns, Churches, Chateaux, etc. even if the names are cut off. The Censorship Regulations do not allow these and even if they were franked by the Commanding Officer they would be destroyed at the Post Office.

Captain R.A.M.C.(T.F.).
Commanding
33rd. Sanitary Section.

Appendix E.

REPORT

on Sanitary Conditions and Water
Supplies of, and Improvements
carried out in Area occupied by
20th. (Light) Division during
period 15/11/16 - 11/12/16.

The Division during the period of this Report has been composed as follows:

1. CORBIE. Divisional Headquarters, one Brigade and portion of another.

2. MERRICOURT.)
   VILLE.   ) One Brigade.
   TREUX.   )

3. Various   ) One Brigade which has been on
   villages.)   the move during this period.

1.

CORBIE.

This Town has been in occupation by Divisional Headquarters Troops, portions of two Infantry Brigades, one Brigade of R.F.A, and Corps Troops.

When this Division was last in occupation of this Town in September 1916 it was necessary to send in a Report on the extremely insanitary state of the Town, the conditions then requiring immediate attention. It was again found necessary to report as, although some improvements had been made, the state of the Town was still far from satisfactory. The latrines are in a dirty condition and urine was generally to be found in pools around the urinals. Most of the small streets and lanes are in a dirty state, excreta lying about every few yards. Owing to its rapidly changing military population and to there being neither a permanent Sanitary Section or Officer or squad of Inspectors, the conditions of the Town are very difficult and if anything like a satisfactory state is to be obtained it

1.

is absolutely essential that a permanent staff of Inspectors shall be allotted to the Town Major. Before the departure of this Division a Town Sanitary Officer had arrived, but there is still not one specialist N.C.O. Inspector.

A thorough inspection of the Town was made twice, first from a general sanitary point of view and then especially to report on all latrines and urinals at the request of the Town Major. A copy of this Report is annexed. Suggestions were made for remedying the defects found and attention was drawn to the lack of public latrines for Officers and the insanitary condition of the Town Dumping ground.

As much assistance in constructional work as it was possible to give was accorded to the Town Major by the Sanitary Section. A cover for the excreta cart was provided enabling the collection of excreta to take place during daylight instead of at night as formerly when excreta was spilled and sometimes buckets not emptied owing to the men being unable to see what they were about.

One new public latrine (12 seats) was constructed, the screen and roof being of corrugated iron and tarred felt. An Officers' latrine (2 seats) was also made.

Apart from these two latrines, the assistance given by the Section consisted in repairing existing latrines and urinals and erecting signboards indicating their position. Corrugated iron was substituted for the perished and dirty canvas screening, corrugated iron roofs were made and many new lids and flaps provided.

Excreta and rubbish is collected daily by the Town Majors Staff and fatigue parties from the Battalion occupying the Town were detailed daily to assist in this and in road sweeping.

WATER: Tests and investigations were made of pumps and supplies in the Town.

The supply from the pump in the yard of the Girl's Primary School (next to Billet No. 20 Rue HERSENT) is an unsatisfactory one.   The pump is 8 yards from a cesspool draining a series of latrines and urinals and during the previous occupation of the premises by a C.C.S. these were used by patients, including infectious cases. A chemical test which I made shewed the water to be markedly contaminated and subsequent bacteriological examination confirmed this. This pump was placed out of Bounds.

The boards on the Towns supplies shating that ½ measure of Bleaching Powder per cart was sufficient were changed to 1 measure.

A notice was affixed to the pump in the Rue AUGUSTE GINDRE prohibiting washing there.

During the occupation of the Town by the Division the construction of a Divisional Laundry has been commenced. Premises (part of which are now used as Baths) near the canal will be used ~~undertaking will be used~~ and washing will be by a rotary reversing washing machine with a centrifugal wringer. This work is being carried on by the 20th. Division R.E. at the present time.

Facilities have been made at the Baths for disinfecting blankets at the rate of 1000 per day and four stoves fixed for the purpose of drying the blankets after spraying.

2.

MERRICOURT.

This village was in occupation by two Battalions.

There are seven existing latrines with a seating accommodation of 78 seats. With one exception these are all permanent fly proof structures built over top of deep trenches In one case there is a pail latrine, the contents of the pails being buried in an adjoining field.   Six incinerators are existing. No new latrines or incinerators have been built, but the Battalions have furnished fatigue parties daily to the Town Major for sanitary work.

WATER: There are two supplies as follows:

        1. Spring supply in courtyard of Town Majors billet.   This is an ample supply and

of good quality, 1 measure of
bleaching powder being required.

2. Limited supply of good quality, requiring
1 measure of bleaching powder per
water cart.

VILLE.

This villages was in occupation by two Battalions,
Brigade Headquarters, a Field Ambulance (less Transport), a
Machine Gun Company and Trench Mortar Battery.

11 latrines are in existence having a seating
accommodation of 71 seats. These are permanent structures,
some being built over deep trenches and some on the pail
system, in which case the contents are buried on adjoining
ground. Three incinerators are existing, two being Public
ones.

No new latrines or incinerators have been constructed by
this Division.

Fatigue parties from the Battalions have been furnished
daily to the Town Major for various sanitary duties.

The Field Ambulance occupying the village has considerably
improved their billet by repairing several of the mud walls
and the construction of an ablution bench.

Water.

The supplies are as follows:

(1). A pump in the Y.M.C.A. yard giving a good supply
of good quality water, 1 measure of bleaching powder per
cart being required. This water was used by Brigade H.Q.

(2). Pump in court yard of billet used for cooking
purposes by the Machine Gun Coy. 1 measure of bleaching pow-
-der per cart required.

(3). Pump in court yard used for cooking purposes by
Trench Mortar Battery 1 measure of bleaching powder per cart
required.

(4). Tanks situated between VILLE and MEAULTE supplying
water carts. The water is pumped from a deep well, a permanent R.E. Staff being i/c under the general control of the

Fourth Army Water Column. 1 measure bleaching powder per cart is required. All drinking water is drawn from these tanks.

There are pumps & wells in other billets, yielding limited supplies for cooking purposes.

TREUX.

This village has been in occupation by several transport lines, an A.S.C.Coy. and part of a R.E.Coy.

There are 7 existing latrines, one being a public one (5 seats.) Some are pail latrines and others boxes over deep trenches. 20th. Division Units have constructed temporary structures. 5 incinerators are existing.

The A.S.C. & R.E.Coys. have very considerably improved their transport lines, the R.E's having roofed the structures over their horse lines.

WATER. The nearest water point is at BUIRE, near Corps Rest Station. Pumps & cisterns in billets supply a limited quantity of water, of good enough quality for cooking purposes.

3. The following villages which have been occupied by various units of one Brigade were merely resting places and were only occupied for a night or so. Obviously, therefore, much in the way of sanitary improvements became impossible. Some villages were occupied for so short a time that no report is sub--mitted.

ALLERY.

This village was occupied by a Machine Gun Coy. and a Field Ambulance.

On arrival no existing sanitary arrangements were found and temporary latrines were provided.

Water Supply: There are pumps at almost every house, the depth of the wells varying, according to the elevation of the soil, from 6 to 60 metres.

LE HAMEL and DREUIL.

These villages were occupied by one Battalion.

There were no existing latrines or incinerators on arrival. 11 latrines were constructed by this Division,

(5).

of the box type with a seating accommodation of 29 seats. Fatigue parties were detailed for cleaning up the main road through the villages.

Water Supply: There are pumps in almost every house.

BETTENCOURT ST OUEN.

This village was in occupation by one Battalion.

On arrival no existing sanitary arrangements were found. Temporary latrines were constructed and one small brick incinerator built on a waste piece of land. Fatigue parties detailed for necessary cleaning up of refuse left by previous occupants.

Water Supply; There is a public pump conveniently situated for filling water carts at the corner of Rue du Marais and the main road. This pump is supplied from a boring in the chalk about 10 metres deep and stands away from the buildings.

BOURDON.

This village was occupied by one Battalion and an A.S.C.Coy.

On arrival no sanitary provision was found (presumably latrines made as mentioned in a previous report having been removed) with the exception of the incinerator on the waste ground. Temporary latrines were made. A good deal of clearing up work was done.

Water Supplies: All the wells are private property, but access is easily obtained to a pump at the rear of Mme. Crampion's house, Chemin d'Hangest, near the church. This is the pump used for filling water carts and 1 measure of bleaching powder per cart is sufficient.

YZEUX.

This village was in occupation for 3 days by a Field Ambulance, a Machine Gun Coy. and a Trench Mortar Battery.

There were 2 ranges of Public Box Latrines existing of 8 seats and a public incinerator to which all refuse was taken. No new latrines or other work was undertaken.

Water Supplies:

Public Supplies:

(a) Well at roadside about 12 metres deep, It is protected inside to the water by brickwork and stands in an isolated position.

(b) Well similarly situated and protected as above but the quality of the water has suffered owing to proximity to crowded billets, wholesale washing taking place at the well and dirty receptacles being lowered.

(c) Pump known as "Pompe Communale" in a remote isolated position in the Rue du Marais, furnishing an excellent supply for water carts, 1 measure of bleaching powder per water being sufficient.

Other Supplies:

There are wells at most of the houses the quality of the water varying according to the number of troops billet--ed in the house and a few borings.

In the yard of the Chateau d'Yzeux is a well fitted with an endless chain on the Lepaitre system, producing a large delivery and enabling water carts to be filled rapidly. This well is 18 metres deep.

SAILLY-le-SEC.

This village was in occupation by one Battalion, Bde. Hd. Qrs., a Field Ambulance and an A.S.C.Coy.

On entry it was found that the existing latrines were in a very foul and insanitary condition, almost without except--ion, the receptacles being full to overflowing and the latrine areas fouled with excreta. The sides of the bye roads and open spaces were also badly fouled. The village was last occupied by French troops.

The latrines used during occupation were of the temporary trench type and the incinerators were also temporary Owing to the shortness of the stay no permanent work could be done. Much road cleaning was done by fatigue parties.

Water Supply:

All the wells are private property except 2 constructed by French Engineers, and two by British Engineers, but not used. The water from the wells in the lowest part of the village is of very poor quality.

At billet 16 a temporary stable was found on unpaved soil within 4 feet of the well. This well was considred by the MAIRE to be the best. At billet 17 the spring was found to be contaminated. This was the alternative supply to that at billet No.16.

The attention of the M.O. of the Battalion was drawn to the need of some form of protection to the well heads to prevent drainage fouling the supplies, but the necessary steps were not taken by him. This an urgent measure.

VAUX-sur-SOMME.

This village was occupied by one Battalion, an A.S.C. Coy. and a Trench Mortar Battery.

Latrines with a seating accommodation of 11 seats have been constructed by this Division and four temporary Incinerators built.

WATER SUPPLIES: In the lower end of the village the wells are too shallow for use and most of the other wells are out of action. Small repairs would remedy this.

Between Billets 13 & 15.   Pump - out of Action. Good position. No apparent contamination.

Billet 15.   Pump - dunghill near.

Billet 13.   Pump; Out of Action. Good position no apparent contamination. requires cleaning.

Billet 21.	Pump. Out of action. Handle removed by occupier.
Billet 22.	Pump. Owing to its being greatly used it runs dry at times.
Billet 3a	Well. Out of Action. Rope broken and well nailed up.
Cafe at corner of Rue des Morts and La Petite Rue.	Pump. Dunghill with 15 feet.
Billet 14c.	Pump. Stable and cattle trough near.
Billet 18.	Well. Dunghill within 10 feet.
Billet 20.	Pump. Large liquid patch of manure within 10 yards.
Billet 11.	Pump. Out of Action Dunghill 10 yards away.
Billet 10.	Pump. In good position.
Billet 9.	Pump. Out of Action. Dunghill within a few yards.
Billet 8.	Pump to well. Out of action.
School.	Boring fitted with a pump.

The village being crowded with troops and most of the wells being out of action the pumps that were in use tended to run dry and the quality of the water to suffer.

OTHER WATER SUPPLIES in area covered by Brigade.

BUSSY-les-DAOURS.

Nearly all the houses are along the three parallel roads and the road which connects them (Cathcart Street).

The villages stands on chalk soil close to a stream and at a slightly higher elevation than the peat bog. As the ground is so low and the water corresponding near the surface (8-10 metres) there are very few windlass wells, pumps being found at most of the houses. About one third of these are out of action.

Borings : At most of the bigger houses borings have been made to tap purer water at about 22 metres. The pumps in these cases are more frequently repaired and only one (at M.Leschus) is out of action. All are accessible to water carts, except No. 6.

Below the Rue d'en Bas the ground is marshy and peat is soon reached. At the "Mill", Mill Road (last door on the right) the water is unfit for drinking. After a small quantity is drawn the water assumes a very dark colour. This house,(The Mill),is partly surrounded by water and stands on a great depth of peat.

There are no public supplies,all the pumps being within private property. The occupiers are reluctant to allow the use of their pumps to water carts owing to the number of times their pumps have been broken.

LALOM.

La Fontine Libertine - This is a fine spring and is supplied by an underground stream running through fissures in the chalk hills and has a very considerable delivery.

AIRAINES.

The feature here is the presence of 3 springs supplying water of excellent quality.

1. Rue Fontaine aux Maladies,but spring is inaccessible to water carts and is away from billets.

2. Fontaine Guillette at the level crossing adjoining the station. It is tapped by a public pump on the roadside but the pump is broken.

3. Opposite Hotel-de-Dieu,but again the pump tapping it is broken.

Capt. R.A.M.C.(T.F.).
O.C. 33rd. Sanitary Section,
attached 20th. (Light) Division.

REPORT

on Public Latrines and Urinals, CORBIE, and
conditions found on inspection, December 2nd. & 3rd. 1916.

Behind billet No.8 Rue Gambetta.

Latrine. 6 seats; urine guides defective, hinge required to flap at front of one bucket; the floor of setts and earth is uneven. The roof is of tarred felt in a dilapidated condition, and the screening is of canvas, which is dirty.
The existing accommodation is insufficient; about 6 more seats are required.

Urinal. Consists of three drums, which are emptied daily; more buckets or drums are required; adjoining ground is saturated with urine.

Rue Bastion.

Urinal. Consists of corrugated iron trough; floor requires paving, being saturated with urine; the urinal requires reconstructing.

Rue Calvaire.

Latrine. 12 seats. In fair condition, except for roof which leaks in places; the floor is composed of old tins; fairly satisfactory in dry weather only but should not be regarded as permanent.

Urinal. Soakage pit type; choked. Should be put out of use at once and a new pit constructed. Drums must be used pro tem. It is possible that the old urine pit may become serviceable again after a rest.

Adjoining 78 Rue Gambetta.

Latrine. 6 seats; floor requires paving; structure in fair condition. Ground adjoining saturated with urine.
Urinal. 1 bucket; more buckets required.

End of passage adjoining 35 Rue Gambetta.

Latrine. 4 seats; 2 lids required; also urine guides throughout. Floor is of trench boards and broken bricks but could be improved; structure in good condition; quantity of urine on adjoining ground. Existing accommodation is insufficient; about 4 more seats are required.
Urinal. Soakage pit type; in fair condition.

End of Rue 14 Juillet.

Latrine. 10 seats; 6 lids required; some of the urine guides defective. The structure is of tarred felt & canvas, & in a perished condition; floor is of earth - fairly dry at time of visit. This & other earth floors become fluid mud in wet times and should be replaced by paving or brick.
Urinal. Soakage pit type; choked; quantity of urine on ground adjoining.

Rue Victor Hugo.

Latrine. 9 seats; quantity of urine on floor, which is in foul condition; the roof is defective and the screening which is of canvas, is in a dirty condition and should be replaced with corrugated iron.

Urinal. Trough & soakage pit type; choked; ground adjoining saturated with urine. Canvas screen in a dirty condition. This pit should be closed at once and replaced by a sufficient number of buckets; floor should be paved and canvas screen replaced with corrugated iron.

Rue de la Digue.

Latrine. 12 seats; in good condition; floor uneven.
Urinal. Soakage pit; canvas screen fouled with urine.

Rue Francisco Ferrer.

(a) Latrine. 6 seats in fair condition.
No urinal adjoining.
(b) Latrine. 6 seats, flaps required behind 3 buckets; otherwise in good condition.
Urinal. Soakage pit type; could be improved by raising the height of the receptacles for the urine.
Note. The latrines marked (a) & (b) are on the same field, about 60 yards from each other.

Behind 71 Rue Leon Cure.

Latrine. 9 seats; 1 lid missing; otherwise in good condition.
Urinal. 1 bucket; more buckets should be provided.

Adjoining 38 Rue Leon Cure.

Latrine. 14 seats; deep trench type; floor requires repairing near bottom of latrine box at level of top of pit. Otherwise in good condition.
Urinal. Biscuit tins.

Latrine. (Sergts.) 4 seats; deep trench type; in fair condition.
Urinal. Soakage pit type; in fair condition.

Opposite 51 Rue Leon Cure.

Latrine. 10 seats; 1 lid required; urine guides defective; the roof and screening required renewal; floor requires paving.
Urinal. Soakage pit type; could be improved by raising the height of the receptacles for the urine. Quantity of urine on adjoining ground.

Place Thiers.

Latrine. 6 seats; 1 lid required; 2 flaps required at rear; structure in fair condition; floor requires paving.
Urinal. Corrugated iron trough and soakage pit; pit choked; floor requires paving; accumulation of urine on adjoining ground. This pit should be closed at once and a sufficient number of buckets substituted.

Rue Charles Ducamps.

Latrine. 4 seats; in fair condition; a quantity of excreta & urine in old brick chamber adjoining. Existing accommodation insufficient; about 4 more seats should be provided.
Urinal. Corrugated iron trough & pit; in fair condition

Rotton Row, (off Rue Pie).

   Latrine.   9 seats; hinges required to flaps at rear; floor composed of old tins; structure in fair condition.
   Urinal.   Soakage pit type; urine on adjoining ground.

Rue Auguste Gindre.

   Latrine.   6 seats; in good condition.
   Urinal.   Soakage pit type; in fair condition.

Passage behind Divn. Hd. Qrs.

   Latrine.   10 seats; urine guides required; floor requires paving; structure in good condition.; 4 or 5 seats required.
   Urinal.   Soakage pit type; in fair condition.

Behind 73 Rue Jules Lardiere.

   Latrine.   4 seats; deep trench type; hinges required to one lid; requires new screen.
   Urinal.   Soakage pit type; in fair condition.

Behind 8 Rue Jules Lardiere.

   Latrine.   2 seats; deep trench type.
   Urinal.   Soakage pit type; in fair condition.

Opposite Divn. Baths.

   Latrine.   11 seats; floor requires paving; otherwise in good condition.
   Urinal.   2 drums; these are insufficient; more buckets or drums should be provided. Large accumulation of urine on adjoining ground.

OTHER REMARKS.

Officers' Latrines.

   There is a great lack latrines for Officers. What few there are existing, are situated away from the main thoroughfares.

General Repairs to Latrines.

   Assistance, such as the provision of lids and flaps, and repairs to roofs and sides, will be given by Sanitary Section.

Divisional Cinema, Grand Place.

   As the existing civilian urinals, adjacent to the above are unsatisfactory, I suggest that a portion of the footpath adjoining (in Rue Sadi Carnot) be screened from public view, and a sufficient number of urine buckets provided. At the conclusion of every performance at the Cinema, soldiers will be found urinating against the wall.

Billet No.3 Band Street - Insanitary Condition.

Part of these premises are occupied by wholesale green-grocers(civilian) and in the yard there is an offensive accumulation of manure, and decaying vegetable refuse. The upper portion of the premises is occupied by troops.

Incinerator.

In the Rue Francisco Ferrer, there is a good incinerator (Horsfall type). This apparently is not being used at present. The Shropshires are billeted in the neighbourhood, and if they could be advised to use this incinerator, and appoint a man to attend same, it would relieve the pressure on the town dump.

Town Dumping Ground.

This is in an objectionable state, there being a large quantity of rubbish deposited, which ought first to be passed through the incinerator. Apparently the existing incinerators cannot cope with all the refuse and it would be advisble for additional ones to be constructed.

The shoot of the big incinerator leaves much to be desired. It should be confined laterally by some form of wall-say-sandbags or corrugated iron, and should be floored with some impervious material.

Appendix F.   Copy No. 5.

SANITARY AND WATER
NOTES OF FORWARD AREA.

----

1. **Disposition & work of Section and attached Personnel.**

Sanitary Section.	Permanently attached Personnel.	Temporarily attached Personnel.	Duties.
Headquarters A.2. d. 9.7.	12 N.C.O's & men as follows:		
	S/Sergt............................		Supervision of work of Section.
	Corporal.) L/Corpl.)................		Office.
	L/Corpl...........................		Inspection of advanced & rear Divn.H.Q., water duties to Divn. troops units & chlorination of GUILLEMONT water Tanks(morning).
	L/Corpl....................	.....	Chlorination of water tanks at TALUS BOISE, BRIQUETERIE & CARNOY.
	L/Corpl........................		Chlorination of water tanks at COSY CORNER CARNOY East & GUILLEMONT. (Afternoon).
	L/Cporl.) L/Corpl.).............................		Carpentry and constructional work -making notice boards for dry--ing sheds and water points.
	Private............................		Storekeeper.
	Private............................		Messenger.
	Private............................		Cook.
	Private............................		Batman.

	Sanitary Section.	Permanently attached Personnel.	Temporarily attached Personnel.	Duties.
Headquarters, A.2.d.9.7.		7 O.R's as Follows: 1.......Pioneer. 1.......Rations. 1.......Cook's assistant. 4.......Assisting in carpentry & odd jobs.		
59th. Brigade. (Billeted at H.Q. 61st. Field Amb. CARNOY-MONTAUBAN Road).		1 Sergt.) 1 Private.) 1 L/Corpl.		Inspection of Camps & Transport lines occupied by Brigade. Water duties with Brigade.
60th. Brigade. (Billeted with H.Q. 61st. Field Ambulance.).		1 Sergt.) 1 L/Corpl.) 1 L/Corpl.		Inspection of Camps and ~~Billets~~ Transport lines occupied by Bde. Water duties with Bde.
61st. Brigade.... (Billeted at Corps Main Dressing Stn. CARNOY.)		1 Sergt.) 1 L/Cpl.) 1 L/Corpl.		Inspection of Camps and Transport Lines occupied by Brigade. Water duties with Bde.
Drying Sheds, TRONES WOOD.		1 L/Corpl.	10 O.R's 1 man from one of the Battns, 5 men from Salvage Coy.	i/c. Billeted in one of the drying sheds at present. When drying stoves (already indented for) arrive Town Major, BERNAFAY and GUILLEMONT will find another billet.
Divn Sock Changing Rooms No.6. (To be used as under-wear drying rooms). A.27.d.3.4. (Behind Y.M.C.A. on MONTAUBAN-BERNAFAY Road).			4 O.R's.	
MONTAUBAN Baths, on Cordoroy Road, South of MONTAUBAN....		1.L/Corpl. 1 O.R.	12 men from various Battns.	

Sanitary Section	Permanently attached Personnel	Temporarily attached Personnel	Duties
Clean Clothes Depot, Camp 21, CARNOY-MONTAUBAN Road, Hut No.1.	1 L/Corpl. 2 O.R's.		i/c. These two other ranks also carry out disinfection of blankets.
Baths, CORBIE.	2 Lorry Drivers.	1 Q.M.S. 13 O.R.	i/c. Including 3 "Baths" Lorry drivers & 2 "FODEN" Disinfector Drivers
CORBIE.	1 Corporal		i/c Sanitation & water duties of Divn. H.Q. details remaining in CORBIE

2. SANITATION.

The problem of Sanitation has been increasingly difficult in the forward area. The Camps occupied by the Divn. are:

    CARNOY EAST, 3 Camps, 21, 22, 23.
    CARNOY WEST, 3 Camps, 17, 18, 19.
    GUILLEMONT 2 Camps "Old" and "New".
    MANSEL CAMP. Occupied by 20th. Divn. Road Battn.

These Camps are not defintely alloted to particulars Units but are occupied for periods varying from 1-3 days by different Battns. A unit vacates its camp & relieves another in the line. The latter generally occupies the camp vacated by the releiving unit but not invariably. Thus there is a constant changing camp population which renders it very difficult to attache the blame for sanitary neglect. Thus no resultant continuous effort at Sanitation answers at CARNOY. The occupying units return from the trenches so utterly worn out that the obtaining of fatigue parties from them is impossible until they have been in occupation for 24 hours, and then the majority of the "fit" men are sent on road repairing work. The pioneers of the Battns. are in the same state as the other men. The system of Brigaded sanitary inspectors is not quite satisafctory under these conditions. It would be better to attach one inspector to each camp and put a standing working party under him.

3. WATER.

The chief water points used by the Division are:

1. GUILLEMONT.   T.25.a.8.8.
2. TALUS BOISE. A.14.b.8.9.
3. BRIQUETERIE. A.4. b.5.1.
4. CARNOY.   A.13.d.6.8.
5. CARNOY, EAST. A.2. d.central.
6. COSY CORNER .S.27.c.

I have not placed my inspectors permanently at these points as other Divisions have done, considering it a waste of good men and as likely to make the water cart men less self-reliant. The usual system was continued of constant inspection of water carts at any place to ascertain that chlorination has been properly carried out.

At these points where drinking water is supplied the tanks have been chlorinated by Sanitary Section men as often as required.

Guillemont.

The supply consists of stand pipes for carts and 2 tanks for filling water bottles, petrol cans, dixies etc. These are respectively of 300 & 400 galls and feed long pipes in which are a numerous taps. Square tank contains a considerable deposit of earthy matter and leaves. The 142nd. Army Troops Coy. R.E. is in charge of this post, and have been asked to clean the tank.

Two, N.C.O's from the Sanitary Section are detailed to chlorinate this supply daily, one N.C.O. each morning and one in the afternoon. Several new taps are needed.

Talus Boise.

The supply is as follows:

1. A 400 gal. tank for water bottles only.
2. A 400 gal. tank for filling petrol cans. This supply is marked "Drinking Water".
3. Three 400 galls. tanks marked, "Cooking only."

One N.C.O. from the Sanitary Section is detailed to chlorinate this supply once daily. It is little used on account of the bad approach.

(4).

Briqueterie.

Supplies as follows:

1. A tank (about 1,000 gals. capacity) filled from deep well on the premises. Tank chlorinated by 1 Sanitary Section N.C.O

2. A 400 galls. tank (over railway) near advanced Divn. H.Q., in BRIQUETERIE-MARICOURT Road. Requires chlorinating every alternate day. One Sanitary Section N.C.O. is detailed for this duty. The C.R.E. has been asked to provide protection for this tank against frost.

Carnoy. (A.13.d.6.8.).

A single tap into a small tank is provided near the water cart stand pipe and a considerable use is made of this for filling petrol tins, dixies and water bottles. This supply is drawn off the main (SUZANNE Supply). Pumping is practically continuous and it is, im possible to chlorinate this supply unless a subsidary tank or tanks with stop cock and key is installed. The C.R.E. (Back areas) has been asked to put this matter in hand.

Carnoy.East.(A.12. A.2. d. central.)

The supply consists of 2 100 gall. tanks, standing on the ground, with no cover. The tanks are filled/twice daily between the hours of 8.30a.m. and 2.30 p.m. One Sanitary Section N.C.O. is detailed to chlorinate this supply daily. The C.R.E. (Back areas) has been asked to put the matter of a stand & taps in hand.

Cosy Corner.

The supply consists of one 400 gall. tank filled twice daily between the hours of 8.30 a.m. and 2.30.p.m. Two brass taps are attached to the tank, one Sanitary Section N.C.O. is detailed to chlorinate supply daily.

PETROL CANS.

Pressure of work in connection with the supply of clean and dry clothes, the drying of gum boots, and the running of baths and laundry has pevented me from completing a scheme for cleaning these cans by steam. They have therefore, been done in the ordinary way under arrangements not under my control. The O.C. 232 nd. Army Troops Coy. R.E. has now placed the steam from two steam-rollers under repair, at my disposal at which stage the matter is handed over to O.C. Sanitary Section 17th. Division.

The C.R.E. has been asked to fix a tank of a few 100 galls. capacity at the new water point on the MONTAUBAN Baths A.27.d. This will enable a supply of sterile/drinking water to be delivered.

It is doubtful whther any of these jobs have been actually started by the C.R.E.

4. BATHS.

The system of supplying clean and dry clothes has been as follows:

This Divn. retained and will retain (under Corps Orders) the CORBIE Baths. The Thresh Disinfector remained at CORBIE and all the dirty clothing was conveyed to there and clean from there by the Sanitary Section and one other lorry. Permission was obtained for the Sanitary Section Lorry to proceed to MONTAUBAN (Fourth Army Hd. Qrs. pass), but the second lorry only proceeded to FRICOURT where clothing was transferred to two G.S. Wagons. A plan of the duties and circuits of the lorries and G.S. Wagons employed on these duties is annexed.

Clothing Exchange.

A NISSON hut (No.1) has been alloted to me for this purpose in Camp 21 on CARNOY-MONTAUBAN Road. All the clean and dirty clothing is collected here and from there distributed or sent to the MONTAUBAN Baths. The clean and dirty clothes are left at opposite ends of the hut. Clothing is here only issued to units returning from the trenches and to no others. 1 N.C.O. from the Sanitary Section i/c assisted by 2 men from attached personnel.

BATHS, MONTAUBAN.

These are situated on the Corduroy Road South of Mon--tauban. They are spray Baths capable of bathing 40 men per hour Clothing is conveyed to and from there to Camp 21 on a G.S. Wagon supplied from Divn. Hd. Qrs. 1 N.C.O. from my attached personnel in charge and the staff consists of 1 O.R. from attached personnel and 12 O.R's from various battalions in the Division.

5. DRYING ROOMS.

The drying rooms are as follows:

TRONES WOOD:

The staff consists of 1 N.C.O from Sanitary Section i/c,
10 O.R's from attached personnel.
5 men from Divn Salvage Coy.
1 man from one of the Battalions.

There are *3 drying huts solely devoted to drying gum boots of which 300 per day can be dried. Coal and wood is supplied by the S.S.O. The huts are situated in an unfortunate position being a considerable distance from the main road.(MONTAUBAN-GUILLEMONT.)

* A fourth hut will be available on receipt of 3 Canadian Stoves already indented for.

Clothes Drying Room No.6. (A.27. d. 3.4.).

(Behind Y.M.C.A. on MONTAUBAN-BERNAFAY Road).

This has just been started and the staff consists of 4 men from my attached personnel. Units desiring to dry clothes there ascertain on the spot when they can be taken in and arrange their own transport both ways.

BRIQUETERIE Drying Room.

This hut, under the supervision of the Town Major BERNAFAY-GUILLEMONT, is available for drying Gum Boots. It is situated on the Corduroy Road South of MONTAUBAN, 100 per day can be dried Fuel is supplied by the S.S.O.

No supervision is carried out by me and none of my N.C.O's and men staff the room. The boots must be taken to the Town Major with four men who must wheel them on the handcars provided to the drying rooms.

GUILLEMONT Drying Room. (at junction of Flers and Morval Road).

This is under care of Town Major of BERNAFAY- GUILLEMONT and is run by the Units themselves.

6 DISINFECTION of BLANKETS.

Some provision has been made for this to be carried out. A NISSON hut (No.2) in Camp 21 has been allotted to me for this purpose.

7. MISCELLANEOUS.

(1) O.C. Sanitary Section is billeted with the Camp Command--and in a NISSON Hut near Rear Divn Hd. Qrs.

(2) The Personnel are billeted in a NISSON Hut in Camp 23.

(3) The Office is in a hut near Rear Divn Hd. Qrs.

(4). A G.S.Wagon is supplied daily by S.S.O. to collect rations from the dump at the PLATEAU.

(5). The Divn. Dump for disinfectants under the charge of the Sanitary Section is at the PLATEAU.

(6) A store of fuel and wood is being left at each dryingroom and baths.

Capt. R.A.M.C.(T.F.).
Commanding 33rd. Sanitary Section.

Copies to:
1. A.D.M.S.
2. O.C.Sanitary Section,17th. Divn.
3. O.C.Baths,17th. Divn.
4. Retained.
5.& 6. War Diary.

EXTRACTS FROM 20th. DIVN. Orders, No. 495 dated 14/12/16 para 1:

(a) A small stock of clean underclothes will be kept in Camp 21 CARNOY-MONTAUBAN Road, Hut No.1, i/c of the O.C.Sanitary Section 33.

(a) It is for the benefit of units returning to Camps on CARNOY-MONTAUBAN Road from the Trenches only. Units may either send for the clothes or may send men there to change their clothes whichever is the more convenient. That dirty clothes are left there by units is essential in order that the supply may be kept up.

(b) There are 4 drying rooms between BERNAFAY & TRONES WOOD. These are now working.

Men may proceed there to get their outside clothing dried and draw clean socks.

At present no stock of clean service dress or greatcoats is available.

(c) There is a Bath House on the Corduroy Road South of MONTAUBAN. This will be available for use on the 16th,-about 40 men per hour.

(d) No drying room is to be used as a billet under any circumstances, except by the Staff in charge.

(e) One of the drying rooms is specially intended for drying Trench Boots.

Rough Sketch Plan showing Traffic Routes.

(Hand-drawn map with the following labelled locations and annotations:)

- **TRONES WOOD** — Drying Room. To take supply of socks kept here.
- **BERNAFAY CORNER**
- **MONTAUBAN**
- **MONTAUBAN BATHS**
- **CAMP 21**
- **MARICOURT** — H.Q. G.S. Wagon. Clean Clothing. Ration Dump. Disinfectants Dump. G.S. Wagon (Rations) starts from and returns to Dump.
- **CARNOY** — Ration Wagon. 2 G.S. Wagons Clean Clothing / Dirty Clothing.
- **FRICOURT** — 2 G.S. Wagons Clean Clothes. 2 G.S. Wagons Dirty Clothes. The Auxiliary Lorry does not proceed beyond Fricourt. Clean clothing is transhipped to and dirty clothing from G.S. Wagons.
- **CORBIE** (Baths and Disinfector) — Auxiliary Sanitary Section Lorry – Clean and Dirty Clothes. Baths Lorry Route.
- **Laundry**

(A.G. Osborne?)
Captain R.A.M.C. (T.F.)
Commanding
33rd SANITARY SECTION
December 1916.

SECRET.   *Appendix G.*

DAILY ORDERS No. 44.   Copy No. 9.

by

Captain A. F. Girvan, R.A.M.C. (T.F.)
Commanding
33rd Sanitary Section.

Thursday 21st December 1916.

1. Move.

21st December. Lce Corporal HAMPSON. I.F. will proceed on lorry with a few stores to CORBIE and a Fatigue.

22nd December. (a) 1 Man from Drying Room TRONES WOOD
1 Man from Baths MONTAUBAN
1 Man from Clothes Exchange, Camp 21
will report at 2 p.m. at Rear Divisional Headquarters to conduct the relieving parties to their destination.

(b) 2 attached men will proceed to CORBIE on the lorry which will return there after bringing up the 17th Divisional Sanitary Section's stores. Men's Kit Bags and other stores will be taken to CORBIE on this lorry.

(c) 3 men from the relieving Section will arrive by this lorry and will be shewn the water points at which chlorination is done. These relieving men will carry on the work starting on the 23rd.

23rd December. (a) The remainder of Sanitary Section and attached personnel (less Staff Sergeant BEAUMONT. A.E. Office Staff, a cook and pioneer and personnel employed at the Baths and drying rooms and clothing exchange area.) will march Heavy Marching Order to FRICOURT leaving Camp at 9 a.m. and will there meet the "Baths" Lorry (11823) and be conveyed to CORBIE. Cooking utensils and cooks will follow later in the day by the Sanitary Section Lorry.

(b) The following temporarily attached personnel will return to their Units on the 23rd:—
Drying Sheds TRONES WOOD.
   5 O.R. from Divisional Salvage Coy.
   1 O.R. from a Battalion.
MONTAUBAN Baths:
   12 O.R. from various Battalions.

24th December. (a) Rations will be drawn in SQUARE CORBIE 8 a.m. by Lce Corporal HAMPSON. F.

(b) Staff Sergeant BEAUMONT. A.E., Office Staff and materials, Officer's Kit, cook and pioneer will be conveyed by Sanitary Section Lorry (or an additional Lorry which has been demanded) to CORBIE.

(c) Baths, Drying rooms and Clothes Exchange will be handed over to 17th Division and receipts obtained for all handed over.

(d) All personnel (except personnel returned to various Units) employed at Baths, Drying Rooms and Clothing Exchange will proceed to Rear Divisional Head Quarters so as to be there by 1.30 p.m. They must convey their cooking utensils etc themselves. They will be conveyed to CORBIE by Lorry.

(e) Pte. BEASLES. A.W. will proceed mounted to CORBIE.

A.F. Girvan.
Captain R.A.M.C. (T.F.)
Commanding
33rd Sanitary Section

Copies to:
1. Staff Sergeant Beaumont.
2. Q.M.S. Hoare.
3. Lce Corporal Pretty. g.h.
4. Lce Corporal Hunting.
5. Lce Corporal Hampson.
6. Lce Corporal Beardsworth.
7/8. Retained
9/10. War Diary.

Appendix H.

SANITARY SECTION REPORT

--for--

fortnight ending 16/12/16.

1. RESERVE AREA.

(a). The usual systematic inspection was rigorously carried out. Units were found satisfactory with the following exceptions:

M.M.P. Rue Victor Hugo, CORBIE. — It was found that the men wash inside the billet and the floor was covered in water, although an ablution bench and drain was provided outside.

Hd.Qrs. Officers' Chargers, 5 Rue Auguste Gindre, CORBIE. — Manure was very slowly removed by civilians.

(b). The usual tests of water carts were carried out and evidence of chlorination found in every case.

The condition of the Divisional Signal Company's water cart, when stationed at CORBIE, left much to be desired. The cart seemed to used as a dining table, and was littered with food - meat, beans, bread, jam, etc. Complaints were made by my water N.C.O. to the Signal Company's N.C.O's with no result.

Pumps, tanks and water points in the Reserve area were tested as customary.

The water cart of the No. 1 Section, 20th. D.A.C. was found to be deficient in equipment as follows:
    Strainer and cage for suction hose.
    1 spanner for wash-out plugs.
    1 curved brush.
    2 disc gauges (Clarifying chamber).
and the following repairs were needed:
    Pumps to be repaired.
    The perforated gauge-holder in the clarifying chamber to be re-soldered.
    Tap-pipe requires refitting (2 taps being out of action.

These defects have been brought to the notice of the Commanding Officer concerned.

(c). Disinfection of blankets and underclothes was carried out, 3132 blankets being done in the week ending 9/12/16 and 9682 articles of underclothing passed through

1.

the Thresh Disinfector.

(d). Number of N.C.O's and men bathed during the period 3/12/16 - 9/12/16:   2753.

Clean clothing issued during the same period:
Shirts. - 5097.
Pants. - 4480.
Socks. - 4580.
Vests. - 2607.
Towels. - 1725.

Dirty clothing received during the same period:
Shirts. - 4597.
Pants. - 3980.
Socks. - 4555.
Vests. - 1907.
Towels. - 1725.

List of disinfectants issued during the same period:
Chloride of Lime.   210 lbs.
Cresol.   75 gals.
Crude paraffin.   15 gals.
Formalin.   4 gals.
Bleaching powder.   34 tins.
Whale Oil.   95 gals.
Anti-Frost Bite
Grease.   106 lbs.

(e). A full report of work done is contained in my S/778/16 dated 19/12/16.

2. FORWARD AREA.

(a). Sanitary conditions have been described in my "Sanitary and water notes of Forward Area" (S/917/16).

The Camps have been frequently inspected and the huts found in satisfactory condition.

The sites of the Camps leave much to be desired as the numerous shell holes and trenches are apt to receive rubbish, the responsibility for which it is difficult to fix. The Camps are extremely muddy and really dangerous on this account at night. Many of the latrines are situated on the far side of an almost impassable quagmire, with the natural result that men are tempted to go elsewhere, particularly at night. Considerable improvement has been effected by the R.E's by laying trench boards.

Ablution sheds or benches are non-existent.

(b).   The various water points mentioned in my S/917/16 have been chlorinated as required.

The customary tests of water carts have been carried out and evidence of chlorination found with the following exception :
> C/92nd. R.F.A. No number to cart. Filled 9 a.m. 12/12/16 and tested 1.30.p.m. same day. The Commanding Officer concerned has been notified of this defect

(c).   Construction work: Very little was done, owing to the Section being fully employed on more important duties.   A number of shelves were put up at the MONTAUBAN Baths to complete the clean clothing room. A number of notice boards, etc. were made for water points and drying rooms.

(d).   Drying Sheds - TRONES WOOD. There was no fuel on taking over from 29th. Division, and only about 140 gum boots. Fuel was obtained and the sheds worked vigorously for the sole purpose of drying gum boots.   300 boots and more per day were dried here.   Each boot takes 48 hours to dry.

Clothes changing Room by Y.M.C.A. BERNAFAY-MONTAUBAN Road - Great delay was experienced in getting fuel to this place. There was none there when taken over from 29th. Division.   Little use has been made of this room, though it has been available for some days. A stock of fuel is left for 17th. Division.

(e).   Baths, MONTAUBAN. - These have been worked since 16/12/16.   Clean clothes have been supplied to most bathers. 460 N.C.O's and men have been bathed.   A stock of fuel is left for 17th. Division.

Clothes Exchange - A Nissin hut was placed at my disposal in Camp 21. A stock of clean dry clothes was maintained here, and every unit returning from the trenches received a change of underclothes. The scheme for providing and maintaining this supply is detailed in my "Sanitary and Water Notes of the Forward Area". This matter I considered the most important undertaken; it was also the most difficult

Clothing issued:
- Shirts. - 2655.
- Pants. - 2755.
- Socks. - 2215.
- Vests. - 1355.

(f). Blanket disinfection - 1500 Blankets have been disinfected by spraying with formalin. A second hut in Camp 21 was used for this purpose.

(g). Number of N.C.O's and men bathed at CORBIE during the period 10/12/16 - 16/12/16: 1772.

Number of articles of underclothing passed through the Thresh Disinfector at CORBIE during the same period : 12986.

Captain R.A.M.C. (T.F.),
Commanding,
33rd. SANITARY SECTION.

Appendix I

WEEKLY REPORT

for week ending 23 December 1916.

1. SANITATION.

The remarks made in my report for fortnight ending 16/12/16 (S/822/16) still hold good. The Camps were frequently and thoroughly inspected and the huts were found to be in a satisfactory condition. Some accumulations of refuse have been dealt with.

2. WATER.

The usual tests of water from water carts have been carried out and evidences of chlorination found in every case with the following exceptions:

Adv. Hd. Qrs.   Cart No.68421   Tested on 19/12/16 @ 3 P.M.   No reaction found.*
Tested every subsequent day and found properly chlorinated.
*This does not necessarily imply that the cart had not been chlorinated.

The various water points mentioned in my S/117/16 have been chlorinated as required.

3. GENERAL.

Troops bathed at Baths MONTAUBAN............1266.

Clean Clothing issued at the same place:

Shirts........	613.
Pants........	753.
Socks........	451.
Towels.......	283.
Vests........	248.

Clothing issued and received at Clothes Exchange Camp 21:

Clean Clothing Issued:		Dirty Clothing Received:	
Shirts.....	6212.	Shirts.....	7225.
Pants.....	5546.	Pants.....	7027.
Socks.....	4881.	Vests.....	7530.
Vests.....	262.	Socks.....	7378.
Towels.....	563.	Towels.....	134.

Blankets disinfected by spraying at Camp 21:   1600.

Articles of underclothing passed through THRESH
Disinfector.....   15,286.

Troops bathed at Baths CORBIE...   2661.

Disinfectants issued...

        Cresol.....   85 galls.
        Whale Oil....   140 galls.

                                      Capt. R.A.M.C.(T.F.).
                    Commanding
                          33rd. Sanitary Section.

Appendix J.

YOUR NEAREST LATRINE
IS No.   SITUATED

YOUR NEAREST
INCINERATOR IS
SITUATED

O.C. SANITARY SECTION.

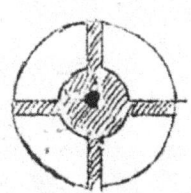

Confidential.

WAR DIARY

—— of ——

Captain A. F. GIRVAN. R.A.M.C. (T.F.)
Officer Commanding

33rd Sanitary Section
1st London (City of London) Sanitary Company
R.A.M.C. (T.F.)

attached
20th (LIGHT) DIVISION.
B.E.F.
FRANCE.

January 1917

Volume 8.

Army Form C. 2118.

War Diary of
Captain AF Sloan Pane (T.F)
O.C. XVth SANITARY SECTION 33.
ATTACHED XVth (LIGHT) DIVISION.

WAR DIARY
or
INTELLIGENCE SUMMARY.
(Erase heading not required.)

Instructions regarding War Diaries and Intelligence Summaries are contained in F.S. Regs., Part II. and the Staff Manual respectively. Title pages will be prepared in manuscript.

Army Form C. 2118.

Place	Date	Hour	Summary of Events and Information	Remarks and references to Appendices
CORBIE	1914 Jan 1		Arranging for move to MINDEN POST. Preparing lecture to 4th Army School of Sanitation	Appendix 1.
	2		Went to ALBERT (5th C.C.S.) and delivered lecture to about 30 MO's drawn from all Divisions of 4th Army. This took about 2 hours in the morning. In the afternoon various wells in ALBERT were visited, sites examined & demonstrations carried out with the Horrocks Test Box.	Appendix 2. Appendix 3. A.F.9.
"	3		Most of section moved to allotted places. Long lorry spring during move	A.F.9.
"	4		2 new front springs fitted to lorry, when repaired moved office etc to MINDEN POST.	A.F.9.
MINDEN POST F19C ALBERT COMBINED SHEET	5		Went BRONFAY Camp 15 where I took over stores from Camp Commans out. Arranged for a large hut to be fitted up as clothing exchange, drying room for boots gum thigh, and eillet. Baths already installed by Guards Div. No information regarding area has been obtainable, except that wells in COMBLES have been tested found good. Blanket disinfector carried out at MANSEL CAMP.	A.F.9.
"	6		Went MANSEL CAMP (FRICOURT ROAD). Arranged for better Seander disinfecting place. Found certain water tanks at entrance had no tops so that water (though chlorinated by San Sec) was spoilt by bucket dipping. Wrote CRE to notify. Visited FRICOURT BATHS to see if available for the Division, they belong to 1st ANZAC CORPS, who nearly have clean under clothes in any quantity	Appendix 4. A.F.9.

Army Form C. 2118.

Captain A.F. STEWART, R.A.M.C.(T)
O.C. SANITARY SECTION 33,
ATTACHED XXth (LIGHT) DIVISION.

WAR DIARY
or
INTELLIGENCE SUMMARY.
(Erase heading not required.)

Instructions regarding War Diaries and Intelligence Summaries are contained in F. S. Regs., Part II. and the Staff Manual respectively. Title pages will be prepared in manuscript.

Place	Date 1917	Hour	Summary of Events and Information	Remarks and references to Appendices
MINDEN POST	JAN 7		Visited Camps 15 and 106 BRONFAY re construction work and sanitary arrangements	Off.
"	8		Visited Arrowhead Copse (aur. Div HQ) and MALTZHORN CAMP (near GUILLEMONT) Inspected dug outs at former with Corpl Gaunt. Conferent latter with Sgt Bauendork	Off
"	9		Delivered Lecture at 5" C.C.S. ALBERT to 4m's at 4" Army School of Sanitation and in afternoon took the party to MEAULTE where some wells were investigated and also the water column lorries. Subject of lecture "Water". Particular stress was laid on the responsibilities of m.o's with regard to water duties.	O & G
"	10		Visited AMIENS to pay laundry and arrange for several improvements there	Off
"	11		Visited COMBLES and inspected each of the eight wells in use there. Also went to fort gun. High fly drying room there. this is doing 200 pairs per day and could do 300 if required. Off Made enq'f from trench foot soap in Soyer stove. Off.	
"	12		Visited camp 15 Bray sur where materials for constructing drying room etc Rare at last arrived after a weeks delay. Also went MEAULTE to draw each from Field Cashier for paying out and for paying laundry to the inferior charges. Off	
"	13		Visited GUILLEMONT to try and find suitable site for erecting baths which at present do not exist at all as far forward, but which are badly needed there	Appendix 5.

Army Form C. 2118.
Major A.F. Sivan RAMC (TF)
O.C. SANITARY SECTION 33,
ATTACHED XXth (LIGHT) DIVISION

WAR DIARY
or
INTELLIGENCE SUMMARY.
(Erase heading not required.)

Instructions regarding War Diaries and Intelligence
Summaries are contained in F. S. Regs., Part II.
and the Staff Manual respectively. Title pages
will be prepared in manuscript.

Place	Date 1917	Hour	Summary of Events and Information	Remarks and references to Appendices
MINDEN POST	Jan 13		continued afternoon soap-making. Received wire from DMS 4th Army ordering me to report at 9.30 a.m. on 15th inst. to take over duties of second in command 4th Army School of Sanitation (held at 5th C.C.S. Albert). Got ADMS to wire back asking whether appointment was permanent or temporary and to whom the duties of O.C. Sanitary Section and O.C. Baths & Laundries was to be handed over, pointing out that the large stocks of clothing, material and stores in my charge in various parts of Divisional Area and outside it could not be checked in less than a week. O.F.G. Collecting papers etc. Paid Section.	
	14	10 p.m.	Handed over duties of O.C. San Sec. and O.C. Baths and the in-but account also the stocks of clothes, stores etc. to Capt SOHIR. DADMS. Owing to the short notice of departure it was found impracticable to check or count the stores etc. which are in various places over a distance of about 35 miles. O.F.G.	
	15	8.45 a.m.	Left for new duties. OFG	

A.F. Sivan
Capt RAMC T.F.
O.C. 33 San Sec 20th Div

Army Form C. 2118.

D.A.D.M.S. A.C.H.Q. Chine,
6. O.C. SANITARY SECTION 3.
ATTACHED XXth (LIGHT) DIVISION

WAR DIARY
INTELLIGENCE SUMMARY.
(Erase heading not required.)

Instructions regarding War Diaries and Intelligence Summaries are contained in F. S. Regs., Part II. and the Staff Manual respectively. Title pages will be prepared in manuscript.

Place	Date	Hour	Summary of Events and Information	Remarks and references to Appendices
MINDEN POST	15/1/17		Took over duties as O.C. 33 San Sect from Capt A.F. GIRVAN - during the latter's absence at 4th Army School of Sanitation ALBERT. Completion of arrangements for new FRENCH Anti-Frenchfort Treatment at BRONFAY. General inspection BRONFAY. Went to AMIENS to pay Laundry Bill. Laundry out of action - for the past	
	16/1/17		2-3 days - No clean clothing being returned. Inspected Baths & Laundry at CORBIE. Found considerable progress had been made - Machines being put into position	
	17/1/17		Heavy fall of Snow. Visited FRENES WOOD A.D.S	
	24/1/17		Handed over to Capt A.F.GIRVAN RAMC(T)	

A.C.T.SUHR
Capt RAMC
O.C. S.S.

A.C.T.SUHR
Capt RAMC
D.A.D.M.S

Army Form C. 2118.

Captain W. F. STEWART R.A.M.C (T.F.)
O.C. SANITARY SECTION 33,
ATTACHED XXth (LIGHT) DIVISION.

WAR DIARY
or
INTELLIGENCE SUMMARY.
(Erase heading not required.)

Place	Date	Hour	Summary of Events and Information	Remarks and references to Appendices
MINDEN POST	18/1/17	3p	Returned from 4th Army School of Sanitation which is closed for time being. Took over command of 33 San Sec. from Capt Suhr DADMS 20th Div. Off.	
"	19		Visited camps 15 and 108. Off.	
"	20		Went to AMIENS to have my eyes examined at No1 New Zealand Stationary Hospital. M.O. said I need not get new Sent-elle glasses than my present ones and said I was a "Six year atom". Visited Casualty AMIENS. Found just re-started. Off.	Appendix 7.
"	21		Morning office work. Afternoon went to CORBIE to buy + bring in construction of laundry. Off.	
"	22		Visited camps 15 and 108 Roadfay. also Mansel camp on FRICOURT road. Off.	
"	23		Went with DADMS to CORBIE to arrange taking Roading over of present area to 1st Div. Arranged with Capt Mathers chief of staff O.C. San Sec 14th Div the date of relief + details. Off.	
"	24		O.C. Batts. 14th Div came to MINDEN POST and was shown round the baths etc by me. Off.	Appendix 8.
"	25		Rode to DADMS to visit O.C. San Sec 29th Div from who we should take over in about a fortnight. There was shown a Letter which stated that Sanitary Sections	

Army Form C. 2118.

Capt W.H. Stewart R.A.M.C. (T.F.)
O.C. SANITARY SECTION 88,
ATTACHED XXth (Light) DIVISION.
Page 6

WAR DIARY
or
INTELLIGENCE SUMMARY.
(Erase heading not required.)

Place	Date 1917	Hour	Summary of Events and Information	Remarks and references to Appendices
	Jan			
MINDEN POST	25		Wrote about to become Army Troops and walked more with Divisions. The letter in Appendix 10 was therefore included	Appendix 9. Appendix 10.
			Went to CORPS WORKSHOPS MAMETZ to try and get boilers made in order to clean out latrine cans for holding drinking water. Failed once more. AHS.	
"	26		Arranging for wire and handing over. On 23rd drafted attached reply to a letter from DADMS asking how latrine cans were cleaned out etc. AHS.	Appendix 6.
"	27		Starting with map of section as per programme except that same staff were sent to take over HEILLY BATHS. AHS	
"	28		Moved to HEILLY sur ANCRE. I had previously made efforts to find out details of this area but nothing at all was handed over to me in the way of information at stores. It is almost impossible to do the work properly without having a car at my disposal, as one cannot visit from the limits even of sanitary area at any but late rare intervals. AHS.	
HEILLY E.1. SE4.17 (AMIENS)	29		Baths begun up at HEILLY but mending of them in hands of Mayhaissey busy acting HEILLY AHS.	
	30		Went with Major Alexander DADMS in car to CARDONETTE + RAINVILLE and villages	

Army Form C. 2118.

War Diary/...
Captain R.F. ELSTON Commd(?)
O.C. SANITARY SECTION 33,
ATTACHED XXth (Light) Division

WAR DIARY
or
INTELLIGENCE SUMMARY.
(Erase heading not required.)

Instructions regarding War Diaries and Intelligence Summaries are contained in F. S. Regs., Part II. and the Staff Manual respectively. Title pages will be prepared in manuscript.

Place	Date 1916	Hour	Summary of Events and Information	Remarks and references to Appendices
HEILLY	Jan 30		in their neighbourhood in order to try & find baths in that area for troops near. Nothing was found except some primitive & dismantled W. baths at TRAMEVILLE which being at the top of a hill is naturally some distance from a water supply. Afternoon walked CORBIE and LA NEUVILLE to try and fix up baths therefor. 10.K.O.R. = dto units within reach. CORBIE is allotted by I.M. Corbie & there is no reason for days. AHANEVILLE there are only two troughs about 8x2x2 feet in a factory so full of steam that view is practically impossible. OM	
"	31		Fixing up baths HEILLY. Lorry sent off at 6.30am to fetch new sprays & boilers from LOOP near CITADEL — Pay Laundry AMIENS. OM	

R.F. Elston(?)
Captain.
O.C. SANITARY SECTION 33.
ATTACHED XXth (LIGHT) DIVISION.

Appendix 1.

Daily Orders No. 49
by
Captain A.F. Girvan. R.A.M.C.(T.F.)
Commanding
33rd Sanitary Section.

Copy No. 7

Monday 1st January 1917.

1. **Disposition**

   (a) The disposition and work of the Sanitary Section and attached personnel is tabulated on the attached sheet. The men who have been attached to Brigades will rejoin their Brigades on the Division moving back into Reserve.

   (b) The following will remain at CORBIE:
   The Baths and laundry Staff as detailed on attached sheet.
   The THRESH Disinfector to be used for clothes from the Forward Area.
   The Sanitary Section lorry and 2 drivers.
   The "Baths" lorry and 3 drivers.
   The above personnel and lorries will be rationed by the Divisional Band remaining at CORBIE.

2. **Move.**

   2nd January. (a) The N.C.O's and men from Sanitary Section and attached personnel detailed for work at Camp 15 (BRONFAY), Camp 108 (BRONFAY), MANSEL Camp, MAULTZHORN Camp, COMBLES and Lce Corporals Spurgeon, Matthew Howes, and Ptes. Gohns and Harrison + Rfns. Scholey + Pettivell detailed for MINDEN POST, will proceed i/c Sergt. Caesar from CORBIE by Motor Lorry leaving CONVENT Wall, BRAY Road, CORBIE at 8 a.m. They will assemble at MINDEN POST at 1 p.m. on the same day where guides from the Guards Division will meet them and conduct them to the Various Camps.

   (b) Certain Mobilisation Stores will be left at the Baths CORBIE, including the bicycles + wheelbarrows. These will be conveyed there on 2/1/17.

   (c) Lce Corporal Mettugh will proceed to COMBLES by car leaving CORBIE Square at 6.45 a.m.

   3rd January. (a) S/Sergt. Beaumont, Corporal Whitlock and Pte. Judd and the Office Staff, Officer's Kit and Kitchen Utensils will proceed to MINDEN POST by the Sanitary Section Lorry leaving CORBIE at 8 a.m. After unloading at MINDEN POST the lorry will proceed to SAPPER CORNER, arriving there at 2 p.m. and take over the load from the "Baths" Lorry.

   (b) The "Baths" Lorry with Lce Corporal Horsley and Ptes. Finch, Payne + Cox (D.C.L.I.) and stores will proceed to SAPPER CORNER leaving CORBIE at Noon. The load will there be transferred to Sanitary Section Lorry.

   (c) Pte. Harrison and Rfn. Scholey will draw rations at the PLATEAU (H.20.c.5.6.) on Wednesday 3rd January at 8 a.m.

   (d) The Sanitary Section Office will close at CORBIE at 7 a.m. on 3/1/17 and re-open at MINDEN POST at 2 p.m. on the same day.

   4th January. Corporal Gaunt will report at Camp Commandants Office, Divisional Headquarters at 8 a.m. and proceed to Divisional Headquarters (Advanced).

2.

3. **Baths.**

The Baths CORBIE will remain working according to the allotment given by Town Major CORBIE, but NO clothing will be exchanged by the Baths Staff Except to 20th Division units and to the parties of Artillery bathing for one hour every other day.

4. **Clean and Dirty Clothing**
   (a) Clean and dirty clothing will be conveyed to and from Clothes Exchange, Camp 15 (BRONFAY) and CORBIE daily by Sanitary Section lorry.
   (b) The "Baths" lorry will carry disinfected dirty clothing to AMIENS from CORBIE and clean clothing from AMIENS to CORBIE daily.
   (c) Daily states of clothing will be rendered as heretofore by Q.M.S. i/c Baths to Sanitary Section Head Quarters by D.R.L.S.

A. F. Girvan
Captain R.A.M.C. (T.F.)
O.C. 33rd Sanitary Section

Copies
1. S/Sergt. Beaumont.
2. Q.M.S. Hoare.
3. Sergt. Caesar.
4/5. Retained
6/7. War Diary. ✓

Disposition of 33rd Sanitary Section and attached personnel.
Work in Forward and Reserve Areas.

Place	Sanitary Section	Attached personnel	Baths Staff	Temporarily attached personnel	Duties
Headquarters MINDEN POST.	S/Sergt. BEAUMONT				Supervision.
	Cpl. WHITLOCK. L/Cpl. HORSLEY				Office.
	L/Cpl. SPURGEON				Water duties and inspection of carts to Divn. Holders and Divn. Troops.
	L/Cpl. MATHER				
	L/Cpl. HOWES				
	Pte. HARRISON				Storekeeper and Rations.
	Pte. JUDD				Cook
	Pte. BEAGLES.				Batman.
	Pte. FINCH.				Messenger.
	Pte. GOHNS				
		Rfn. PAYNE. Rfn. SCHOLEY			Rations
		Rfn. PITWELL			Cook's Assistant
		Pte. COX (D.C.L.I.)			Pioneer.
Divn. Hd.Qrs. (Adv.) ARROW HEAD COPSE	Cpl. SAUNT.				Sanitary Inspections.
Camp 15 (BRONFAY.)	Sergt. CAESAR				To supervise construction of drying Room in hut C32.
		Pte. COX (S.L.I.) Pte. MITCHELL Rfn. TAYLOR Pte. PRICE			Construction of drying Room.
	Sergt. HARDCASTLE L/Cpl. HAMPSON				Inspections of Camp. Supervising Working party of 11 for Camp Duties.
				11 O.Rs.	Working party.
	L/Cpl. EDE				Water duties & inspection of carts of 61st Brigade. Chlorination of Camp water points (if any) General water supervision in vicinity.
	L/Cpl. HUNTING				To work Clothes Exchange in hut C32.
			Rfn. FISHWICK Pte. LAMB		
			L/Cpl. BEARDSWORTH Rfn. HILLIER Rfn. THOMPSON Pte. CRISFORD Pte. LEA Pte. RUSH Pte. SHAIL Pte. HARRINGTON		To work Baths in hut C32.
Camp 108 (BRONFAY).	L/Cpl. NICHOLLS Pte. BARENTS.				Inspections of Camp. Supervision of working party of 6 for Camp Duties.
				6 O.Rs.	Working party.
MANSEL CAMP	L/Cpl. OTTERWAY				Inspections, etc

Place	Sanitary Section	Attached personnel	Baths Staff	Temporarily attached personnel	Duties
MAULTZHORN CAMP	Sergt. BALMFORTH Pte. CLOAKE }				Inspection of Camp. Supervision of working party of 12 for camp duties.
				12 O.R's	Working party.
	L/Cpl. GRAY L/Cpl. WILSON }				Inspection of carts and water duties to respective Brigades. Chlorination of water points.
COMBLES. Drying Rooms.	L/Cpl. McHUGH				Supervision of work at four boot drying rooms. Keep records of boots issued and received with receipts in all cases.
				59th Bde. 1 L/Cpl. 3 O.R's 61st Bde. 1 L/Cpl. 6 O.R's }	11 O.R's to work drying rooms.
COMBLES. Catacombes.	L/Cpl. HILL				Inspection of Catacombes and other Divisional Billets in Combles.
CORBIE. Baths.			Q.M.S. HOARE		I/c Baths.
			L/Cpl. Taylor. Pte. PRAHSNELL Pte. THOMPSON }		"Baths" lorry drivers. 1 on leave.
			Pte. STEVENS. Pte. POWELL }		Sanitary Section lorry drivers.
			Pte. CLAYTON Pte. FOSTER. }		"Foden" drivers. 1 on leave.
			Pte. WHITLOCK. Rfn. ALLCOCK. Rfn. SIMPSON. Pte. BOULTER. Pte. LOVELL. Pte. ROBINSON }		To work Baths.
			Pte. WRIGHTSON " ROGERS. " WILLIAMS. Rfn. WALTERS. }		On leave.
		Rfn. CROCKER			On leave.
			Pte. STOREY. Pte. LIDDLE }		Sick. Corps Rest Station.
VILLE. Baths.			Pte. PORTER		I/c clothing.

A.F. Girvan

Captain R.A.M.C.(T.F)
O.C 33rd Sanitary Section

Appendix 2.

DAILY ORDERS NO. 50
-by-
Capt. A.F.GIRVAN, R.A.M.C.(T.F)
Commanding 33rd. Sanitary Section.
Tuesday 2nd. Jan.1917.

---

1. **GOOD CONDUCT BADGE.**

The following man having served 2 years with the colours without an entry in his A.F.B.18A is granted permission to wear one Good Conduct Badge.

    16th.(Service) Battn. The King's Royal Rifles Corps.
        No.166 Rfn. CROCKER,G.

2. **MOVE.**

Daily Order No. 49 para. commencing "3rd.Jan.1917" dated 1/1/17 is cancelled and the following substituted:

3rd.January:-

    (a) S/Sergt BEAUMONT and Ptes. JUDD,COX (D.C.L.I.) & PAYNE and stores and kitchen utensils will proceed to MINDEN POST by the Sanitary Section Lorry leaving CORBIE at 8 a.m.
    (b) The Baths lorry will proceed to VILLE and afterwards to AMIENS as customary.
    (c) Pte. HARRISON and Rfn. SCHOLEY will draw rations at the BEAZEN PLATEAU (A.xx.D.S.S.) on Wed. Jan. 3rd. at 8 a.m.

4th. January:-

    (a) Corpl. WHITLOCK, L/Cpl.HORSLEY and Pte. FINCH and the office staff and officer's kit will proceed to MINDEN POST by Sanitary Section lorry leaving CORBIE at 8.30 a.m.
    (b) The Sanitary Section office will close at CORBIE at 7 a.m. on 4/1/17 and re-open at MINDEN POST at 4 p.m. on the same day.
    (c) Pte.BEAGLES will proceed mounted to MINDEN POST from CORBIE.

A.F.Girvan

Capt. R.A.M.C.(T.F.)
O.C.33rd. Sanitary Section.

Appendix 3.

WEEKLY REPORT
FOR WEEK ENDING 30th. DEC. 1916.

1. **SANITATION.**

Inspections have been made daily of Units in the Division by Inspectors detailed for this work.

The conditions found were as follows:

Unit.	State of Camps and Billets.	Remarks.
G.O.C. & No.1 Mess.	Satisfactory.	
No. 2 Mess.	Satisfactory.	
No. 3 Mess.	Satisfactory.	
D.A.D.O.S.	Satisfactory.	
M.M. Police.	Satisfactory.	
Traffic Police.	Satisfactory.	
Salvage Coy.	Satisfactory.	
Divn. Band.	Satisfactory.	
Divn. Baths.	Satisfactory.	
Divn. Hd. Qrs.	Satisfactory.	New urine pit made.
H.Q. Transport.	Satisfactory except;	No attempt made to burn or remove manure.
H.Q. Chargers.	Satisfactory.	New grease pit made. Manure being removed by civilians.
H.Q. Signal Coy. R.E.	Satisfactory.	
do do Transport.	Satisfactory.	Manure being burned daily.
C.R.E.	Satisfactory.	New grease pit and ablution pit made.
Divn. School of Instruction.	Satisfactory.	

(1).

Units.	State of Camps and Billets.	Remarks.
C/91st. R.F.A.	Satisfactory.	Manure is being placed in rear of lines and covered with mud.
D/92nd. R.F.A.	Satisfactory except	A collection of tins & other refuse near incinerator but is being disposed of.

59th. BRIGADE.

Units.	State of Camps and Billets.	Remarks.
59th. Brigade Hd.Qrs. and Signals.	Satisfactory.	
10th. K.R.R. and Transport.	Satisfactory.	
11th. K.R.R. and Transport.	Satisfactory.	
10th. R.B. and Transport.	Satisfactory.	
11th. R.B. and Transport.	Satisfactory.	
59th. Trench Mor. Battery.	Satisfactory.	
59th. Machine Gun Company.	Fairly Satisfactory.	Special report submitted. Latrine condemned & another made. Incinerator set going.
88th. Field Coy. R.E.	Satisfactory	
169th. Coy. A.S.C.	Satisfactory.	
60th. Field Amb.& Transport.	Satisfactory.	Manure deposited on manure dump on outskirts of town.

60th. BRIGADE.

Units.	State of Camps and Billets.	Remarks.
60th. H.Q. & Transport.	Satisfactory.	
60th. Bde. Signals & Transport.	Satisfactory.	
60th. M.G.C. and Transport.	Satisfactory.	
6th. K.S.L.I. and Transport.	Satisfactory.	Town incinerator & waste pits used. Assistance given by unit to Town Major's Staff to work these.
6th. Oxon. & Bucks.L.I. & Transport.	Satisfactory.	

Units.	State of Camps and Billets.	Remarks.
12th. K.R.R. & Transport.	Satisfactory.	Public latrines are being used. New public latrine in course of construction by this Unit.
12th. R.B. and Transport.	Satisfactory.	Public latrines are used. Two new ones (1 for Officers) being erected. New urinal dug at one billet.
60th. Trench Mor. Battery.	Satisfactory.	
160th. Cy. A.S.C.	Satisfactory.	
61st. Field Amb.	Satisfactory.	
61st. BRIGADE.		
61st. Bde. Hd. Qrs. and Transport.	Satisfactory.	
12th. King's (L'pool) Regt. & Transport.	Satisfactory.	
7th. K.O.Y.L.I. & Transport.	Satisfactory.	
7th. D.C.L.I. & Transport.	Satisfactory.	
7th. Somerset L.I. & Transport.	Satisfactory.	Billets very dirty when taken over.
61st. M.D.C.	Satisfactory.	
61st. Trench Mor. Battery.	Satisfactory.	
84th. Field Coy. R.E.	Satisfactory.	

All the billets occupied by this Brigade were in a dirty condition when taken over and a good deal of hard work has been put in to make them satisfactory. The billets of the Somerset L.I. were particularly bad owing to the quantity of refuse left by previous unit. The destruction of refuse and the draining of back yards has occupied a great deal of time and the K.O.Y.L.I. have also executed repairs to the fabric of their billets.

WATER.

Divn. Hd. Qrs. & Divn. Troops.

The water from the following two carts was tested for free chlorine with the results shown:

Divn. Hd. Qrs.   Cart No.70593.   Tested 27th. Dec. 10 a.m.
                                     No blue coloration.*

Divn. Signal Coy.   Cart No.86421.   Tested 27th. Dec.10a.m.
                                     Found chlorinated.

* Cooks from Hd. Qrs. and also cooks from Divn. Troops use water for cooking direct from the pumps on or near their billets "Horrocks" Test shews these sources to be good.

20th. D.S.C. use water from a 200 gallon tank. The water from this tank was tested on 27th. Dec. at 2.30 p.m. and shewed a faint blue. It has been tested daily since together with the water carts and other sources.

59th. Brigade.

Tests for free chlorine have been carried out from the water in the carts of the Brigade with the following results:

10th. K.R.R.   Cart no.E65656.   Tested daily from
                    do   E73692.   26/12/16 to 30/12/16.(inc)

11th. K.R.R.   Cart No.E63621.   Tested daily from
                                      24/12/16 to 30/12/16
                                      except 25/12/16.

10th. R.B.   Cart No.E131272. Tested daily from
                                      26/12 16 to 30/12/16
                                      except 24/12/16.

11th. R.B.   Cart No.N73657
                    do   N70294.   Tested daily from
                                      24/12/16 to 30/12/16
                                      except 25/12/16.

59th. M.G.C.   Cart No.E65265.   Tested daily from
                                      26/12/16 to 30/12/16.

189th. Coy. A.S.C. Cart No.E70255.   Tested daily from
                                      26/12/16 to 30/12/16.

80th. Field Coy.   No number   Tested daily from
R.E.   (1915 pattern).   27/12/16 to 30/12/16.

Other Units draw their water from pumps which have been tested daily.

60th. Brigade.

Tests for free chlorine have been carried out from the water from the carts in the brigade with the following results

12th. K.R.R.	Cart No. E27507	Tested 26/12/16)	Found
	do E130885.	28/12/16)chlorinated
		29/12/16)	
12th. R.B.	Cart No. E7.636	Tested 26/12/16)	Found
	do E65273.	28/12/16)chlorinated
		29/12/16)	
6th.Shropshire L.I.	E69615.	Tested 26/12/16)	Found
	E70325.	30/12/16)chlorinated
60th. M.G.C.	Cart No. E100584.	Tested 28/12/16)	Found
		30/12/16)chlorinated

Bde. Hd. Qrs.and Transport,Bde. Signals R.E., and Trench Mortar Battery,have all drawn their cooking water from pumps direct. The water from these pumps has been tested and is quite good.

61st. Brigade.

Tests for free chlorine have been carried out from the water in the carts of the brigade with the following results:

7th. K.O.Y.L.I.   Cart No. 70268   Tested 24/12/16 no colora-
                              2 3/4 hrs after filling   -tion.

12th. King's
(L'pool) Regt.   Cart No. 68164   Tested 24/12/16 light blue.

7th. D.C.L.I.   Cart No. 70332   Tested 24/12/16 Light blue.
                 do   68349   Tested 24/12/16 Blue.

62nd Field Amb. Cart No. 64366 Tested 29/12/16 Light blue.

Bde. Hd.Qrs. and the Trench Mortar Battery have either drawn their water from other Unit's carts or from a boring in MEAULTE at Billet No.86,High Street. This water is good, not being fouled like the majority of the wells in the village. Manure heaps have accumulated to an unusual extent owing to the difficulty the farmers experience in getting it away. Wells so fouled have been placed out of bounds but only a few bear notices to this effect. Strict instructions have been given that all water not drawn from water carts must be boiled before use.

GENERAL WORK.

Supervision of pumping out of cesspool at Billet no.18 Etinehem Road MEAULTE.

Numerous notice boards made for Town Sanitary Officer CORBIE.

Disinfection.

Number of Blankets Disinfected...... 2,631.
Number of Articles of Underclothign passed through "Thresh"
Disinfector for Laundry....... 19,857.

List of Parties Bathed at CORBIE Baths:

    10th. K.R.R..... 345.
    11th. K.R.R..... 465.
    10th. R.B..... 520.
    11th. R.B.... 576.
    59th. Trench Mor. Battery... 45.
    80th. Field Ambulance..... 30.
    96th. Field Coy. R.E.... 180.
    20th. Divn. Signal Coy... 20.
    20th. Divn. Hd.Qrs. 100.
    R.F.A.Rest Camp.... 207.
    R.G.A.Rest Camp... 55.
    German Prisoners... 200.
        Total 2443.

Clean Clothing Issued:		Dirty Clothing Received:	
Shirts.....	3432.	Shirts....	4562.
Pants....	4655.	Pants....	5487.
Socks........	4753.	Socks..	6114.
Vests...	1316.	Vests...	1752.
Towels....	3168.	Towels...	3572.

Clean Clothing Received from Store, Camp 21 CARNOY

    Shirts... 900.
    Pants... 100.
    Socks.. 5200.
    Vests... 400.

R.L.Gorran

      Capt. R.A.M.C.(T.F.)
      O.C.Sanitary Section.

Appendix 4.

SANITARY AND WATER

REPORT

for week ending 6th. January 1917.

1. SANITATION.

On entering the forward area the system of certain N.C.O's and men of the Sanitary Section being attached to Brigades was temporarily discontinued. Each Camp in the area has one or more N.C.O's permanently resident there and they are responsible for the sanitation of their camp alone. A more satisfactory state of sanitary supervision is thus possible and as each camp has a permanently attached working party, sanitary measures are enabled to be carried out.

The sanitary conditions and work done at the various is as follows:-

Divisional Headquarters, Advanced.
        Arrowhead Copse.

The sanitary conditions are in a fair condition. The trench system of latrines is in use and I consider this insanitary under the conditions there prevailing. I have drawn the attention of the Camp Commandant to this and I have suggested a system of fly-proof pail latrines or if this is impracticable the trench latrine system might be safely employed in the space outside the dug-out system. New grease pits have been made and a new urine pit. No ablution arrangements are in existence but an ablution bench will be made as soon as the necessary materials are available.

C.R.E.

The dug-out and cookhouses were left in a very bad state by the previous occupants, GUARDS DIVISION.

These are being cleared, but slowly as NO fatigue party has been available. Efforts are being made by the M.O. to get a permanent party detailed and the C.R.E. has personally promised to get things put right.

Divn. Signal Coy.

The sanitary arrangements are fair order. New grease pits, urine pits, and latrines are being dug and the camp site cleared up as fast as one man can do it.

KALTZHORN CAMP.

The general conditions at this camp are very bad, as regards mud, water supply and shelter.

My N.C.O. has supervised the work of the permanent working party, which has consisted of cleansing of latrines and the building of incinerators, digging of grease pits, and the removal of rubbish deposited in shell holes in and adjoining the camp left there by previous occupants.

As soon as the rubbish is cleared it is proposed to proceed with cutting new drains in the camp.

CAMP 13, BRONFAY.

The conditions are fairly satisfactory at this camp and are improving.

My N.C.O's have supervised the work of the permanent working party and the vast accumulation of refuse left by the previous occupants of the GUARDS DIVN. has either been burned or buried. An old incinerator has been demolished a 4 new ones erected. The latrines have also been thoroughly cleansed.

There is an enormous collection of horse manure between the camp and the road, which will have to be removed before the fly season begins. There are no proper ablution arrangements, except as regards foot washing for the camphor anti trench foot treatment.

CAMP 108.

The sanitary conditions here are fairly satisfactory.

Much work by the permanent working party has been supervised by my N.C.O., including the following:-

Digging of 2 Urinals.
" " 2 refuse pits for small cookhouses.
" " 1 soakage pit.

Various paths have been made to the latrines and incinerator.

The latrines are satisfactory with the exception of a few minor defects which are being remedied. The excreta is buried.

The camp is without a supply of washing water, the nearest being at Camp 15, fully ½ mile away. This has already been reported, vide my S/26/17, and a suggestion made to tap a pipe line which supplies camp 15.

MANSEL CAMP.

Conditions here are quite satisfactory.

An ablution bench and shed has been built; also N.C.O's latrine and an incinerator.

290 blankets sprayed and various huts etc. disinfected Arrangements have been made for disinfecting a large number of blankets daily.

WATER.

(a) Tests for free chlorine have been carried out from water from the following water carts and the results shewing satisfactory chlorination.

Divn. H.Q.	1 cart.
Divn. Signal Coy.	1 cart.
10th. K.R.R.	2 carts.
11th. K.R.R.	1 cart.
10th. R.B.	2 carts.
11th. R.B.	2 carts.
159th. Coy. A.S.C.	1 cart.
96th. Field Coy. R.E.	1 cart.
60th. Field Ambulance.	1 cart.
12th. K.R.R.	2 carts.
12th. R.B.	2 carts.
61st. Field Ambulance.	2 carts.

(b) The following tanks for filling water bottles, dixies etc. regularly chlorinated by my N.C.O's detailed for this work:

> MINDEN POST.
> BRONFAY FARM.
> MARSEL CAMP.

At the latter camp the R.E's have been requested to carry out some improvements to the water point.

(c) Some of the Divnl. water carts fill at the BRIQUETERIE and GUILLEMONT supplies, both of these being chlorinated by the 17th. DIVISION.

(d) A special report has been submitted on the water supply at COMBLES, vide my S/56/17.

2. GENERAL WORK.

(a) At camp 15 BRONFAY Baths and a clean clothing exchange are in operation. 630 troops have been bathed.

(b) At COMBLES I have an N.C.O. supervising the work at the Gum Boot drying rooms and 2965 pairs were dried up to mid-night 10/11 January.

(c) Plans were made for constructing a gum boot drying at Hut C.32 Camp 15. The indent for the material was sent off the day after arrival in this area.

List of Clean Clothing issued:-   List of Dirty Clothing Rec:-

Shirts.	2730.	Shirts.	3826.
Pants.	3115.	Pants.	3801.
Socks.	3306.	Socks.	4240.
Towels.	2727.	Towels.	1908.
Vests.	1052.	Vests.	1381.

No. of articles passed through "THRESH" Disinfector for Laundry....   15,256.

List of parties bathed at CORBIE.

10th. R.E.	132.
A.S.C. 14th. Corps.	20.
London R.E.	23.
20th. Divn. Salvage Coy.	20.
159th. Coy. A.S.C.	17.
No.9 Field Ambulance.	30.
Irish Guards.	372.
Scotch do.	580.
Gren. do.	345.
Cols. do.	650.
R.F.A. Rest Camp.	50.
R.G.A. Rest Camp.	80.
Total	2329.

Disinfectants Issued.

    Chloride of Lime.   20 lbs.
    Cresol..   30 galls.

A.L.Girvan

    Capt. R.A.M.C.(T.F)
    O.C. 33rd. Sanitary Section.

Appendix 5.

SANITARY AND WATER
REPORT OF 33rd. SANITARY SECTION
for week ending 13th. JAN. 1917.

----

1. DISPOSITION.

A Disposition list of the Sanitary Section and attached personnel is annexed hereto.

2. SANITATION.

The Sanitary Conditions of and the sanitary work done in the various camps is as follows:-

Divn. Hd. Qrs., Advanced.

The dug-outs occupied by Adv. D.H.Q. are overcrowded and the ventilation is bad; in the men's dug-outs the space works out at 85 cubic feet of air space per man which is far too little. The latrines, which are defective, have already been condemned and they were reported in my Sanitary Report (S/85/17) for the week ending 6th. January 1917.

All dug-outs, offices and staircases have been sprayed with formaldehyde. The men's dug-outs have been thoroughly cleaned and 10 large sacks of rubbish burned. New grease pits, urine and waste-pits have been made; also a new ablution bench and soakage pit. Shell holes have been filled in and drainage channels cleared.

Divisional Signal Coy.

Satisfactory.

G.S.E. Camp.

Satisfactory. A large amount of rubbish has been collected and burned. Waste pits have been dug and new latrines made. Several shell holes full of rubbish have been filled in.

(1).

MANSEL CAMP.

This camp is in occupation by the 4th. Works Battn, the Divn. Salvage Coy. and small units of the 17th. Divn. Conditions are satisfactory. Disinfection of blankets is carried out at this camp and 1084 have been done during the week.

Camp 15 BRONFAY.

Conditions here are satisfactory. Inspection of the transport lines has been carried out. The following work was supervised by my N.C.O. detailed for this work.

Clearing waste water drain from Bath to rear of Camp.
Construction of grease pit for cookhouses.
Cleansing of drains in transport lines.
Construction of urine pit.

Camp 108 BRONFAY.

Sanitary Conditions are satisfactory. The Units who have vacated the Camp during the week have left their portions of the Camp in a clean condition. The 12th. King's (Liverpool) Regt. have improved the latrines by adding sheets of iron to prevent fouling of the ground. The work of enlarging of the holes of the latrine seats to prevent fouling -has desired been commenced. Two new urinals and new paths have been made.

MALTZHORN CAMP.

The ordinary work of camp sanitation, under the supervision of my Sergt. i/c, has been carried on. The working party has emptied the latrines, cleared out the incinerators and cleaned up a large portion of the camp site. One man has been stationed permanently at each incinerator to ensure cleanliness of the incinerator site. The construction of permanent latrines has been commenced and the 11th. R.E's pioneers are engaged on the construction of ablution benches.

D.A.C.

No. 1 &c Sections- Satisfactory.

Divn. Train.

Satisfactory. The camp of the No.3 Coy. was left in a very bad state by the previous occupants and great improvement has been effected by the present occupants.

COMBLES.

61st. Brigade Headquarters.)	In Catacombs.
84th. Field Coy. R.E.)	Satisfactory.
96th. Field Coy. R.E.)	
B.Coy. 11th. Durham L.I.	Satisfactory.
114th. Siege Battery R.G.A.)	These Batteries are in
88th. " " " ")	XIVth. Corps Heavy Artillery
136th. " " " ")	group and were visited at
8th. " " " ")	the request of the Town Major
145th. " " " ")	Sanitary arrangements satisfactory.
Hd.Qrs. 232nd. R.F.A. (Signallers only).	Satisfactory.

The public latrine accommodation in COMBLES is nil and trench latrines are in use. I am endeavouring to create a Sanitary Section Workshop, vide my S/14/17, and as soon as this is a working concern the latrine problem in COMBLES will be tackled. Meanwhile arrangements have been made for the erection of one public latrine at the corner of the Rue de FREGICOURT and Rue de GUILLEMONT.

2.WATER.

The following water carts were tested for free chlorine and evidence of efficient of chlorination found as stated:-

Divn. Hd. Qrs.	1 cart.	Tested daily. Found Chlorinated.
Divn. Signal Coy.	1 cart.	Tested daily. Found chlorinated, with following exceptions When tested on 14/1/17 no reaction was found from the water from this cart. The cart was filled on 15/1/17 at 11.30 a.m. and tested at 12 noon on the same day. A ½ measure added and the water tested again at 3 p.m. when a good reaction was observable.
No.1 Section D.A.C.	1 cart No.7,332. Found chlorinated.	This cart is deficient in filter cloths and gauzes and the attention of the O.C.S. has been drawn to this for his necessary action.
No.2 Section D.A.C.	1 cart. No.7,321.	When tested on the 11/1/17 no evidence of chlorination was found. The cart was filled on 11/1/17 at 1.30 a.m. and tested at 2 a.m. on the same day the cart was deficient in cloths & had no good chloride. It appears that no experienced man is in charge of this cart.

Divn. Train
   2nd. Coy.   1 cart No.70293.   Filled 11 a.m. on
                                       12/1/17 and tested at 11.30 a.m. on the
                                       same day when no evidence of chlorination
                                       was found.

Divn. Train.
   3rd.& 4th. Coys.   2 carts. Nos.70323.   Tested 12/1/17.
                                  70331.   Found Chlorinated.

11th. Rifle Brigade.   2 carts. Nos.70294.
                                  70557.   Tested daily found
                                                Chlorinated.

64th. Machine Gun Coy. 1 cart No. 60883.   Tested 11/1/17 &
                                                    12/1/18 found
                                                   chlorinated.

90th. Field Coy. R.E. 1 cart.   Tested daily &
                                                    found chlorinated

60th. Field Ambulance. 2 carts. Nos.70318.   Tested daily and
                                  70330.   found chlorinated.

12th. K.R.R.   3 carts. Nos.12683.   Tested 8/1/17,
                                     67567.   10/1/17 and 11/1/19
                                               Found chlorinated.

6th. K.S.L.I.   2 carts. Nos.69615.   Tested 12/1/17
                                  70323.   Found chlorinated.

83rd. Field Coy. R.E. 2 carts. No. 34222.   Tested 8/1/17,
                                                 9/1/17 and 10/1/17
                                               Found chlorinated.

61st. Field Ambulance. 2 carts. Nos.70317.   Tested 7/1/17,
                                  70330.   9/1/17 & 14/1/17.
                                               Found chlorinated.

7th. K.O.Y.L.I.   2 carts. Nos.70705.   Tested 8/1/17 and
                                  70348.   11/1/17 found
                                               chlorinated.

12th. King's (L'pool)
   Regt.   1 cart. No. 68164.   Tested 8/1/17 and
                                               11/1/17 .Found
                                               chlorinated.

61st. Machine Gun Coy. 1 cart No.10030.   Tested 9/1/17 and
                                               11/1/17. Found
                                               chlorinated.

7th. Somerset L.I.   1 cart No.70691.   Tested 11/1/17.
                                               Found chlorinated.

7th. D.C.L.I.   1 cart No. 70332.   Found chlorinated.

11th. Durham L.I.   2 carts. Nos.68163.
                                  67712.   Found chlorinated.

GENERAL WORK.

(a) No. of troops bathed at Camp 13 during the
week......   2272.
No. of troops bathed at CORBIE during the
week......   2014.

(b) Clean Clothing Issued.   Dirty Clothing Received.

    Shirts.   5845.   Shirts.   4538.
    Pants.   4840.   Pants.   3044.
    Socks.   6721.   Socks.   5318.
    Vests.   0123.   Vests.   225.
    Towels.   4231.   Towels.   108.

It will be noticed that the amount of dirty clothing received does not equal the clean clothing and that there is a big deficiency. It is found that Quartermasters of Units are not carrying out the provisions of 55th.Divn. Order No.543 para. 3 dated 27/12/16.

(c) No. of articles of underclothing passed through the Thresh Disinfector....   1825.

(d) Disinfectants issued:-

    Chloride of Lime....   48 lbs.
    Cresol....   160 galls.
    Crude Paraffin....   40 galls.
    Formalin....   14 galls.
    Bleaching Powder....   74 tins.
    Whale Oil....   155 galls.

4. DISINFECTION.

The Disinfection of the dug-out of Capt.THORNTON, (removed to hospital and suffering from quinsie) was carried out on the night of 9th.January. The same dug-out was occupied by some other officers whose bunks and bedding were sprayed.

5. ANTI TRENCH FOOT SOAP.

All the camphorated soap required by the Division was made by the Sanitary section.

80 lbs. of soft soap was melted in a SOYER stove, the camphor and borax stirred in little by little, and the mixture then poured into empty biscuit tins ready for issue.

400 lbs was prepared.

Capt. R.A.M.C.,
O.C.55rd. Sanitary Section.

Appendix 6.

To.
   A.D.M.S.,
      20th. Division.

I think it is purely Divisional though it should be Corps in my opinion so as to have continuity.

Water is an A.S.C. supply.

At present the cans are drawn from the S.S.C. at Grovetown - uncleaned - and the Brigades do the cleansing. I have already written to them for exact details but the replies are not yet to hand.

Formerly the S.S.C. cleaned the cans by the help of various fatigues, such as the Divn. Band, detailed by "Q", for purpose. They were inefficiently done.

The cans are filled from GUILLEMONT, BRIQUETERIE and COMBLES. The latter point alone being in the Divisional Area and arrangements for chlorination have been made there.

I have frequently complained about the lack of cleanliness of the cans and have made numerous attempts to get the matter into my own hands.

In the last area after much trouble I obtained the promise of steam from a broken down steam roller but by the time I got it we were on the point of vacating the area and I handed over the promise to the 17th. Division.

At the present moment I am endeavouring to get some small boilers made out of oil drums and have written to the O.C. Wilts. A.T.Coy. R.E., SWINDON CAMP asking him to do it.

Give me a good boiler and I will undertake to clean all the cans needed by the Division and to mark them cleaned by Sanitary Section.

As regards wells I have written the Brigades exact details of the solution to be used and given them the alternative of drawing the solution ready made by me.

I do not know whether the wells not mentioned in Divn. Orders have been closed.

the stoppers -. The screw-on ones cannot be secured by wire in such a manner as to be detachable easily. Wooden ones cannot be regarded as bacteriologically sound.

The whole principle of using petrol cans for water supplies is thoroughly bad. Indeed in a previous report on this matter I compared it with the scarcely more dangerous practice of keeping poisons in wine bottles. Special cans with flap stoppers are needed.

If the Hun thinks it worth while to use glass bottles why shouldn't we do something better than use second hand cans?

Capt. R.A.M.C.(T.F.).
O.C. 53rd Sanitary Section.

Appendix 7.

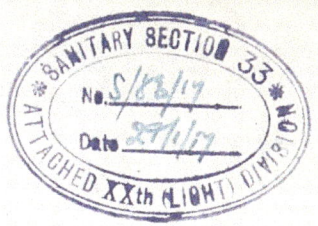

SANITARY AND WATER

Report for week ending 20th. January 1917.

----

1. DISPOSITION.

A Disposition List of the Sanitary Section and attached personnel is annexed hereto.

2. SANITATION.

The sanitary conditions of and the sanitary work done in the various Camps is as follows:-

Divn. Hd.Qrs. Advanced. Satisfactory. Dug-outs, Staircases, etc. sprayed with a Formalin Solution.

Divn. Hd.Qrs. Rear. Satisfactory with the exception of the M.M.P. stables, outside of which there is a considerable quantity of manure, the accumulation of both previous and present occupants A start has been made at removing this.

Divn. Signal Company. Satisfactory. New latrines constructed.

C.R.E.Camp. Satisfactory. New latrines constructed. Camp site thoroughly cleaned up.

Camp 15 BRONFAY. Satisfactory. The following work has been carried out under the supervision of my N.C.O.:
    Construction of two incinerators.
    Road to latrines and excreta pit relaid.
    Old incinerator dismantled.

Camp 108 BRONFAY. Conditions satisfactory. The following work has been carried out under the supervision of my N.C.O:-
    Gutter made to one hut and three large barrels sunk into the ground to catch water for washing.
    Construction of an incinerator.
    Completion of work of enlarging latrine seats to prevent fouling.

MALTZHORN Camp. Conditions satisfactory. The following new work has been carried out under the supervision of my N.C.O.:
    Large tins provided for camp refuse, these being emptied twice daily and the contents burnt in the incinerator.
    Construction of grease and urine pits.
    One cookhouse and two permanent latrines constructed.
    Notice boards marking "Foul Ground" put up.

TASSEL CAMP. Conditions Satisfactory. The
following work has been carried out under the
supervision of my R.C.O.:
    All huts occupied by 9th. Horse Batts.
        sprayed with solution of Cresol.
    New latrine erected.
    Numerous notice boards made for use in Camp.
    Drainage work still being carried on.
    Disinfection of blankets is carried out at this
        Camp and this were done during the week.

BILLETS.

        21st. Bde. Hd.Qrs.
        98th. R.E. Section.   ) In CATACOMBS.
        84th. R.E. Section.   )   Satisfactory.
        61st. Field Ambulance.)

        11th. Durham L.I.   Satisfactory.

        22nd. R.F.A. Signallers. Old Latrine filled in
            and new one provided. Satisfactory.

        One public latrine has been erected on waste land
            at corner of Rue de FREDICOURT and Rue de
            GUILLEMONT. One urinal made by the side of this

Other units.

    Divisional Train.   Satisfactory.

    Mobile Veterinary Section.   Satisfactory.

    Divisional Amn. Column.   Satisfactory.

4.   WATER.

        The customary surprise tests of water carts to
ascertain efficient chlorination have been carried out
and all the carts tested showed evidences of having
been chlorinated with the following exceptions:

        64th. Divn. R.F.A. Hd.Qrs. Cart No. T.9148.
            Filled 3p.m. 15/1/17 and tested at 3.30 p.m
            on the same day. Water not chlorinated.

        3rd. Company Divn. Train. Cart No. T9...
            Filled 7 a.m. on 15/1/17 and tested at
            9 a.m. on the same day. Water not
            chlorinated. One Company of the Divn. Train
            (No. 3.) was reported for insufficient
            chlorination in my last week's report.
        61st. Company A.S.C. Cart No. T.9...
            Filled 9.30 a.m. 15/1/17 and tested at 1..
            a.m. on the same day. Water not chlorinated
            The water was to be used for sick horses. x

        The water bottle point on the GUILLEMONT-AIRCOURT
Road in the 55th. Division area, does not appear to be
dealt with by the 55th. Divisional Sanitary Section.

        It was found that the well in RED FAY FARM was being

used by troops for filling water bottles. The water gave a reaction in the second cup of the Horrock's Test and a temporary notice "Unfit for drinking" was affixed.

The water bottle points at HILDEN POST and BRICKFAY have been chlorinated twice daily.

4. GENERAL WORK.

List of Disinfectants Issued:-
    Chloride of Lime.............. 10v.
    Cresol........................ galls.
    Crude Paraffin................ galls.
    Bleaching Powder.............. tins.
    Clarifying Powder............. tins.
    Whale Oil..................... 125 galls.

No. of men bathed at COMINES.. 2271.

No. of men bathed at Camp 15 BRICKFAY.. 2121.

List of Clean Clothing Issued:-

    Shirts..   740.
    Pants..
    Socks.
    Vests..
    Towels..

List of Dirty Clothing Received:

    Shirts.
    Pants...   2217.
    Socks...
    Vests...
    Towels...

No. of Articles passed through Thresh Disinfector
    for laundry.............. 12,000.

No. of Gum Boots dried at Drying Room at
    COMINES....   4,496 pairs.

A new gum boot drying room capable of holding 400 pairs has been constructed in hut C 32 Camp 15. A clothing exchange has also been made there, also a billet for the bath staff.
All the work has been done by the San. Section

R.F. Girvan
Capt. R.A.M.C.(T.F.)
O.C. 3rd. Sanitary Section.

Appendix 8. Copy No. 6.

NOTES ON SANITATION, WATER
AND BATHS IN
FORWARD AREA

1. Disposition and Work of Section and attached personnel:

San.Sec.	Permanently attached Personnel.	Temporarily attached Personnel.	Duties.
Headquarters, MINDEN POST	15 N.C.O's and men as follows:		
	S/Sergt.............................		Supervising work of Section
	Corpl.) L/Cpl.)		Office.
	L/Cpl.............................		Water duties & inspections of Divn Troops' carts, D.A.C. etc. & sanitary inspections of D.H.Q Rear, Mob.Vet.Sec. Salvage Coy. & D.A.C
	L/Cpl.............................		Chlorination of water at MINDEN Post & BRONFAY.
	L/Cpl.) Pte.)		Construction work.
	Pte.............................		Cook.
	Pte.		Batman.
	Pte............................)	1 O.R.)	Rations & making of Anti-Trench Foot soap & powder.
		1 O.R...............	Pioneer
		1 O.R...............	Cook's Assistant
		1 O.R...............	Messenger.
		1 O.R...............	Assisting in carpentry and odd jobs.
Divn.Hd.Qrs. Adv. ARROWHEAD COPSE.	Corpl.		Sanitary inspection of Camp of D.H.Q.Adv. and C.R.E. & water duties thereto
Camp 15 BRONFAY.	Sergt............)	4 O.R's)	Construction of drying room at Hut C.32.
	Sergt) L/Cpl.)		Inspections of camp & supervision of working party of 5 O.R's for camp duties.
		5 O.R's.	Working party.

	San. Sec.	Permanently attached personnel.	Temporarily attached personnel.	Duties.
Camp 15 BRONFAY. (contd.)		L/Cpl		Water duties to 61st. Bde. Chlorination of Camp water points & water supervision in immediate vicinity of camp.
VILLE		L/Cpl) 2 O.R's)		Working clothing exchange in hut C.32.
		L/Cpl) 8 O.R's)		Working baths in hut C.32.
Camp 108 Bronfay		L/Cpl		Inspections of camp & supervision of working party of 6 O.R's for camp duties.
			6 O.R's from one of the Battns.	Working party.
LANSEL CAMP.		L/Cpl		Inspections of Camp & supervision of blanket disinfection room.
MALTZHORN CAMP.		Sergt.) Pte.)		Inspections of camp & supervision of working party of 12 O.R's for camp duties.
			12 O.R's from Salvage Coy.	Working party.
		L/Cpl.) L/Cpl.)		Water duties to 59th & 60th. Bdes. Water supervision in immediate vicinity of camp.
COMBLES Drying Room.		L/Cpl		Supervision of drying rooms.
			11 O.R's from Bdes.	To work drying rooms.
COMBLES Catacombs		L/Cpl		Sanitary inspections of Catacombs & other Divn. Billets in Combles; inspection of XIV Corps Heavy Art. & making up of stock solution for chlorination.
CORBIE Baths.		2 lorry drivers		Drivers of San Sec. Lorry.
			Q.M.S.	i/c Baths.
		2 Foden Drivers		Drivers of Foden Disinfector.
			14 O.R's	To work baths; incl. 3 drivers of "Baths" Lorry.
VILLE.			1 O.R.	i/c Clothing issued to Art.

2. SANITATION.

In order to satisfactorily cope with the sanitary conditions of the Forward area I recalled the Brigades Squads on taking over the area and alloted certain N.C.O's and men to each camp. Their duties consisted of supervising the sanitation and work at their own particular camp and that alone and a working party for each camp was arranged. Thus continuity of work and sanitary effort was arrived at.

The camps occupied by the Divn are:
- Forward: FREGICOURT.
- Resting: Camp 15 BRONFAY.
  - Camp 108 BRONFAY.
  - MALTZHORN Camp.

These N.C.O's and men and working parties live in the camps and are either rationed by the Town Major or by the rear parties of the Battns.

An N.C.O. was also detailed to work at MANSEL CAMP occupied by the 20th.Divn.Works Battn. and 17th.Divn. details.

At MALTZHORN camp one man from the working party has been placed i/c of each incinerator and made responsible for that, thus ensuring cleanliness of the incinerator site.

No other point calls for special mention except:- the latrines(or lack of) at COMBLES.

There is only one public latrine at COMBLES -erected by my L/Cpl. at the Catacombs-. It has been impossible to erect any more owing to the lack of labour ~~available~~.

WATER.

The chief water points used by the Division are:
- a COMBLES.
- b GUILLEMONT.
- c BRIQUETERIE.
- d BRONFAY.
- e MINDEN POST.
- f French Hospital BRAY-MARICOURT Road.
- g MANSEL CAMP.

(a) COMBLES.

There are 8 wells here (see map Appendix) all within a radius of a few hundred yards. These are of the deep type and apparently of good quality. Some copies of Chemical analyses made by the GUARDS Divn. San.Sec. are annexed "B". 6 of these wells are fitted with pumps on the dredger system and 2 with bucket and windlass. The supply is ample but the waste is excessive. When I took over from the GUARDS Divn there was no provision for chlorination, except in water carts, and only in 2 cases would it be easy to fix tanks owing to the fact that the water is delivered by the pumps at a height of only 1 foot & 18 inches above the ground. I personally fully investigated the supply and reported to A.D.M.S. suggesting that water be drawn only from certain wells and that a man be detailed at each point to chlorinate each patrol can as it was drawn. I also suggested that a guard would be necessary at each point but that all wells could be used for cooking purposes; at the same time I stipulated that I was unable to supply either chlorinators or guards from my personnel.

At this time there was a certain amount of diarrhoea in the area which would certainly be attributed to the water and therefore it was necessary to take some immediate measures.

The result was the following order in Divn. Orders:-

"In view of the fact that there is a certain amount of diarrhoea in COMBLES the following arrangements will be made to regulate the water supply.

"Water will be drawn only from four wells shown in sketches forwarded to left and right groups respectively, to whom all units must apply for location.

"Guards will be placed on these wells, and necessary steps must be taken to ensure that every petrol tin of water from these wells is chlorinated before it is taken away. It is suggested that this be done by the provision of a standard chlorinating solution of which a measure is tiped into each tin before removal.

"The left group will be responsible that this precaution is taken at wells numbered 5 and 6, and the right group that it is taken at wells numbered 2 and 4".

The present position is that my L/Cpl. stationed at the Catacombs makes up the following solution as required by the Staff Capts. of the Bdes. and all the rest is done under Bde. arrangements.

Solution:

15 scoops of bleaching powder made into a thin cream, and diluted up to a Winchester Quart (2700 c.c.). One scoop of this solution to each petrol can giving a dose of about 2 part per million of free chlorine. The Winchester Quart bottle used is an empty Formaldehyde bottle and a scoop from a bleaching powder tin is tied to each bottle.

- (b) GUILLEMONT) These sources are under the control
- (c) BRIQUETERIE) of the 29th. Division.

- (d) BRONFAY) These sources consist of a series of tanks
- (e) MINDEN POST) for filling water bottles and dixies etc. The ones at MINDEN POST are situated at Rear Divn. Hd. Qrs. One L/Cpl. from the Sanitary Section is detailed to chlorinate them twice daily. At BRONFAY there is a further supply consisting of 2 regxgull. 400 gallon tanks at rear of Camp 15. These are chlorinated by the water N.C.O. at Camp 15.

- (f) French Hospital
  Bray-Maricourt Road.
  The water is pumped from a well into 2 tanks by a small motor. "Eau de Javelle" is discharged into tanks. A board has been affixed here stating that chlorination is unnecessary.

- (g) MANSEL CAMP.

There are a series of small tanks here chlorinated daily by my N.C.O. at the Camp. On entering the area the tanks were standing on the ground but I requested the Engineers to place them on stands. The stands have arrived but the tanks have not been fixed on them yet and still stand on the ground.

Other Particulars.

(1) Petrol Cans:- Owing to the fact that all my efforts at getting a steam boiler have failed up to the present no cans have been cleaned under the supervision of the Sanitary Section, but they are done under Bde. arrangements. Several complaints have been received of their dirtiness.

(2) Maltzhorn Camp is supplied by a Bttn water cart. The cart stands by the water towers at the railhead and water taken by hand to the cart.

(3) C.R.E.Camp (WEDGWOOD Camp) is supplied by water carts of the units there. The M.O. has made several good arrangements there.

(4) D.H.Q.Adv. is supplied by the Hd.Qrs.cart which refils t twice daily.

(5) Camp 108 Bronfay has no washing water supply nearer than Camp 15. A suggestion was sent in to Headquarters to tap the pipe line to Camp 15 at about L.4 .b.5.7. (Albert combined sheet) on the railway line, which at this point is only a few hundred yards away from Camp 108. At this time the men were using absolutely filthy water to wash in. A reply was received that this suggestion was embodied in a scheme of the Town Major BRONF -FAY and approved by the XIVth. Corps. Nothing has been done. Meanwhile my N.C.O. at the Camp has fixed a gutter to one hut and has sunk 3 large barrels in the ground to catch the water nad this isused for washing.

(6) At BRONFAY FARM there is a well and troops were found to be filling their water bottles there. On testing by the Horrock's test a blue was obtained in the second cup. A board has temporarily been affixed marking the water as unfit for drinking. Apart from the organic matter the water is of good chemical quality.

4. BATHS.

The system obtaining for supplying clean and dry clothes is as follows: The Divn.retained and will retain the CORBIE Baths. Here all disinfection of underclothing is carried out. The clean and dirty clothes are conveyed between there and Camp15 Two lorries were used - the Sanitary Section lorry and one from the Divn.Supply Col. detailed on request by the O.C.M.T.XIVth. Corps. No passes are required for these lorries to travel in the prescribed area, as the area is easily avoided by their return -ing via SUZANNE.

One hut, C.32, is allotted to me in Camp 15 and in it are Baths, Clothing Exchange, Gum Boot Drying Room and men's billet.

(a) A spray bath is fitted up capable of bathing 90 men per hour. The allotment of Baths is done by me.

(b) Clothing Exchange:- The only thing needing special mention is the fact that owing to the hut being so very far from the road a fatigue party is needed daily to load and unload the clothing lorries. This party has been obtained from one of the resting Battns through the Town Major BRONFAY.

(c) Drying Room:- This was constructed by me and was finish -ed a few days ago. It has now been handed over to one of the Bdes. and is worked under Bde. arrangements. I exercise no super -vision over it at all. It can hold 400 pairs of Gum Boots thigh A supply of fuel is left at this hut for handing over to the 17th.Division.

5. DRYING ROOM COMBLES.

This was formerly supervised by one of my N.C.O's but is now being worked under Bde. arrangements. It has been improved by my N.C.O. there.

6. DISINFECTION OF BLANKETS.

A blanket disinfecting station has been arranged by me at MANSEL CAMP. It consists of (a) a spraying room (b) a drying room The former is a tarpaulin-covered shed with a floor of trench- boards. The latter is an "elephant hut" i.e. a semi cylindrical dug out. It has been fitted with a stove and trench boards. The blankets are sprayed with 20% solution of "formalin".

Units were informed in Divn.Orders that the station was ready. The allotment was made by me. 500 blankets are disinfec ted and returned the same day.

7. MISCELLANEOUS:

(a) O.C. San.Sec. is billeted with D.A.D.M.S. xx in an Division Armstrong Hut.
(b) The personnel at MINDEN POST are in various huts and dug outs.
(c) The hut used as Office will be handed over.
(d) The Divn. dump for Disinfectants under the charge of the San Sec. is at the PLATEAU.

8. Manufacture of Anti Trench Foot Soap and Powder.

The whole of the soap and powder required by the Division is made and supplied by the San. Sec. from ingredients supplied by the S.S.O.

The soap is melted in a SOYER stove, the camphor and borax added and stirred in, and then ladled into biscuit tins ready for issue.

A.F. Gorvan
Capt. R.A.M.C.(T.F.)
O.C. 33rd Sanitary Section.

Copies to:

1. A.D.M.S. 20th. Divn.
2. O.C. San.Sec. 17th. Divn.
3. O.i/c. Baths 17th. Divn.
4. Retained.
5/6 War Diary. ✓

Appendix A.

WATER SUPPLIES.

Water supplies round about MINDEN POST used for filling water bottles.

MINDEN POST.

    5 - 400 gallon tanks; chlorinated twice daily. One of these is out of order and cannot be used.

BRONFAY FARM.

    2 - 400 gallon tanks; chlorinated twice daily.

CAMP 15.   At rear of camp; (not far from BRONFAY FARM.)

    2 - 400 gallon tanks; very little used.

MANSEL CAMP.

    4 - 200 gallon tanks; chlorinated twice daily.

Water Supply of Combles –
Rough Sketch Plan showing Wells.

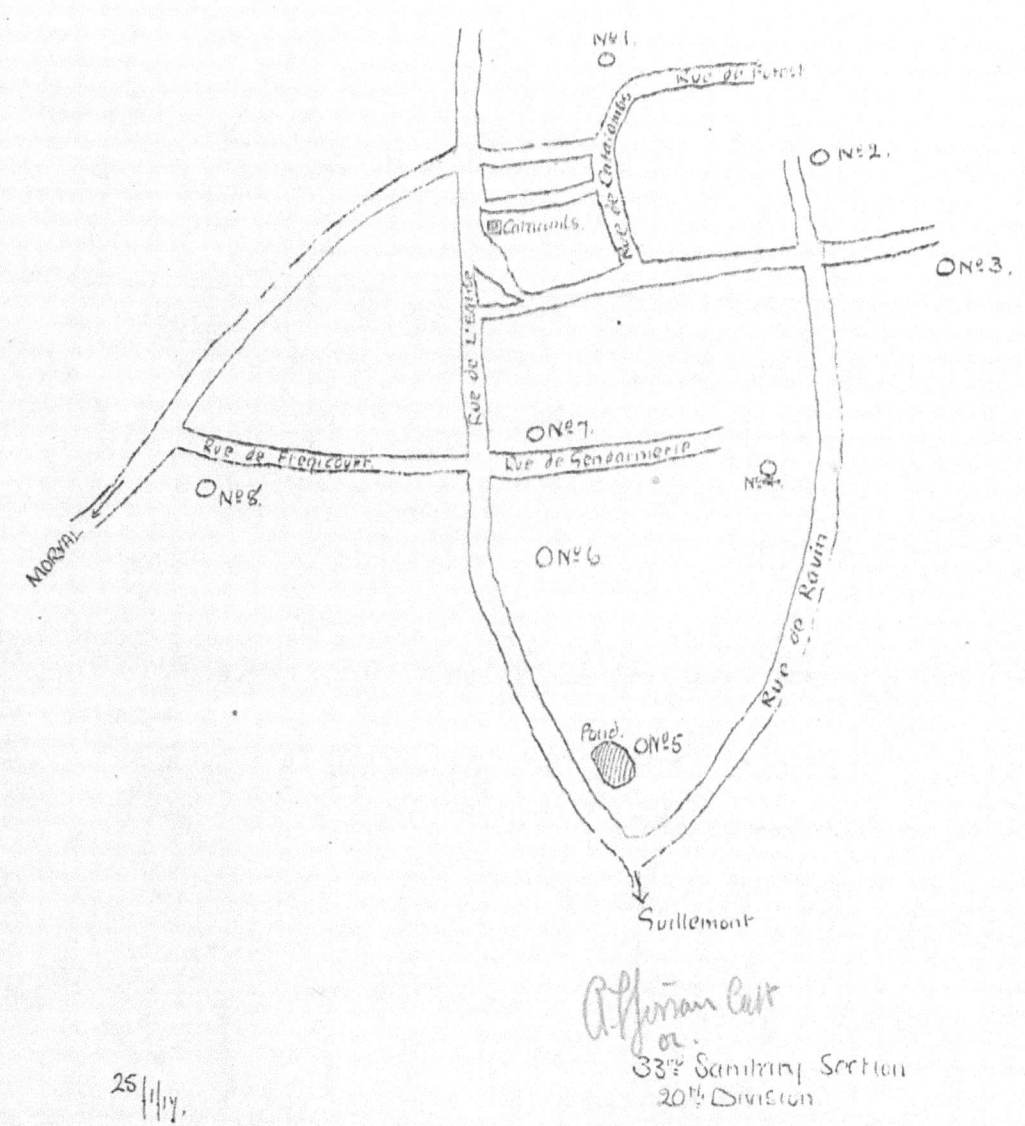

25/1/17.

A. Herman Capt
OC.
33rd Sanitary Section
20th Division

Appendix B.   Copy.

COMBLES.

Well No.1 - Near Pond - Opposite Rue de Sailly.

Colour.   -   Colourless.

Turbidity.   -   Clear and Bright.

Odour.   -   None.

Reaction.   -   Neutral or alkaline.
  Residue left   ) White - Chalky.
  on evaporation) No charring.

Free Ammonia.   No evident trace.

Chlorine.   About 2 parts per 100,000.

Equivalent Nacl.   About 3.3 parts.

Nitrites.   None.

Nitrates.   None.

Hardness.   About 10°.

Lead, Zinc, Copper
  and Iron.   Trace of Iron.

Oxygen absorbed in) Less than 0.1 parts
  15mms. at 212 F.) per 100,000.

Horrock's Test.   Colour remains in 1st. cup.

Arsenic Mercury.   None.

Cyanides.   None.

From examination of source and results obtained by analysis, I am of the opinion that this is suitable for drinking or cooking purposes after being previous--ly boiled or chlorinated. 1 scoop of C.of L. to cart.

J.G.ORTON R.A.C.
A.PECK M.P.S.

APPENDIX B.   Copy.

COMBLES.

Well No.2   -   Opposie Gendarmerie Ruins.

Colour.	-	Colourless.
Turbidity.	-	Clear and Bright.
Odour.	-	None.
Reaction.	-	Neutral or alkaline.
Residue left on evaporation.	)	White - Chalky / No charring
Free Ammonia.		Appreciable trace.
Chlorine		About 3 parts per 100,000.
Equivalent NaCl.	-	About 5 parts.
Nitrites	-	None.
Nitrates.	-	None.
Lead, Zinc, Copper and Iron		Trace of Iron.
Oxygen absorbed in 15mms. at 212 F.	)	Less than 0.1 per 100,000 parts
Horrock's Test.		Colour remains in 1st Cup.
Arsenic Mersury.		None.
Cyanides.		None.
Hardness	-	About 9°.

From examination of source and results obtained by analysis I am of the opinion that this water is suitable for cooking or drinking purposes after being previously boiled or chlorinated. 1 scoop of C.eof L. to cart.

A.N.PECK
M.P.S.

APPENDIX B.   Copy.

COMBLES.

    Well No.3 - Rear of Gendarmerie Ruins.

Colour.	Colourless
Turbidity.	Clear and bright.
Odour.	None.
Reaction.	Neutral or alkaline.
Residue left on evaporation)	White - Chalky No charring.
Free Ammonia.	No appreciable trace.
Chlorine.	About 5 parts per 100,000.
Equivalent Nacl.	About 8 parts.
Nitrites.	None.
Nitrates.	None.
Hardness.	About $10°$.
Lead, Zinc, Copper and Iron.	Trace of Iron.
Oxygen absorbed in 15 mins. at 212 F.	Under 0.1 parts per 100,000.
Horrock's Test.	Colour remains in 1st Cup.
Arsenic Mercury.	None.
Cyanides.	None.

    From examination of source and results obtained by analysis, I am of the opinion that this is a suitable drinking or cooking water provided it has been previously boiled or chlorinated. 1 scoop C.of L. per water cart.

                                         A.N.PECK   M.P.S.

APPENDIX B.   Copy.

COMBLES.

Well no. 4 - Opposite corner of Rue de la Gare.

Colour. — Colourless

Turbidity. - Clear and bright.

Odour.   None.

Reaction. — Neutral or alkaline.

Residue left) White - Chalky.
on evaporation.) No charring

Free Ammonia. No evident trace.

Chlorine. About 8 parts per 100,000.

Equivalent Nacl. About 13 parts.

Nitrites. None.

Nitrates. None

Hardness. About 10°.

Lead, Zinc, Copper and Iron. Trace of Iron.

Oxygen absorbed in 15mms. at 212 F. Less than 0.1 parts per 100,000.

Horrock's Test. Colour remains in 1st. cup.

Arsenic Mercury. None.

Cyanides. None.

From examination of source and results obtained by analysis, I am of the opinion that this water is suitable for cooking and drinking purposes after being previously boiled or chlorinated. 1 scoop of C. of L. per cart.

A.N. PECK   M.P.S.

Appendix 9.

SECRET.

Daily Orders No 57
by
Captain A.F. Girvan. R.A.M.C.(T.F.)
Commanding
33rd Sanitary Section.

Copy No 10.

Thursday 25th January 1917.

1. **Disposition.**

   (a) The Headquarters of the Sanitary Section will be at HEILLY. The Sanitary Section Lorry will rejoin the Section and park at HEILLY on the 28th January.

   (b) The men who have been allotted to Camps and who were previously attached to Brigades will rejoin their Brigades under the arrangements tabulated below.
   The Brigades will be concentrated as follows:

59th Inf. Bde. Group.	FRANVILLERS, BONNAY, La HOUSSOYE,
+ 84th Field Coy. R.E.	HEILLY.
60th Inf. Bde. Group.	MEAULTE and MEAULTE huts.

61st Inf. Bde. Group	La NEUVILLE, COISY, CARDONNETTE,
including 11th D.L.I.	BUSSEY-les-DAOURS.
but less 84th Field Coy R.E.	

   The Field Ambulances will be situated as follows:
   60th Field Ambulance. FRANVILLERS.
   61st Field Ambulance. MEAULTE.
   62nd Field Ambulance. CARDONNETTE.

   (c) The following will remain at CORBIE:
   The Baths and Laundry Staff.
   The Thresh Disinfector.
   The "Baths" Lorry and 3 drivers.
   The above personnel and lorries will be rationed by S.O. 91st Bde. R.F.A. as before.

2. **Move.**

   (1). 26th January. The following NCO's and men will meet the relieving details as shewn at BRONFAY FARM at 11 a.m. and conduct them to their stations, where they will be initiated into the work there:
   L/Corpl Spurgeon will meet details for COMBLES.
   L/Corpl. Johns   "   "   " BRONFAY Camps.
   Pte. Cloake   "   "   " MALTZHORN Camp and ARROWHEAD COPSE

   One man from
   MINDEN POST   "   "   " MINDEN POST and MANSEL Camp.

   27th January. (a) The N.C.O's i/c Camps, Baths, etc. will hand over to the relieving details, carefully taking receipts in duplicate for all stores handed over.

   (b) The Sanitary Section personnel from Camps 15 and 108 BRONFAY, MALTZHORN Camp, ARROWHEAD COPSE and MANSEL Camp will proceed to MINDEN POST and will be conveyed to CORBIE Baths by the Sanitary Section Lorry leaving MINDEN POST at 3 p.m. excepting the 60th Brigade Squad, i.e. Sergt. Hardcastle, L/Corpl Wilson and L/Corpl. Barents who will alight at MEAULTE and rejoin the 61st Field Ambulance.

27th January. (c) The Baths details from Camp 15 will proceed to Town Mayor's Office, BRONFAY Camp 15 to meet Lieut JAMES from Divisional Headquarters at 1 p.m. They will be under the charge of L/Cple. Beardsworth. Each man will carry full pack, 2 blankets and 2 days rations.

28th January. (a) The "Baths" lorry will proceed to MINDEN POST via MEAULTE, SAPPER CORNER and PLATEAU to reach MINDEN POST at 10 a.m. and will take Staff Sergeant Beaumont and all men and stores at MINDEN POST (Except Office Stuff and personnel and Officers Kit) to HEILLY.

(b) The Sanitary Section lorry will proceed to MINDEN POST reaching there at 11 a.m. and will convey Officers Kit and Office Stuff and personnel to HEILLY.

(c) Pte. Beagley will proceed mounted to HEILLY.

29th January. The Sanitary Section lorry will proceed to CORBIE reaching there at 9 a.m. and will then convey the 59th and 61st Brigade Squads to FRANVILLERS and CHARDONNETTE respectively. On its return journey to HEILLY it will bring back a load of stores from CORBIE.

(2) Staff Sergeant Beaumont will arrange carriage of all stores either to CORBIE or HEILLY between the 25th - 28th January by lorry as convenient.

(3) The Baths personnel proceeding with the Divisional Details from BRONFAY to HEILLY will on arrival at HEILLY, and after reporting to Sanitary Section Office at Divisional Headquarters, proceed to CORBIE and rejoin the Baths Staff.

(4) The various working parties at Camps 15, 108 and MALTZHORN, COMBLES, etc. act under the orders of O.C. Salvage Company.

A.T. Gowan
Captain R.A.M.C. (T.F.)
O.C. 33rd Sanitary Section.

Copies to:
1. S/Sergt. Beaumont.
2. Q.M.S. Hoare.
3. Sergt. Caesar.
4. Sergt. Bulmforth.
5. Sergt. Handcastle.
6. Cpl. Garrat.
7/8. Retained
9/10. War Diary.

Disposition of Sanitary Section and
attached personnel in Reserve Area.

Place.	Sanitary Section.	Attached personnel.	Baths Staff.
Headquarters HEILLY.	S/Sergt. Beaumont Corpl. Gaunt Corpl. Whittock. L/Cpl. Horsley. L/Cpl. Hampson. L/Cpl. Spurgeon. L/Cpl. Heather. L/Cpl. Howes. L/Cpl. Hunting. L/Cpl. McHugh. L/Cpl. Hill. Pte. Harrison. Pte. Judd. Pte. Beagles. Pte. Finch. Pte. Stevens. Pte. Powell.	Rfn. Scholey. Rfn. Crocker. Rfn. Payne. Rfn. Pitwell. Rfn. Taylor. Pte. Cox. (D.C.L.I.) Pte. Mitchell Pte. Price. Pte. Cox.	
FRANVILLERS 60th Field Ambulance	Sergt. Balmford. L/Corpl. Gray. Pte. Cloake.		
MEAULTE 61st Field Ambulance	Sergt. Hardcastle. L/Cpl. Wilson L/Cpl. Barents		
CARDONNETTE 62nd Field Ambulance	Sergt. Caesar. L/Cpl. Otterway. L/Cpl. Gohns.		
CORBIE Baths.			Q.M.S. Hoare. L/Corpl. Beardsworth Pte. Harrington. Pte. Whittock Pte. Wrightson. Pte. Storey. Pte. Lamb. Rfn. Allcock. Rfn. Mansell. Rfn. Fishcock. Rfn. Simpson. Rfn. Hillier. Rfn. Walters. Rfn. Thompson. Pte. Rogers Pte. Williams. Pte. Lovell. Pte. Knock. Pte. Doulton. Pte. Shail. Pte. Denney. Pte. Crosford. Pte. Robinson. 2 Foden Drivers 3 Baths lorry drivers.
VILLE Baths.			Pte. Porter.

Appendix 10.

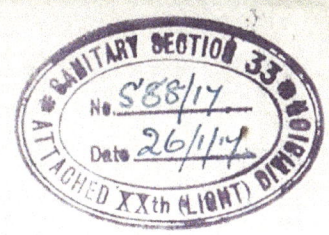
No. 588/17
Date 26/1/17

To.
 A.D.M.S.,
  20th. Division.

The following is submitted in view of the probability of Sanitary Sections becoming Army Troops in the near future.

The work of the Sanitary Section falls mostly under one of the following headings:-

1. Inspection of and advice to units as regards sanitary matters.
2. Inspection of and advice to units as regards water duties & chlorination of all water used by them.
3. Inspection of water points in Divn. area and arranging for chlorination there.
4. Training of water-cart and regimental sanitary men in their duties.
5. Disinfection of blankets.
6. Disinfection of billets from vermin or after infect-ious disease.
7. Spraying of billets and messes with fly-killing mixture.
8. Manufacture of Anti Trench Foot Soap and other mixtures as required from time to time.
9. Construction work on a small scale e.g. latrines incinerators, notice boards, purification plants for ablution sheds, baths etc.
10. Construction work on a large scale e.g. Baths, Laundries, ablution sheds etc, or advice thereto.
11. Running of established baths.
12. Running of established laundries.
13. Establishing of clothing exchanges in new area and keeping them a going concern when established.
14. Supplying all disinfectants, whale oil, latrine paper etc. to the Division.
15. Cleaning petrol cans for holding drinking water. This has not been done by the Sanitary Section but I am of the opinion that it should be.

The work under headings 1,2,3,6,7,8 and perhaps 15 should be capable of being carried out by each sanitary section for the Division in its area. 11,12 will probably in most cases be carried on by a Divisional or Corps Baths Officer.

No.1 will certainly require supplementing by some Divisional Staff, otherwise the different ideas of successive O.C. Sanitary Sections will tend to confuse those responsible for the sanitary efficiency of units.

The attaching of one R.A.M.C. man to each Battalion providing him with a S.M.P. armlet and working him under the D.A.D.M.S. would seem to be the method likely to combine greatest efficiency and minimum of trouble for the D.A.D.M.S.

It will obviously be necessary to select such men with the greatest care to train them in their new duties, seeing that the men they are to replace were in most cases chosen for their qualifications and then had special training at the H.Q. of a Sanitary Coy. in England.

This particularly applies to their water duties, as the men in charge of water carts will probably be more experienced than the inspectors and will probably be likely to resent the inspections of the newcomers.

No.4 will presumably fall to the lot of the D.A.D.M.S.

No.2 do   do   do   do do do do do do do

No.13 will probably require a Divn. Officer or an N.C.O. acting under orders from Q.

No.14 will have to be undertaken by the S.S.O.

The Foden Disinfector belongs to the Div. Supply Col. and moves with the Division when the Supply Column moves. At present it is attached to the Sanitary Section, presumably some other arrangement will be made under the new scheme.

Capt. R.A.M.C.(T.F.)
O.C.33rd Sanitary Section.

CONFIDENTIAL

WAR DIARY

– of –

Captain A. F. GIRVAN,

R.A.M.C.(T.F.).

Commanding,

33rd. SANITARY SECTION,

1st. London (City of London) Sanitary Company,

R.A.M.C.(T.F.).

attached

20th. (LIGHT) DIVISION.

B. E. F.

FRANCE.

February – 1917.

Volume 9.

Army Form C. 2118.

WAR DIARY
or
INTELLIGENCE SUMMARY.
(Erase heading not required.)

War Diary of
Captain R.F. STEVAN D...... S.(T.F.)
O.C. SANITARY SECTION 38,
ATTACHED XXth (LIGHT) DIVISION
Vol. 9.
Page 1.

Place	Date Feb 1919	Hour	Summary of Events and Information	Remarks and references to Appendices
HEILLY	1		Reorganize tofey together 2Off. Inspected billets & latrines etc in HEILLY. Aff.	J.I.d. ALBERT Combriship 1:40000.
"	2		Visited DDMS XIV Corps HQ MEAULTE with regard to the scheme of making Sanitary Sections into Army Troops. He had no more information on the subject than I knew except that the scheme had not actually come into operation. Visited baths MEAULTE also HRBs at BONNAY the other side of HEILLY. Aff.	Appendix A.
"	3		Visited Laundry Amiens to arrange about higher prices for washing and also to try and get more washing done there. Also visited Schools Instruction DAOURS to inspect it + arrange for instruction there by our guy Sgts Off	
"	4		Went to forward area to see O.C. San Sec 24th Div (Capt CRAWFORD). He was on leave but DADMS was active. Arranged plans for taking over from him. Off.	
"	5		Various inspections + office work. No more Off.	Appendix B.
"	6		Inspected billets of 11th RB at BONNAY after vacation. Left clean. Off.	
"	7		Staff of men to forward area according to Appendix B.. Off.	
"	8		All Section except office moved to forward area. 4 Off.	
"	9		Moved to A2 A.Q.Y. Rear Div HQ. A tent covered sheet Off.	
ARMY A2 A.Q.Y	10		Visited baths Maricourt. All boilers in burst condition + frozen up. This has forced	

Army Form C. 2118.

WAR DIARY
or
INTELLIGENCE SUMMARY.
(Erase heading not required.)

War Diary of
Captain A.F. SIDNAN Ram:(T.F.)
O.C. SANITARY SECTION 33,
ATTACHED XXth (LIGHT) DIVISION
Vol. 9.
Page 2.

Place	Date 1917	Hour	Summary of Events and Information	Remarks and references to Appendices
CARNOY A.2.d.9.7 after Cordwainer shut	Feb 10		about a fortnight before the 29th. Div vacated area. Apparently no effort had been made to get the drainage put right. I have written to CRE to put right at once so that Cooking may start as soon as main pipe is thawed. Inspected a number of public latrines, they were mostly in foul condition & need immediate attention. Inspected latrines etc in Camps 1, 2, 3, 4, 5, 6 nearly all of them are badly in need of attention. All camps including Adv D.H.Q & near D.H.Q very untidy. All this is interesting in view of remark in report of D.A.D.M.S. 29th Div that "little now remains of an insanitary nature in the Divisional Area". Clothing exchange Camps H and blanket disinfecting hut Camp 4 in full working order today. A.f.	
"	11		Went BRAYTOWN to see if future can cleaning was being properly carried out there. It was not, so gave instructions as to future treatment. Went LOOP SIDING & tackle Valley to arrange for steam from a steam roller to be available for cleansing extra Camp. A.f.	
"	12		Went GUILLEMONT CAMPS. Met Major B. Hamilton D.A.D.M.S on way round with him. These camps need a lot of attention. Also inspected more public Latrines also in need of renewal. A.f.	
"	13		Went to Advanced H.Q. re various Sanitary matters. Afternoon to AMIENS to pay Laundry. A.f.	

WAR DIARY or INTELLIGENCE SUMMARY.

Army Form C. 2118.

War Diary of Captain A.F. SIRAN, R.A.M.C.(T.F.)
O.C. SANITARY SECTION 33,
ATTACHED XXth (LIGHT) DIVISION.

Vol. 9.
Page 20

Place	Date Feb 1917	Hour	Summary of Events and Information	Remarks and references to Appendices
CARNOY Az dQ.	14		Various inspections. Lt Ottaway complained of Sgt Botanjuk for using insulting language to him. This necessitated an enquiry in which the language was admitted but statings said to be of a character usually employed in the section & army generally. A.Y.	
"	15		Went around HQ to see if any action was being taken with regard to a shortage of socks which was pointed out to AA+QMG yesterday which was urgent. AA+QMG was out. Went round Camps 1 & 2 and visited Corps Main Dressing Station re footwashing soap. A.Y.	
"	16		Went to GINCHY to examine all public latrines from there (where duckboards to front line begin) back to CARNOY. Large ammunition dumps at MARICOURT bombed by the enemy, with result that a series of terrific explosions has been proceeding all day. So far no projectiles have reached as far as this camp, though several men were have been knocked over in their huts by the most violent explosion. A.Y.	
"	17		Examined incinerators in camps 2,3,4,5 & generally inspected articles of camps Offr	Appendix C.
"	18		Inspected camps 1 & 2. Also went BRIQUETERIE. A.Y.	
"	19		Had interview with Divisional Commander on A. incinerators B. Formation of Sanitary Section Workshp (C) General matters. Inspector large number of latrines in camps. Went Guillemont to water dump there. A.Y.	

Army Form C. 2118.

War Diary of Captain A.F. STEWART Ra--C.(T.F.)
vol. 2 O.C. SANITARY SECTION 33,
Page 4. ATTACHED 22th (LIGHT) DIVISION.

WAR DIARY
or
INTELLIGENCE SUMMARY.
(Erase heading not required.)

Instructions regarding War Diaries and Intelligence Summaries are contained in F. S. Regs., Part II. and the Staff Manual respectively. Title pages will be prepared in manuscript.

Place	Date	Hour	Summary of Events and Information	Remarks and references to Appendices
CARNOY A2day Albert Combined St. et	1917 Feb 20.		Paid Laundry at AMIENS and settled as to reason why some 11,000 socks were being held up there. 5 punctures and a broken spring hence 15 hours occupied on journey. A.Y.	
	21		Arranged with Col DUNDAS (AAQMG 20th Div) for baths to be erected at GUILLEMONT. Trissen huts to be used if possible thus :— [sketch: Bath House, Dressing Room, Exit, Undressing Room, Entrance, Clean Clothes Store] XIV Corps however refused permission for these to be put up as being too visible to the enemy. A.Y.	

Army Form C. 2118.

War Diary of
Captain AF STEVEN R.A.M.C.(T.F.)
O.C. SANITARY SECTION 33.
ATTACHED XXth (LIGHT) DIVISION

Vol. 9.
Page 5.

WAR DIARY
or
INTELLIGENCE SUMMARY.
(Erase heading not required.)

Instructions regarding War Diaries and Intelligence Summaries are contained in F. S. Regs., Part II. and the Staff Manual respectively. Title pages will be prepared in manuscript.

Place	Date 1917	Hour	Summary of Events and Information	Remarks and references to Appendices
CARNOY A2d9	Feb 22		Owing to suspension of traffic for the Thaw that set in some days ago, there is a vast accumulation of dirty clothes at my clothes exchange. This means overflowing into the next hut (which is used as Blanket disinfecting Stean) and temporary shifting of the latter to smaller camps.	
"	23		Arranged with AAPQMG & CRE for construction of baths at GUILLEMONT from an existing wood and peat structure and "elephant" huts. It will be a makeshift arrangement but is all that can be done under the circumstances. Work is handicapped by fact that neither the Division nor Corps has any timber, corrugated iron, canvas or felt. Water will be conveyed by pipe from the GUILLEMONT water point which is only a few hundred feet away. This site is as near to the round (two way) as can be managed, an important point frequently overlooked.	
"	24		Arranged with CRE to take on the job of finishing Laundry at CORBIE. AJF. Inspected camps 6, 5 and 2. AJF.	
"	25		Paid Section. Various inspections AJF.	
"	26		Socks coming up very insufficiently. Wrote Mons BACAUT AMIENS to expedite same. AJF.	
"	27		Thaw precautions now over for GS wagons. Clothing therefore can be delivered to	

Army Form C. 2118.

War Diary 26
Capln A/ SURGN Rawes
Capln " O.C. SANITARY SECTION 33,
Vol. 7. O.C. SANITARY SECTION 33,
Page 6. ATTACHED XXth (LIGHT) DIVISION

WAR DIARY
or
INTELLIGENCE SUMMARY.
(Erase heading not required.)

Instructions regarding War Diaries and Intelligence Summaries are contained in F. S. Regs., Part II. and the Staff Manual respectively. Title pages will be prepared in manuscript.

Place	Date 1917	Hour	Summary of Events and Information	Remarks and references to Appendices
CARNOY And At (ALBERT combined sheet)	Feb. 27		MONTAUBAN BATHS. Visited CORBIE LAUNDRY which is now almost ready to start work, though not at quite full pressure, the necessary men have been demanded, and as soon as full corps save 30 nuns will be secured to do the mending ironing of garments. A full description of laundry will be given in next volume of war diary. A.G.	
"	Feb 28		Visited DAOURS MARICOURT sanitary clothing and materials for laundry. Many days are frequently wasted owing to the lack of a cur a yet but could be put in hand with a delay of only one day if a car were always available nor will there be risks days to get started while violets etc are going slowly through "the usual channels". A.G.	

A.G. Gunton
Capt. RAMC. T.F.
O.C. SANITARY SECTION 33,
ATTACHED XXth (LIGHT) DIVISION

End of Volume 9.

No. 33
SANITARY
SECTION.
No. 28/2/17
Date

War Diary of Captain A.F. SIRVAN. R.A.M.C.(T.F.)
O.C. SANITARY SECTION 33,
ATTACHED XXth (LIGHT) DIVISION
Vol.9. Appendix A.

No. 33
SANITARY
SECTION.
No. S119/14
Date 6/2/17

SANITARY AND WATER REPORT
FOR FORTNIGHT ENDING 3rd. FEB. 1917.

FORWARD AREA.

(a) Sanitation

Conditions at Divn. Hd. Qrs. Advanced and Rear and at all the Camps were satisfactory.

The following new work has been carried out:-

Construction of Incinerator and digging of excreta pit at Camp 15 DAOURAY.
Large additional incinerator built in MALTPORT Camp.
Ablution shed and bench, new latrines with 14 seats, water tanks fitted with taps and into stands and cookhouses repaired at MANSELL Camp. 1000 blankets sprayed at this camp.
Public latrine erected at COMBLES.

(b) Water

The usual chlorination of water tanks and surprise tests of water carts were carried out. Insufficient chlorination was found in the following instances:

C/122nd.R.F.A. No. number to cart.
Filled at ____ on 2/21/17 and tested 11a.m. on same day.
No coloration resulting from tests — thus showing inefficient chlorination.
The stock solution for use when chlorinating petrol cans at COMBLES was made up by the Sanitary Section.

RESERVE AREA.

(a) Sanitation.

Sanitary conditions in the area are on the whole satisfactory. In many cases the billets and lines were left in a bad state by the previous occupants and a lot of cleaning up has been done.

The Hd. Qrs. Divn. Train.

This billet No.55 occupied by 21 and was found to be insanitary owing to proximity of the urinal of an Estaminet and civilian manure heap. This was reported to the Sanitary Specialist Officer of the Division, (who was notified of same).

Attention is being paid to the Divn. School of Instruction and I have detailed one of my Sgndet. N.C.O's to visit it daily and give the necessary advice and if possible construct some simple cheap sanitary appliances.

(b) Water.

Owing to the freezing of supplies, in some case river water was used.

Particular attention is drawn to the inconvenience & possible danger which arises when water carts have to be sent for repair. The unit is left with no cart or with only one. It is highly desirable that a reserve of carts should be held to replace those temporarily out of action for any reason.

The usual surprise tests of water carts to discover efficient chlorination were carried out.

My Water N.C.O's have inspected and tested many pumps and supplies in the Reserve Area.

(c) General

Disinfection of Blankets has been carried out at [?].

Water Cans:- Arrangements have been made for securing better cleaning of petrol cans for holding drinking water. This will be supervised by Sanitary Section personnel.

Capt. [signature]
O.C. XIIth Sanitary Section.

Vol. 9. War Diary of Capt. A.F. GIRVAN. R.am.c(T.F)
O.C. SANITARY SECTION 33,
ATTACHED XXth (LIGHT) DIVISION.
Copy No. 11.

Appendix B.

DAILY ORDERS No. 59
by
Captain A.F. GIRVAN. R.a.m.c. (T.F.)
Officer Commanding
33rd Sanitary Section.

Monday 5th February.

Reference maps FRANCE 62D and ALBERT Combined Sheet.

1 Disposition

(a) The Headquarters of the Sanitary Section will be at Divisional Headquarters (Rear) A.2.d.9.7. The disposition of the personnel is tabulated on the annexed Disposition List. The THRESH Disinfector Sanitary Section and "Baths" lorries will remain at CORBIE. The personnel and lorries remaining at CORBIE will be rationed by S.O. 91st Brigade R.F.A. as before.

(b) The following N.C.O's attached to Brigades will rejoin the Sanitary Section at HEILLY under the arrangements tabulated below:
  Sergt. BALMFORTH.
  Sergt. HARDCASTLE.
  Corpl. GAUNT.
  Lce.Corpl. OTTERWAY.
  Lce.Corpl. BARENTS.
Lce. Corporals GRAY, WILSON, CLOAKE and JOHNS will remain attached to their respective Ambulance.

(c) The various Battalions in the Division will, when in rest, occupy the following Camps:
  Camps 1, 2, 3, 4 and 26 on CARNOY-MONTAUBAN Road.
  GUILLEMONT Camp.
A working party of 8 men per Camp for Camps 1, 2, 3, 4 and 26 have been arranged for.

2. MOVE.

(1) 7th February. (a) The N.C.O's returning from Brigades will rejoin the Section on the morning of the 7th February after making any necessary vacation inspections of their Brigades.

(b) Lce.Corporal MATHER. T.J. will report at General Staff 20th Division with full kit and come under the orders of Divisional Headquarters

(c) An advance party consisting of Sergt. BALMFORTH, Lce.Corporals HAMPSON, McHUGH & SPURSETT and Pte's. HARRISON & CRISFORD, together with some stores, will proceed to Divisional Headquarters (Rear) on the Sanitary Section lorry leaving HEILLY at 8.30 a.m.
Sergt. BALMFORTH will take over the Sanitary Section Camp at A.2.d.9.7. Lce.Corporal HAMPSON the Clothing Exchange and Pte. CRISFORD will proceed to the Baths and take over the Baths. They will be careful to take copies of all receipts for stores handed over to them.

The Sanitary Section lorry will, on its return journey, bring back a load of men and stores of the 29th Divisional Sanitary Section.

(d) Sergt. HARDCASTLE and Lce.Corporals OTTERWAY and BARENTS and some stores will proceed to the Forward area on the 29th Divisional Sanitary Section lorry on its return journey there in the afternoon. Lce.Corpl. OTTERWAY will take over the Blanket Disinfecting Shed (in NISSEN hut close to Clothing Exchange now in use by 29th Division as a dirty clothes store) carefully taking copies of all receipts given for stores taken over.

(c) Ptes. HARRINSTON and RUSH will proceed to Baths CORBIE for duty and Ptes. ROGERS, STOREY, ROBINSON, WALTERS and WILLIAMS will report at Baths HEILLY. They will make their own way to these places arriving there at 9am. Rfn. ALLCOCK will return to Baths CORBIE from Baths MEAULTE.

8th February S/Sergt. BEAUMONT and all the remaining NCO's and men of the Sanitary Section and attached and Baths personnel and remaining stores (with the exception of the Office staff and personnel and Officer's Kit and Batman) will proceed to the Forward area on the Sanitary Section and "Baths" lorries leaving HEILLY at 10am. On their return journey these lorries will bring back loads of men and stores of 29th Divisional Sanitary Section.

9th February (a) Corporal WHITLOCK and Office staff and personnel and Officers Kit will proceed to the Forward area in the Sanitary Section lorry leaving HEILLY at 10am. The Sanitary Section lorry will afterwards return and park at the Baths CORBIE.
(b) Pte. BEASLES will proceed mounted to the Forward Area.

(2) S/Sergt BEAUMONT will arrange the carriage of all stores to the Forward area.

3. Baths.

The Baths CORBIE will remain working according to the allotment given by the Town Major CORBIE but no clothing will be issued by the Baths Staff except to 20th Division units and to the parties of Artillery bathing for one hour on every other day.

4. Clean and dirty Clothing

(a) Clean and dirty clothing will be conveyed daily between the Forward area and the Baths CORBIE by the Sanitary Section lorry. The driver of this lorry is always to carry with him the special pass of the Fourth Army.
(b) The Baths lorry will carry clean and disinfected dirty clothing between Baths CORBIE and AMIENS daily.
(c) Daily States of clothing will be rendered as heretofore by the QM.S. i/c Baths CORBIE to Sanitary Section Hd.Qrs. by D.R.L.S.

5. Reinforcement

The following man reported his arrival for duty with the Section this day:
No 1270. Pte. DEWHURST. J.T.

Captain Rannie (T.F.)
O.C. 33rd Sanitary Section.

Copies to:
1. O.C. San.Sect. 29th Divn.
2. S/Sergt. BEAUMONT.
3. QM.S. HOARE.
4. Sergt. CAESAR.
5. Sergt. BALMFORTH.
6. Sergt. HARDCASTLE.
7. Corpl. GAUNT.
8. L/Corpl. BEARDSWORTH.
9/10. Retained
11/12. War Diaries ✓

Disposition List of Sanitary Section and attached personnel in Forward Area.

Place.	Sanitary Section	Permanently Attached Personnel	Baths Staff.	Temporarily Attached Personnel	Duties
Hd. Qrs. (Rear) R.2.d.9.7.	S/Sergt. Beaumont	—	—	—	Supervision.
	Sergt. Balmforth	—	—	—	I/c Sanitation Camp 1.
	Sergt. Hardcastle	—	—	—	I/c Sanitation Camp 2.
	Corpl. Whitlock }	—	—	—	Office.
	L/Corpl. Horsley }				
	L/Corpl. McHugh	—	—	—	I/c Sanitation Camp 3
	L/Corpl. Hunting	—	—	—	I/c Sanitation Camp 4
	L/Corpl. Spurgeon	—	—	—	Inspection of rear D.H.Q. Water duties to Own Troops. Daily chlorination of water tanks at CARNOY & CARNOY EAST.
	L/Corpl. Barents	—	—	—	
	L/Corpl. Hale	—	—	—	I/c Sanitation Camp 2E
	L/Corpl. Ottoway	—	—	—	I/c Blanket disinfector
	Pte. Harrison	—	—	—	Stores & rations.
	Pte. Judd	—	—	—	Cook.
	Pte. Beagles	—	—	—	Ratman.
	Pte. Finch	—	—	—	Construction work.
		Rfn. Scholey	—	—	Messenger
		Rfn. Crocker } Pte. Nuttall } Pte. Price } Rfn. Player }	—	—	Blanket disinfector
		Rfn. Pickwell	—	—	leave.
		Rfn. Taylor	—	—	Cook's Assistant
		Pte. Cox (DCLI)	—	—	Pioneer
		Pte. Cox (Somerset)	—	—	Rations
Divn. H.Q. Adv. BRIQUETERIE.	Corpl. Garnet	—	—	—	I/c Sanitation Corpl. SAUNT le Eve at Rear. H.Q. (A.2.d.9.7.) with Section
TRONES WOOD Dressing Station. 60th F.A.	L/Corpl. Cloake	—	—	—	I/c Sanitation GUILLEMONT Camp
	L/Corpl. Gray	—	—	—	Water duties to 59th Brigade. Daily Chlorination of tanks at BRIQUETERIE
H.Q. Collecting F.H. (A.2.0.S.S) 61st F.H.	L/Corpl. Wilson	—	—	—	Water duties to 60th Brigade. Daily Chlorination of tank at COSY CORNER.

Place	Sanitary Section	Permanently attached personnel	Baths Staff	Temporarily attached personnel	Duties
Corps Main Dressing Station. 62nd F.A.	L/Corpl. Gohns	— — — — — —	— — — — — —	— — — — — —	Water duties to 61st Brigade. Daily Chlorination of Tanks at TALUS BOISE
SUILLEMONT Petrol can Water Dump.	L/Corpl. Harris	— — — — — —		— — — — — —	Chlorination of tanks at SUILLEMONT. Daily. Supervision of clean of petrol cans.
		Rfn. Dunn. Pte. Hardy. Rfn. Soebominco. Rfn. Ayers. Rfn. Blenkisop. Pte. Slate.			Cleaning of petrol cans for water
Clothing Exchange Camp ( ) (formerly Camp 21.)	L/Corpl. Hampson	— — — — — —		— — — — — —	i/c
			Rfn. Fishwick Pte. Rogers.	— — — — — —	to work Clothing Exchange
Baths MONTAUBAN.			L/Corpl. Bandsworth Pte. Storey Pte. Wrightson Rfn. Hillier Pte. Denny Pte. Ensford Pte. Robinson Rfn. Walters Rfn. Thompson Pte. Williams	— — — — — — — — — — — —	i/c to work Baths
CORBIE Baths.	Sergt. Caesar	— — — — — —		— — — — — —	i/c Divn. Laundry & Sanitation & School of Instruction DAOURS
	Pte. Stevens. Pte. Powell	— — — — — —		— — — — — —	Sanitary Section Lorry Drivers.
	Pte. Clayton. Pte. Foster.	— — — — — —		— — — — — —	Tender lorry, driver
			Q.M.S. Hoare Pte. Whitehead Pte. Harrington Pte. Arenk Pte. Mansell Rfn. Simpson Pte. Porter. Pte. Rush. Pte. Lovell. Pte. Boulter. Pte. Shail Rfn. Allcock. 3 lorry drivers	— — — — — — — — — — — — — — — — — —	i/c Baths to work Baths & disinfection of underclothing. Baths lorry

Vol. 9.
Appendix C

War Diary of Captain H.F. SIRVAN. R.A.M.C. (T.F.)
O.C. SANITARY SECTION 33,
ATTACHED XXth (LIGHT) DIVISION.

SANITARY SECTION REPORT

for period of ten days ending
17/2/17.

No. 33
SANITARY
SECTION.
No. S154/17
Date 22/2/17

1. **SANITATION.**

Progress is being made in regard to sanitary measures in the Camps on the CARNOY-MONTAUBAN Road and at CUILLEMONT, for, despite the vacation Report of the outgoing Sanitary Section which stated that little that was insanitary remained in the Area, it was found on investigation that a vast amount of work was required to render this statement correct. Practically every latrine in the Area requires attention, some of them being in a very bad state and a thorough investigation has been carried out by me assisted by my N.C.O's. The result is the annexed statement marked "A" showing the condition of each latrine and the amount of work necessary to render it sanitary.

I have detailed one of my N.C.O's to supervise the work of each Camp thus ensuring continuity of supervision and work. The difficulty has been that the permanent fatigue parties supplied by the Town Major CARNOY have not been "permanent", there being different men each day and on some days no men at all, and urgent work has had to be neglected owing to the absence of a working party. I have written to the various Adjutants concerned and expect greater regularity in the future.

A statement is annexed showing approximately the amount of work (apart from latrines) required in each Camp.

A detailed statement of sanitary conditions is as follows:

Divisional Headquarters, Advanced.	Conditions satisfactory with the exception of ablution arrangements, of which there is an entire absence. A new grease trap and pit have been made and new latrines are in course of construction.
Divisional Headquarters, Rear.	In fair condition with the exception of a large accumulation of manure outside the stables. Apart from this accumulation, manure is now being daily dumped in shell holes.
Divisional Signal Coy. (D.H.Q. Adv.).	Conditions satisfactory with the exception of ablution arrangements, of which there is an entire absence. A new grease pit has been made and new latrines constructed.
C.R.A.	Satisfactory.
11th. Durham L.I. Hd.Qrs. and Transport.	Satisfactory.
60th. Machine Gun Coy. No. 2 Camp BERNAFAY.	Satisfactory. A fatigue party of 20 men has filled in old latrines, made new ones and has cleaned up the Camp.
D.A.D.O.S. MARIC URT BOIS.	Satisfactory.
Camp adjoining D.H.Q. Rear, CARNOY, occupied by	
(a) 60th. Bde. Hd.Qrs.	There was no sanitary orderly with the unit and the camp site is in a dirty state, there being no grease trap to cook-house, etc. The Staff Captain has been asked to detail a "Pioneer", which he has done.
(b) 14th. Corps Heavy Artillery H.Q.	This area is in a very dirty state. The ground behind the Counter Battery Officers' Mess Cook-house is in a filthy state. Several shell holes behind the latrines contain a large amount of excreta and foul rubbish. Men are urinating behind the latrines and there is no urine pit. A complaint was made to the Sergt. Major by my N.C.O. who promised to have the defects remedied at once.
CARNOY Camp 1.	The amount of work done in this Camp has been fairly satisfactory, but the frost and the lack of permanent working parties has caused necessary work to be held up - such as the waste water pits near the ablution bench. The following work has been done: New Grease traps made. Incinerator repaired. A new urine pits dug. A new incinerator built. Rubbish removed from space underneath huts and floors of several huts repaired to prevent men sweeping the rubbish underneath the floors.

CARNOY Camp 2.   Camp is in a fair condition, but the
                        remarks made reference to permanent
                        working parties at Camp 1 and the result-
                        -ing delay of work equally applies here.
                        The following work has been carried out:-
                            Latrines removed and re-erected.
                            1 incinerator removed and refuse
                              around and in Trench adjoining
                              dealt with.
                            2 Grease pits made for Cook-houses.
                            New incinerator constructed at S.E.
                              of Camp.
                            Soakage pits constructed for ablution
                              shed.
                            Old incinerator cleaned out.
                            Urine pit dug.

CARNOY Camp 3.   Satisfactory. The following work has been
                        done:-
                            Accumulation of rubbish around the
                              incinerator burnt.
                            2 new grease pits constructed.
                            One horse buried.

CARNOY Camp 4.   Satisfactory. On vacation on the 14th.
                        instant the 12th. Rifle Brigade left the
                        Camp in a very dirty condition. The
                        attention of the Commanding Officer was
                        called to this and he was requested to
                        take steps to prevent a reoccurrence.
                        The following work has been carried out:
                            2 incinerators constructed.
                            1 Grease pit made.

CARNOY Camps 5 and 6.   Conditions in these Camps on entry were
                        unsatisfactory and work was held up owing
                        to the absence of a working party.
                        Improvements have now been carried out
                        and the following work has been done:-
                            Rubbish cleared from Camp site
                              and excreta lying in trenches covered.
                            Incinerators cleared of rubbish
                              left by previous occupants.
                            Old latrine filled in.
                        Scarlet fever contacts are now being
                        employed as a working party

MONTAUBAN Camp 20.   This is a one Battalion Camp occupied only
                        at present by the Salvage Company. On
                        entry this Camp was found to be in a
                        most unsatisfactory condition. A working
                        party was obtained and several improve-
                        -ments have been carried out. It was
                        reported that my work here was rendered
                        more or less useless by reason of the
                        fact that after my men have left troops
                        come and knock down wooden structures and
                        cart them away - presumably for firewood.
                        This was attributed to the Anzacs and a
                        report of this was sent to the Town Major
                        of MONTAUBAN for his information and
                        necessary action. The following work

has been carried out:
- Old incinerator pulled down.
- Accumulations of burnt refuse buried in shell holes.
- 2 old latrines filled in.
- New latrine (5 seats) erected.
- Urine pit dug.

GUILLEMONT.   On entry these Camps presented a difficulty as Battalions only occupy the Camps for 24 hours before moving into the line and there were no permanent staffs. The work of sanitation was therefore performed more or less feebly by the various Battalion "pioneers", who frequently were not up to full strength as some were left at Camps lower down. The Camps were in urgent need of a thorough clean up and after some trouble a permanent working party was obtained to work under my N.C.O's. The following work has been done:

Camps 1 and 2.
- The four incinerators have daily been dealing with the large accumulations of tins left by the previous occupants.
- Ground around cookers, which was littered with cook-house debris, has been cleared.
- 3 urine pits and 2 latrine pits dug.
- Latrine pails and tins emptied twice daily.
- Tins for refuse placed outside huts

Camp 3.
- Old latrine filled in and new pit dug.

Mobile Veterinary Section) The sanitary arrangements of these
Hd.Qrs. D.A.C.   ) Camps are satisfactory. In the case
No. 2 Section, D.A.C.   ) of the Mobile Veterinary Section and
No. 4 Section, D.A.C.   ) the No. 2 Section D.A.C. there are
A/82nd. R.F.A.   ) accumulations of old manure near the
C/82nd. R.F.A.   ) stables.

B/82nd. R.F.A.   ) The condition of these Camps were bad,
D/82nd. R.F.A.   ) excreta being in the trenches unburnt
                              for some time past and also much
                              rubbish of all kinds. My N.C.O.
                              complained to the senior N.C.O's at the
                              Camps and immediate steps were taken
                              to improve matters.

Divisional Train:) Conditions here are satisfactory with
  No. 159 Company.   ) the exception of the latrine
  No. 160 Company.   ) arrangements near the stables and the
  No. 161 Company.   ) necessary changes are promised in
                              respect of this. There are
                              accumulations of old manure near the
                              stables also.

20th. Divisional School   ) Sanitary conditions here are good and my
  of Instruction.   ) supervising N.C.O. has given sanitary
                              instruction to the "pioneer" N.C.O.
                              Two model incinerators have been
                              erected and a scheme of work has been
                              mapped out so as to provide model
                              Camp sanitary appliances. This work
                              will be carried on as material for it
                              arrives

4

Other sanitary work.   A new public latrine has been
                                        erected at [illegible] near the
                                        Town Majors office.

Camps generally.   More labour is needed for drain
                                        -age work and for clearing away
                                        carts of accumulations of mud.
                                        Many latrine buckets are needed
                                        for use at night arrivals in some
                                        of the Camps.They should be
                                        obtained from the Town Major.
                                        Biscuit tins are a bad substitute.

2. WATER.

    (a). The ordinary surprise tests of water from water
          carts have been carried out and all found
          efficiently chlorinated with the following
          exceptions:-
          60th. Machine Gun Company.
                        Water obtained from [illegible].
                        Cart filled [illegible] a.m. on 10/3/17
                        and tested at [illegible] a.m. on the
                        same day. No reaction resulted.

          Hd.Qrs. [illegible].
                        Cart No. [illegible]. Filled 8.45 a.m.
                        on [illegible] and tested at 3 p.m. on
                        the same day. No blue coloration.
                        This cart was reported for a
                        similar occurrence on the 14/2/17,
                        vide my S22/17 of 14/2/17 and 2 th.
                        Division No. [illegible].

    (b). The water tanks at GUILLEMONT, [illegible]
          [illegible] [illegible] Road , CROIX [illegible] and
          CARNOY CAMP have been chlorinated as required.
          At the first three mentioned places it has been
          arranged for T.M.B.C. personnel to be on duty
          continuously to ensure efficient chlorination.

    (c). PETROL CANS FOR WATER FOR FRONT LINE.-
          Two men from Salvage Company are from Sanitary
          Section are still and at GUILLEMONT Dump and very
          entirely at cleaning out the cans by boiling water
          in them until they are free from smell.
          Four men from Salvage Company are and one C.E.O. from
          Sanitary Section are stationed at the water Dump
          at GUILLEMONT and re-examine all the cans from
          GREYSTONE and if necessary, boil them out again.
          The clean cans are stencilled "Drinking Water"
          and are filled with chlorinated water from water
          carts at the Dump.
          Many more cans are issued than are returned.
          Many cans previously cleaned are returned in a dirty
          state (inside), being fouled with tea leaves or
          paraffin. Other cans are badly damaged, holes
          being made in the side, presumably to allow the
          water to be poured out more rapidly. Some are,
          of course, are damaged by shell fire. The screw
          caps are scarcely ever returned even if wired.
          The same applies to wooden plugs, which presumably
          are used for firewood.

3. **Disinfections.**

    CARNOY Camp 6.   15/2/17.   Disinfection following case of Scarlet fever from 7th. Somerset L.I.

    CARNOY Camp 6.   16/2/17.   Disinfection following cases of Scarlet fever from 7th. K.O.Y.L.I.

    CARNOY Camp 5.   17/2/17.   Disinfection following case of German Measles from 6th. Oxon and Buck. L.I.

    CARNOY Camp 5.   18/2/17.   Disinfection following case of Scarlet fever from 6th. Oxon and Bucks. L.I.

    Trenches.   17/2/17.   Disinfection carried out at Headquarters of Left Battalion when Officers', mens' and Signallers' quarters were sprayed.

4. **General Work.**

The usual general work, such as the supply of Disinfectants and anti-trench foot soap and ointment, constructional work and disinfection of underclothing, has been carried on.
No Baths are yet available, the R.E's not having finished the necessary repairs.

CLOTHING EXCHANGE - This has been carried on and Battalions supplied with clean clothing as stocks have permitted.

BLANKET DISINFECTION - 4044 blankets have been disinfected.

DRYING ROOMS - 350 pairs of S.D. Trousers have been brushed.

                              Captain R.A.M.C.(T.F.).
                      O.C. SANITARY SECTION 33,
                        ATTACHED XXth (LIGHT) DIVISION.

Report on Latrines "A"

Position	Used by	Type	Defects. Remarks.	Labour required
CARNOY Camp 1.				
N.E. Side.	Men.	Deep trench. 24 seats.	No lids to seats; otherwise good.	2 men days.
do.	do.	Deep trench. 14 seats.	No lids to seats; screened but without roof. Will require new trench in very few days.	20 men days.
do.	Sergts.	Deep trench. 6 seats.	Will require new trench very shortly; otherwise good.	10 men days.
West side.	Men.	2 latrines. Deep trench.	Require new pits and roofs to structures.	20 men days
Divn. H.Q. (Rear)				
N.E. side.	NCO's & men.	Deep trench. 4 seats.	Will require new trench very shortly; one of latrines requires attention; structure in good condition. A separate latrine for Sergts. is suggested.	8 men da.
Corps Hy. Arty H.Q. (adj. D.H.Q. Rear)				
N.E. side.	Men.	Bucket. 2 seats.	Front of seat structure is of canvas; without lids.	2 men days.
do.	N.C.O's.	Bucket. 1 seat.	do.	1 man days.
CARNOY Camp 2				
N.E. side.	Sergts	Deep trench. 6 seats.	In good condition	—
do.	Mens.	Deep Trench. 14 seats	No lids to seats; otherwise good. The provision of a few trench boards leading to and inside latrine would be an improvement.	2 men days.
S.E. sides.	Men.	Buckets. 25 seats.	No back, front or lids to seats; otherwise good.	30 men days.
do.	do.	Deep trench. 7 seats.	No back or lids to seats; otherwise good.	1 man day.
CARNOY Camp 3				
S.W. Side.	Sergts	Buckets. 4 seats	No lids or back to seats; otherwise good.	8 men days
do.	Mens.	Bucket. 40 seats.	Not fly-proof; otherwise good.	40 men days.
CARNOY Camp 4.				
E. side.	Officers.	—	Very good.	—
W. side.	Officers.	—	Structure good but trench full.	8 men days.
E. side	NCO's & men	4 latrines. 10 seats each.	Congestion now. Trenches full and foul. No urinals. Fly-proof seats.	60 men days.

Position	Used by	Type	Defects. Remarks.	Labour required.
CARNOY Camp 5				
N.W. Side.	Mens.	3 latrines. 10 seats each. Deep Trench.	Wants moving only.	} 50 men days.
	Officers.	Deep Trench 10 Seats.	To be converted to mens' latrine.	
	Officers.		Latrines wanted nearer their Quarters.	20 men days.
CARNOY Camp 6.				
N.E. side.	Men.	4 latrines. 6 seats each. Buckets.	Require converting to trench type. Trench already dug. No urine pits.	40 men days.
MONTAUBAN Camp 26.	Men.	–	Very bad Trench. I have had these removed & reconstructed.	–
GUILLEMONT Camps.	–	–	Very fair.	–
PUBLIC LATRINES				
GINCHY. By A.D.S.	–	–	Good.	
GUILLEMONT. (Junction of GUICHY-LONGUEVAL Roads).	–	–	Bad. Trench full. No seats. Urine pit required.	8 men days.
GUILLEMONT. (Junction of COMBLES-LONGUEVAL Roads)	–	–	Bad. No urine pit	8 men days.
TRONES WOOD.	–	–	Bad. Trench full. Approach a Quagmire	8 men days.
BERNAFAY WOOD (near Town Major)			Very bad. Trench full. (This is now renewed).	–
BERNAFAY - MONTAUBAN Road (nearly opposite Y.M.C.A.)	–	–	Bad. No seats.	8 men days.
MONTAUBAN - CARNOY Road. (in Camp 1.)	1 latrine.	–	Structure requires repairing	} 10 men days.
	1 latrine	–	Bad. Trench full.	
MONTAUBAN - CARNOY Road. (by Rear D.H.Q.)	–	–	New trench required.	6 men days.
MONTAUBAN - CARNOY Road. (opp. No.3. Camp)	–	–	Not fly-proof.	8 men days.

Position	Used by	Type	Defects	Remarks	Labour required
CARNOY - MINDEN POST ROAD (by Railway)	-	-	Very insanitary		8 man days.
CARNOY CORNER	-	1 seat	Very bad. Requires demolishing.		1 man day.
					Total - 391 men days

Note:-

The term "1 man days" signifies 1 man working 1 day.

The term "8 men days" signifies 8 men working 8 days
or 4 men working 2 days.
or 1 man working 8 days

as most convenient.

A.F. Girvan.

Captain R.A.M.C. (T.F)
O.C. 33rd Sanitary Section.

Report on Incinerators.

Place.	Type.	Condition	Surroundings.	
CARNOY Camp 1.	1. Corg⁴ iron. 2. do.	Good.	Very fair.	
do. Camp 2.	Biscuit Tins.	Good.	Very fair.	
do. Camp 3.	Biscuit Tins.	Good	Very fair.	
do. Camp 4.	1. Corg⁴ Iron. Square. 2. Corg⁴ Iron. tubular. 3. Expanded metal.	Very fair. — Poor.	Good. Good. Very fair.	
do. Camp 5.	Corg⁴ Iron.	—	Very fair.	This incinerator is too small and is worn out. A new one of biscuit tins is to be made.
do. Camp 6.	Expanded metal.	Very fair.	Good.	
SUILLEMONT Camps.	Various.	All working vigorously.	Very fair.	
MONTAUBAN Camp 26.	Corg⁴ Iron.	—	—	Just made by Sanitary Section.

Captain R. Auml. (T.F.)
O.C. 33rd Sanitary Section.

WORK REQUIRED TO BE DONE.

CARNOY Camp 1.

Cover over wash bench.
Cover over one of latrines.
New grease pits) In hand.
New Incinerator)
Floors of several huts require repairing to prevent rubbish being swept underneath.

CARNOY Camp 2.

Waste pits to Mens' and Officers' cookhouses.
Urinals - one at bottom of Camp.
Wash-house pit.
Incinerator - one to clean out.
Night urinals - 12 pails required.
Public latrine - 4 seats.

CARNOY Camp 3.

Soakage pit for ablution bench - under construction.
2 grease traps.
1 large manure incinerator.
30 night latrine buckets required.

CARNOY Camp 4.

1 latrine.
2 urinals.
Signs for huts - "Refuse bags" and "Urine tins".
2 signs - "No rubbish to be thrown into shell holes".
2 signs - one for urinal and one for grease trap.
10 night latrine buckets required.

CARNOY Camp 5.

Small heap of manure to be moved to trenches and covered.
1 grease trap.
1 soakage pit.
2 urine pits.
1 latrine to be filled in and new pit dug. — *already included.*
Fixing of ablution benches and making covers.
Filling in shell-holes and trenches.
40 night latrine buckets required.

CARNOY Camp 6.

Moving 5 latrines - new pits already dug. — *already included.*
2 urine pits.
1 soakage pit.
Ablution benches and covers.
Filling in of large trenches.

MONTAUBAN Camp No.

  2 mens' latrines.
  1 Officers' latrines.
  Incinerator.
  Grease pit.
  Repairs to ablution bench.
  Soakage pit to ablution bench.
  1 latrine to be filled in.

CAILLEMONT Camp.

  2 pits for burial of excreta.
  4 grease traps.
  1 latrine structure.
  10 latrine buckets.
  Latrine canvas for repairs.
  Large shelter for Company cookers at corner
   of COBBLED Road.

Rear Divisional Headquarters.

  Accumulation of manure to be dealt with.

Confidential

ORIGINAL

140/2043. 06/17

WAR DIARY

COMMITTEE FOR THE MEDICAL HISTORY OF THE WAR
Date 11 MAY 1917

— of —

Captain A. F. GIRVAN. R.A.M.C.(T.F.)
Commanding

33rd Sanitary Section
(1st London [City of London] Sanitary Company.
R.A.M.C.(T.F.))

attached

20th (Light) Division
B.E.F.
FRANCE.

March 1917.

Volume 10.

Army Form C. 2118.

War Diary of
Captain H.F. GIVEN[?] Sanitary Officer
O.C. Sanitary Section 33.
Attached 18th (LIGHT) DIVISION.
Volume 10 [pages?]

WAR DIARY
or
INTELLIGENCE SUMMARY
(Erase heading not required.)

Instructions regarding War Diaries and Intelligence Summaries are contained in F. S. Regs., Part II. and the Staff Manual respectively. Title pages will be prepared in manuscript.

Place	Date MARCH 1919	Hour	Summary of Events and Information	Remarks and references to Appendices
CARNOY	1		Rode to GUILLEMONT baths to see how their construction was proceeding. Went round Carnoy Camps. A.f.g.	
A2 d 9 4 (ALBERT Combined Sheet)	2		Rode GUILLEMONT baths and water point, also AAHQ and DADOS (MARICOURT BOIS)	
"	3		Went round CARNOY CAMPS. A.f.g. Rode to GROVETOWN to see how petrol can cleaning was proceeding (L7 a 32) Paid the men there. Found them about to move forward to PLATEAU (MARICOURT) Roads near BRAY and at FORKED TREE [cnt?] near GROVETOWN in exceedingly bad condition owing to thaw. A.f.g.	Appendix A.
"	4 5 6		Various office work and inspections [?], including new Baths GUILLEMONT and Dis Dugout [?]. office work all day. A.f.g. Visited CORBIE and spent all day arranging details of completion of Divisional Laundry there	Reconn. A.f.g. Appendix B.
"	7 8		Materials required etc f.t.f. and started washing a few hundred garments - A.f. met M2QMG to arrange for starting CORBIE laundry off. Went to AMIENS to [buy?] laundry and to purchase a number of fittings etc required for CORBIE LAUNDRY. Returned at CORBIE for a few days to start CORBIE Laundry. A.f.g.	
CORBIE	9		Visited Mere Corlande Orphelinage de CORBIE to arrange for girls to work at mending room at CORBIE LAUNDRY. fat Laundry going well. Everything works excellently. A.f.g.	
"	10		16 girls start work at CORBIE Laundry under SOEUR MARIE CLEMENT. 3000 garments washed	

Army Form C. 2118.

War Diary of Captain A.F. SWAN R.amc(T.F.)
O.C. Sanitary Section 38,
ATTACHED 20th (LIGHT) DIVISION.
Vol ..... to Page ....

WAR DIARY
or
INTELLIGENCE SUMMARY.
(Erase heading not required.)

Instructions regarding War Diaries and Intelligence Summaries are contained in F.S. Regs., Part II. and the Staff Manual respectively. Title pages will be prepared in manuscript.

Place	Date	Hour	Summary of Events and Information	Remarks and references to Appendices
CORBIE	1917 MAR. 10 (continued)		Purchased a number of small fittings such as reducing sockets, elbows, nipples (for fitting) clock thermometer. AFS.	
	11		Tried up fine weather, made arrangements for emergency exit for girls etc. French mission came and inspected arrangements made for the girls and expressed themselves as highly pleased with everything. Returned to 20th CARNOY Rear Div. HQ. AFS.	
CARNOY A2dQ7	12		Visited AMIENS to report on laundry, office work. AFS.	
	13		Rode to GUILLEMONT water-point and baths. Tested water sample from R. SOMME as being used at Carnoy in order to calculate amount of soda to add. AM. AFS.	
	14		Horse shed. Taken by Col Dundas (AA+QMG) to CORBIE LAUNDRY. Col Dundas expressed satisfaction	
	15		Visited AMIENS (w DADMS on arm other duty) to arrange w Madame BRGAULT to cease employing for laundry there. AFS. At 6 p.m an old mine exploded in Camp 4 CARNOY (a few hundred yards from this office) and wrecked every hut in the camp + caused about 60 casualties. They blamed disinfection huts were completely flattened + my clothing - exchange hut was half-wrecked being the least damaged hut in the camp. No casualties were suffered by any of my men + useful help was rendered by Cpl Whitworth, Lt McHugh, L/Cpl Ottaway + others. AFS.	

Army Form C. 2118.

War Diary of ?ansm H.F. Sta??
?ann?(?F)
O.C. Sanitary Section 33.
ATTACHED XXth (LIGHT) DIVISION.
Volume ? Page 3

WAR DIARY
or
INTELLIGENCE SUMMARY.
(Erase heading not required.)

Instructions regarding War Diaries and Intelligence Summaries are contained in F. S. Regs., Part II. and the Staff Manual respectively. Title pages will be prepared in manuscript.

Place	Date 1917	Hour	Summary of Events and Information	Remarks and references to Appendices
CARNOY Rear Hdqrs Adqy Adlnt Combined	March 16		Clothing exchange was carried out as usual, though a forgotten lot of the clean clothing had to be rejected as it was coated with dirt. Fresh huts have been secured. Transference to new site will be made tomorrow morning. Off.	Appendix "C"
Sheet	17		Various wishkins clothing are clothing exchange. Off.	Appendix "D"
"	18		Captured German water cattle forwarded to me for examination. It was found to contain coffee free from arsenic or metallic poisons. Off.	
"	19		Route march to BRIQUETERIE but 3 decided to stay at 2 d 97 owing to see the activities near such as blanket disinfecting huts, clothing exchange etc. 3 samples of water from captured villages sent me for Watson for poisons. all free from appreciable contamination. Off.	
"	20		Went to CORBIE in Ambulance Car C, ADMS to buy military & civil staff at Laundry. Found all places in dying room in breaking up condition owing to ordinary bricks having been employed. Off.	
"	21		Wrote GUILLEMONT BATIN which start to day. Analysed 3 samples of water for metallic poisons. Off.	
"	22		Analysed a water for poisons. Visited ADMS. Off.	
"	23		Sent out 6 men of Section, 2 to each Brigade M.M.	

Army Form C. 2118.

War Diary of Captain A.F. SIRIAN
R.A.M.C. (T.F.)
O.C. SANITARY SECTION 33
Vermin STOPPING 20th (LIGHT) DIVISION.

WAR DIARY
or
INTELLIGENCE SUMMARY.
(Erase heading not required.)

Instructions regarding War Diaries and Intelligence Summaries are contained in F.S. Regs., Part II. and the Staff Manual respectively. Title pages will be prepared in manuscript.

Place	Date	Hour	Summary of Events and Information	Remarks and references to Appendices
	1917 MARCH			
CARNOY	24		Made several sani[tary] questionnaire lists with orders and got out a pamphlet on the subject for circulation to all the m.o's of the Division. See "Appendix E." Was organising tests of Appendix E	Appendix E
Billon Carnoy Sk[.]	25		Analysed a water. Road good GUILLEMONT BRISISTAFF. AG	
"	27		Went AMIENS on leave. Road good to settle with Laundry as to amount of clothing they still have there to deliver. Also arranged about testing pulp for arsenic testing, and gauge glasses for some of the CABLE Laundry machines. AG	
BOQUETERIE A.A.D.S.2	28		Road Sailly Aff- and clothing exchange to BRIQUETERIE CARNOY - MARICOURT Road A.A.D.S 2. 1/2 Nissen hut. Clean G glazy for my billet and Lieutenant's. Some huts for offices. Rose Box to 15 to sent came Renee D again was with box M/N ?	
			Tested 6 waters for Jawas. Road burnt in part small. AG	
"	29		Analysed the seven la Lieut from St HUDULY AG	
"	30		Inspection of CARNOY CAMPS AG	
"	31		Rode LE TRANSLOY to see conditions generally its back for a site for D.R. Baths AG. Inspected MARICOURT Bois by order of DDMS XV Corps - Dirty - Guards Refreshed AG	

A.Girvan
Head Quarters
20° Division
31/3/17

A.Girvan
Captain R.A.M.C (T.F)
Commanding 33 Sanitary Section
20 Division

War Diary of Captain A.F. SIRVAN. R.a.m.c.(T.F.)
O.C. SANITARY SECTION 33,
ATTACHED ___ (LIGHT) DIVISION.
Volume 10. Appendix "A"

No. 33
SANITARY
SECTION.
No. S184/14
Date 8/3/17

SANITARY SECTION REPORT
for
period of fourteen days ending 3rd. March 1917.

1. The work of the Sanitary Section and attached men has kept the undermentioned concerns in full working order:

    a. Sanitary and water cart inspections and water point chlorisation.
    b. Supervision of working parties for sanitary duties at all the camps.
    c. Supervision of petrol can cleaning for drinking water for the line.
    d. Baths MONTAUBAN.
    e. Baths CORBIE.
    f. Clothing Exchange CARNOY Camp 4.
    g. Blanket disinfecting room CARNOY.
    h. Drying Rooms, MONTAUBAN.
    i. Disinfection of all underclothing for laundry AMIENS.
    j. Completion of new machine Laundry CORBIE.
    k. Distribution of disinfectants, etc.
    l. Manufacture of all anti-trench foot soap and powder required.
    m. Disinfecting huts, etc. after cases of infectious disease.

2. SANITATION.

Conditions are on the whole satisfactory.

CARNOY Camps - The chief defects in these Camps are:

    a. Lack of water at ablution benches. Even where stand pipes are erected no water is available.
    b. Some of the latrines of the trench type are full up. A number of them have been re-constructed under my supervision and the work is being continued as fast as the available labour and other sanitary duties permit.
    c. Biscuit tins are used to replace latrine buckets as night urine pails in some cases, as buckets are not available at the Camps in sufficient numbers. These tins soon leak.
    d. Trenches and shell-holes on the outskirts of the Camps are often used as latrines by individuals who cannot be traced.
    e. Lack of scrupulous tidiness. Match boxes, pieces of paper, etc. are generally to be found in each Camp near the huts, particularly near any canteen. Although this is unpleasing to the eye it is not a sanitary matter but is purely an affair for regimental discipline.

Very little has been done to any of the latrines mentioned in my Appendix "A" to my Sanitary Report S184/17 of 22/2/17 except such as are mentioned in this Report.

A detailed statement of sanitary conditions is as follows:-

Divisional Headquarters, Advanced.	Satisfactory. The following work has been done: 2 new grease pits constructed 8 latrines (9 seats) made. New urine pit dug. New ablution pits made. Shell holes filled in.
Divisional Headquarters, Rear.	Satisfactory. The latrine pit became flooded and a new pit has been dug. Other work done has been: 4 new grease pits made. Manure being rapidly disposed of by being put into shell-holes and covered with earth.
C.R.A.	Satisfactory. An accumulation of manure arose in the transport lines and the attention of the Staff Captain was drawn to this with the result that manure is now being buried in shell-holes and a great improvement in the lines has been effected.
Divisional Signal Company.	Satisfactory.
59th. Brigade Hd.Qrs. (adjoining rear D.H.Q.).	Satisfactory.
11th. Durham L.I., Hd.Qrs. and Transport.	Satisfactory. Manure is being removed daily by a fatigue party of 20 men. New grease pits have been dug.
Corps Heavy Artillery H.Q. (adjoining rear D.H.Q.).	Satisfactory. Since my last report a great deal of work has been put into this Camp, such as the digging of grease pits and urine pits; the covering over of the filth in the shell-holes and generally the cleaning up of the Camp site, with the result that sanitary conditions here now are satisfactory.
59th. Brigade Machine Gun Company.	Satisfactory; New latrine pits have been dug and old ones filled in. New grease pit dug.
D.A.D.O.S., MARICOURT LOIS.	Satisfactory.
CARNOY Camp 1.	The condition of this camp is Satisfactory. The following work has been done by the fatigue party under the supervision of my N.C.O.: 5 new latrine pits dug, old ones filled in and structures removed. 3 grease pits dug. 2 urine pits dug. Daily collection of Camp refuse and incineration thereof.

                                          A soakage pit and a drain made from the ablution bench to the large trench East of the Camp.
One old incinerator demolished and two grease pits filled in.
Boards fixed marking foul ground.

CARNOY Camp 2.   The condition of this Camp is fairly good. The following work has been carried out by the fatigue party under the supervision of my N.C.O.:
- The burial of excreta, burning of Camp refuse and the cleaning of ground and drains adjoining the huts.
- 1 new incinerator constructed
- New urine and grease pits dug
- Trench dug for disposal of excreta.
- Pit dug for waste water at wash-bench.
- A considerable amount of old equipment which had been deposited on the ground at East side of Camp disposed of to Salvage Company.
- Lines between the huts have been kept in a clean condition and the drains cleansed

CARNOY Camp 3.   Camp satisfactory. Work done:
- 2 new incinerators erected and path of burnt tins made to them.
- New urine and grease pits dug.

CARNOY Camp 4.   Camp satisfactory. Work done:
- 1 latrine removed, new pit dug and old one filled in.
- Grease and urine pits dug.

CARNOY Camp 6.   General sanitary conditions fair. Much untidiness is caused by the men throwing refuse down outside huts or dumping it into the nearest shell-holes, thus causing extra work for the Sanitary squads. The N.C.O's i/c of huts have been warned of their responsibility for general tidiness in this respect. The drainage pits between the huts were being used as refuse pits and were being filled in with burnt tins and covered with earth. An ablution shed has been constructed by the R.E's and also two new cooking sheds.
The following work has been carried out by the fatigue parties working under the supervision of my N.C.O.:

	2 latrines moved, new pits being dug and old pits filled in.
	New urine pit and grease pit dug.
	Soakage pits made to new ablution shed.
	Refuse boxes placed outside huts.
	Trench clearing work carried on.
CARNOY Camp 6.	The condition of this Camp is fairly satisfactory. The following work has been done:-
	Latrine moved, new pit dug and old pit filled in.
	New grease and urine pits dug.
	Trench clearing work carried out.
MONTAUBAN Camp 26.	The condition of this Camp is now satisfactory. The following work has been done:
	New incinerator erected.
	Grease and urine pits dug.
GUILLEMONT, Camps 1, 2, 3 and 4.	These Camps are in an improved condition. The following work has been carried out by the fatigue-parties working under the supervision of my N.C.O's:
	Accumulations of refuse and tins around incinerators and excreta lying about have been deposited in shell-holes and in pits dug specially for this purpose and covered with earth.
	Drainage channels made.
	Several latrines have been moved, the old pits being filled in and the new pits dug.
	New pit boards and duck boards laid down leading to mens' latrine.
	Refuse and tins from incinerator burnt daily.
	At Camp 4 – which is a large dug-out holding one battalion and with cook-houses and messes for Officers – the mens' latrine is 50 yards away and over very rough ground and men have been using old dug-outs near the entrance as latrines. A large pit has therefore been made and the old latrines closed down
R.E. Camps. 53rd, 54th, and 55th. Field Companies, R.E.	Satisfactory.

Divisional Train.	
Headquarters Camp.	Satisfactory.
No. 1 Company.	Satisfactory.
No. 2 Company.	Satisfactory with the exception of ablution arrangements which are to be improved.
No. 3 Company.	Satisfactory with the exception of an accumulation of refuse in trench which is being dealt with.
No. 4 Company.	Satisfactory.
Divisional Ammunition Col.	Satisfactory.
81st. and 82nd. Brigades R.F.A.	Satisfactory, with exception of A/81st. R.F.A. where there is an unsatisfactory latrine. The Q.M.S i/c has promised to remedy this defect.
Mobile Veterinary Section.	Satisfactory.
12th. King's Royal Rifles. Transport.	Satisfactory.
60th. Machine Gun Coy. Transport.	During the first part of the period under review the state of affairs here was very unsatisfactory. There was no specially detailed sanitary Orderly. The attention of the responsible officer was called to this and conditions are now satisfactory.
Divisional Supply Column.	Satisfactory.
Divisional School of Instruction.	Satisfactory. 2 model incinerators have now been erected.

From now onwards the Supply Column and the School of Instruction can be inspected only very rarely. I have no man to spare for the duty nor can I myself visit either except at long intervals.

CARNOY COLISEUM.	Old craters and a mine shaft have been made into urinals of such capacity that they should last indefinitely in spite of the big demands on them.

5. WATER.

(a). The customary water tests from carts have been carried out and all found efficiently chlorinated with the following exceptions:

C.R.A.
Cart No. 1674. Filled 10.30 a.m. on 15/2/17 and tested at 11 a.m. on the same day.

54th. Machine Gun Company.
Cart No. 85903. Filled at PRIQUE FRIE at 11 a.m. on 2/3/17 and tested at 11.15 a.m. on the same day. No re-action resulted.

No. 2 Coy. Divn. Train.
Found unchlorinated on 22/2/17 and orderly admitted that cart was not chlorinated.

5.

No. 4 Section R.A.C.
  Cart No. 10247. Filled noon 23/2/17 and tested at 2.30 p.m. on the same day. There was no orderly in charge of the cart and the driver was apparently quite inexperienced in the chlorination of water.

C/61st. R.F.A.
  Cart No. 6122. Filled 9 a.m. on 21/2/17 and tested at 10.30 a.m. on the same day.

53rd. Field Coy. R.E.
  Cart No. 3452. Filled 1.15 p.m. on 21/2/17 and tested at 1.40 p.m. on the same day.

In every case the attention of the responsible officer has been called to these defects with a request for him to take sufficient measures to ensure efficient chlorination in the future.

(b). The water tanks at GUILLEMONT, COSY CORNER and CARNOY EAST have been chlorinated as required.

(c). Petrol cans for water for Front Lines – As mentioned in the previous Report the cans have been cleaned at GROVETOWN by boiling them out under the supervision of one of my men. They are then taken to GUILLEMONT where every can is examined and if free from smell is filled with chlorinated water and issued. If any smell is detected the cans are again boiled out until they are quite clean.

(d). Opposite TRONES WOOD there are some large uncovered canvas tanks erected for the purpose of supplying water to the railway. Owing to their accessibility troops are using these for drinking water and I have therefore called the attention of the C.R.E. to this and requested him to erect some suitable tanks with taps near to the standpipe there. These will be chlorinated under my supervision.

(e). A new tank with tap and fixed on a proper stand has now been fixed by the D.C.R.E. at the water point opposite CARNOY Camp 2. My requests regarding this point have therefore now been fulfilled satisfactorily.

(f). The water point in CARNOY at entrance to TALUS BOISE is being put in order in a similar manner.

4. GENERAL WORK.

MONTAUBAN Baths.

Mass troops have been bathed and clothed during the last fortnight. The baths have been kept working at the highest pressure from 7 a.m. to 7 p.m., but many more applications are received than can be dealt with. The frost and subsequent thaw, regulations and the damaged condition of the baths when handed over to the Division proved a considerable handicap at the beginning of the period under review. The allotment is made by me and the greatest care is taken to give first choice to those who need baths most. The new GUILLEMONT Baths under construction will help matters but even then the bathing accommodation will be insufficient.

CORBIE Baths.

> These are worked by a portion of the 20th. Division Baths Staff for XVth. Corps Troops (Allotment by Town Major). Fuel is obtained whenever possible from the Division using the Baths. In future I propose to refuse to bathe a Division unless it supplies its own coal.

Clothing Exchange. CARNOY Camp 4.

> The maximum amount of clothing which can be obtained from the Laundry AMIENS is brought here daily. The whole of it is always issued every day to the Baths and also to units applying for it. The greatest care is taken to issue to those most in need. There are always many more applications than can be satisfied. 26691 Clean garments were exchanged during the period under review. It is of interest to note that the Exchange was kept working during the whole of the period of Thaw precautions, by means of daily lorry passes obtained from Army. The work was very laborious for the lorry drivers as devious and daily changing routes had to be followed on account of the very bad roads. As far as can be ascertained no other Division in the Corps was able to do this.

BLANKET Disinfection.

> 5485 blankets have been dealt with at CARNOY Camp 4. A few have been sent to CORBIE for passing through the Thresh Steam Disinfector.

Drying Rooms MONTAUBAN.

> The work of drying and cleaning S.D. clothing has been carried on continuously at the two rooms ("No. 6" and "BRIQUETERIE"). It is slow and very dirty work. Fortunately the demand for dry S.D. clothing has been small (less than 1000). A big demand could not be met with the means available.

Disinfection of Underclothing.

> Disinfection of underclothing for laundry by Thresh Steam Disinfector has been carried on, 35,565 garments having been dealt with. For a time the machine was kept working from 6 a.m. until midnight.

Completion of new Machine Laundry CORBIE.

> I took this piece of work over from the C.R.E., obtained tools from LOOP SIDING CITADEL and MERICOURT (on authority of C.R.E. and Corps) and completed the Laundry. A large amount of washing should be forthcoming when the work there has been properly organised.

Anti-trench Foot Soapex

> About 600 lbs. have been made and issued. 7300 lbs. of powder

Disinfection.

Disinfection of huts, etc. has been carried out promptly on notification of all cases of infectious disease.
All the huts at HARGEL Camp occupied by the 20th. Works Battalion were sprayed on 1/3/17 with a cresol solution on the request of the M.O.

[signature]

Captain R.A.M.C.(T.F.).
Commanding,
33rd. Sanitary Section.

War Diary of Captain A.F. SIRVAN. R.A.M.C.(T.F.) Copy No. 14
O.C. SANITARY SECTION 33,
ATTACHED XXIII (LIGHT) DIVISION.

SECRET. Volume 10. Appendix "B"(i) 53rd. Sanitary Section.
S165/4/17.

SCHEME FOR COLLECTION AND CUSTODY OF STORES OF 53rd. SANITARY SECTION AND BATHS etc. IN THE EVENT OF A SUDDEN ADVANCE.

On receipt of Order "Prepare for sudden advance"

1. The mobilization stores of the Sanitary Section will be collected at Section Headquarters by Staff Sergeant BEAUMONT.

2. Surplus stores including the second blanket per man will be collected at the CARNOY COLISEUM by Staff Sergeant BEAUMONT. No. 673 Pte. FINCH. A. will be left in charge of these stores under the orders of the O.C. Salvage Company.

3. The personnel of the Section will be distributed as follow: N.C.O's and men will proceed as soon as possible to the Units to which they are to be attached.

   Divisional Headquarters.

Unit	Personnel
11th. Durham L.I.	Corporal GAUNT. E.L.
10th. King's Royal Rifles.	Pte. HARRISON. T.O.
11th. King's Royal Rifles.	Sergt. BALMFORTH. A.J
10th. Rifle Brigade.	Lce Corp. HUNTING. E.A.
11th. Rifle Brigade.	Lce Corp. HOWES. A.E.
12th. King's Royal Rifles.	Lce Corp. HILL. E.
12th. Rifle Brigade.	Lce Corp. HAMPSON. F.
6th. Oxon & Bucks. L.I.	Lce Corp. McHUGH. P.
6th. Shropshire L.I.	Lce Corp. OTTERWAY. A.F.
7th. Yorkshire L.I.	Pte. DEWHURST. J.T.
7th. Somerset L.I.	Lce Corp. BARENTS. A.J.
7th. Cornwalls L.I.	Pte. PARKER. T.F.
12th. King's (Liverpool) Regt.	Lce Corp. HORSLEY. A.E. Reinforcement.

   For duties (water etc.) in the Brigades:

Unit	Personnel
59th. Brigade Hd.Qrs.	Sergt. HARDCASTLE. L.
60th. Brigade Hd.Qrs.	Lce Corp. WILSON. J.A.V.
61st. Brigade Hd.Qrs.	Lce Corp. SPURGEON. T.G.

   Sanitary Section Hd.Qrs.
   S/Serg. BEAUMONT. A.E.
   Corporal WHITLOCK. J.W.
   Pte. BEAGLES.
   Pte. JUDD. A.
   Reinforcement.
   Rfn. SCHOLEY. W.
   Pte. COX (D.C.L.I.)

   When Battalions are in the Line the personnel will remain behind with the details.
   All the attached men, except those mentioned, will remain behind and come under the orders of the O.C. Salvage Coy.

4. Baths and Laundry CORBIE will continue as at present.

5. The Staff and stores at GUILLEMONT Baths will remain as at present.

6. The clothing and stores at MONTAUBAN BATHS and DRYING ROOMS (No. 6 and BRIQUETERIE) will be conveyed to Huts 1 and 2 Camp 4 CARNOY under the supervision of Lce Corporal BEARDSWORTH by arrangement with the O.C. Salvage Company. Lce Corporal BEARDSWORTH will then remain in charge of the stores in these huts. Lce Corporal CRISFORD will remain in charge of the Baths.

The remainder of the staff will act according to the orders of the O/C Salvage Company.

7. Approximate number of details left behind will be as follows:

		At present rationed by
GUILLEMONT Baths.	8.	
MONTAUBAN Baths.	8.	O.C. Salvage Coy.
DRYING ROOMS.	5.	Town Major BERNAF Y.
Clothing Excahnge and Blanket Disinfection, CARNOY Camp 4.	11.	Sanitary Section.
Men attached to Sanitary Section (Camp 2).	2.	Sanitary Section.
GUILLEMONT Water Dump.	4.	Divn. Grenade Officer.

Captain R.A.M.C.(T.F.).
Commanding,
33rd. Sanitary Section.

6/3/17

Copies to

1. "Q" 20th. Division.
2. A.D.M.S.
3. Staff Captain 59th. Brigade.
4. do.   60th. Brigade.
5. do.   61st. Brigade.
6. Staff Sergeant BEAUMONT.
7. Q.M.S. HOARE.
8. Sergeant CAESAR.
9. O.C. Salvage Company.
10.)
11.)
12.) Retained.
13.)
14/15. War Diary.

War Diary of Captain A.F. SIRVAN. R.a.m.c.(T.F)
O.C. SANITARY SECTION 33,
ATTACHED XXIII (LIGHT) DIVISION.

Q.M.S. HOARE. G.G.   Volume 10. Appendix "B"(2) S16 C/5/14.
Sergt.   CAESAR. F.S.
Lce Cpl. BEARDSWORTH. H.
Lce Corpl CRISFORD. H.A.
Pte.   FINCH. R.

On receipt of the Order "Collect Stores forthwith"

1. Q.M.S. Hoare will collect washed clothing from AMIENS and get all dirty clothes washed and stored at CORBIE. The Baths and Laundry CORBIE will continue as at present.

2. Lce Corporal Beardsworth will arrange with O.C. Salvage Company (who will be at BRIQUETERIE) for conveyance of all underclothing and service dress from Baths and Drying Rooms to Huts 1 and 2 Camp 4 CARNOY and will come under the orders of O.C. Salvage Company.

3. Lce Corporal CRISFORD will remain in charge of the Baths.

4. Pte. Finch will remain in charge of all surplus Sanitary Section stores and will come under the orders of the O.C. Salvage Company.

No. 33
SANITARY
SECTION.
No............
Date............

A Sirvan
Captain R.a.m.c.(T.F)
Commanding
33rd Sanitary Section.

War Diary of Captain A.F. SIRNAN. R.a.m.c.(T.F.)

Volume 10. Appendix "B"(3)

No. S165/6/17.

To
33rd Sanitary Section

You will proceed on ———— to the ———— ———— and report to the ————
You will take full pack and one blanket and ———— days rations. You will be attached to this Unit for rations, billets and transport only.

You duties will be to daily (or more frequently as the case may require) inspect all the Sanitary arrangements of the Unit to which you are attached. To help them by your advice but you are **not** expected to do unskilled manual labour. If any defects are found which cannot be remedied (by going to the R.M.O. or other sources) in 2 or 3 days at most you must report the matter to me. You are to send me a weekly report to be despatched every Saturday night. You are still under my orders and for discipline and are only attached to the Unit for purposes of convenience of work. You must endeavour to get into frequent touch with me.

A.F.Sirnan
Captain R.a.m.c.(T.F.)
Commanding
33rd Sanitary Section.

No. 33
SANITARY
SECTION.
No. ....
Date ....

War Diary of Captain A.F. SIRVAN, R.a.m.C.(T.F.)
O.C. SANITARY SECTION 33,
ATTACHED ——————— DIVISION.
Volume 10. Appendix "B". No. S.165/7/11

No. 33
SANITARY
SECTION.

TO.

33rd Sanitary Section

You will proceed on _____ to the _____
Brigade Headquarters and report to the Staff Captain.
You will take full pack and one blanket and ____ days
rations. You will be attached to Brigade Headquarters
for billets, rations and transport only.

Your duty is to ensure that all water that is
drunk in your Brigade is properly sterile. To see that all
water carts are in a proper condition and properly
cleaned and sterilised. If units have NO water carts you
are to report if conditions are unsatisfactory. You are to
know of small sources for filling water bottles. You are
not to do any work which will prevent your keeping
all units under frequent observation from a water
point of view. Whenever the Brigade moves you will
invariably accompany the Brigade billeting party in
order to give any required advice reference to water
supplies.

You are to send me a weekly report to be
despatched every Saturday night. In this report you
are to shew the sources from which each unit is
supplied. You are still under my Orders and for
discipline and are only attached to Brigade
Headquarters for purposes of convenience of work.
You must endeavour to get into frequent touch
with me.

A.F.Sirvan.

Captain R.a.m.C.(T.F.)
Commanding
33rd Sanitary Section.

War Diary of Captain A.F. GIRVAN. R.A.M.C (T.F.)
O.C. Sanitary Section.

Volume 10. Appendix "C"

S T A N D I N G   O R D E R S

- for -

CORBIE   LAUNDRY.

N.o. 33
SANITARY SECTION.
No............
Date............

1. <u>DRYING ROOM</u>.
    a. The Drying Room is <u>NEVER</u> to be left unoccupied.
    b. No accumulation of fluff is to be permitted. The floor will be swept every Sunday morning or more often if necessary.
    c. 12 full buckets are to be kept in the room and are to be replenished every Sunday morning or more often if necessary.
    d. The hatch to the Mending Room will be kept closed except when actually in use.

2. <u>MENDING ROOMS</u>.
    a. No fluff is to be allowed to accumulate. The floor will be swept after each shift and the sweepings removed outside the building.
    b. 6 full buckets will be kept in each room and are to be replenished every Sunday morning or more often if necessary.
    c. The hatch to the Drying Room will be kept closed except when actually in use.

3. <u>WASH-HOUSE</u>.
    a. 12 empty pails will be kept in the Wash-house.
    b. The steeping tanks will be filled with water (but no clothes) on work ceasing for the day.

4. <u>SMOKING</u>.
    a. Smoking is absolutely forbidden at all times in the Laundry premises except in the Wash-house and Engine Room.
    b. No man on the Drying Room Staff may smoke <u>AT ALL</u> during his shift.

5. <u>MERRYWEATHER PUMP</u>.
    a. The fire will never be drawn.
    b. The fire hose will be coupled to the engine as soon as the day's work ceases.

6. <u>FIRE REGULATIONS</u>.
    a. <u>Alarm</u>. The N.C.O. or man discovering an outbreak of fire will immediately ring the Alarm Bell and then proceed to warn the N.C.O. i/c Laundry, who, on arrival will assume full control of the proceedings. In his absence the next senior N.C.O. will assume such control.
    b. <u>Proceedings</u>. On the alarm being given each man will spring to his allotted post according to the Fire Drill Regulations. Each man must be thoroughly acquainted with this Drill
    c. Every man will be detailed for his post for the week by the N.C.O. i/c Laundry.
    d. <u>Practice Drill</u>. A practice drill for a fire will be

STANDING ORDERS FOR CORBIE LAUNDRY.
Page 2.

held every alternate Saturday (for the Drying Room) at 5 p.m. and for a fire in the Mending Room on the intervening Saturdays at 1 p.m. The drill will be complete in all respects ~~except that the fire hose will NOT be filled with water.~~

7. **DUTY OF N.C.O's.**
An N.C.O. of the Laundry will always remain on the Laundry premises according to a Roster to be arranged by the N.C.O. i/c.

8. **FIRE INSTRUCTIONS.**
Detailed instructions as to practice and drill are appended

[signature]

Captain R.A.M.C.(T.F.).
Commanding,
33rd. Sanitary Section.

16th. March 1917.

FIRE DRILL REGULATIONS FOR CORBIE LAUNDRY.

> No. 33
> SANITARY SECTION.
> No ....
> Date ....

The Alarm MUST be sounded as soon as the smallest fire is discovered, even if it is thought that one bucket of water will suffice.

ON THE ALARM OF FIRE:

1. **DAY.**
   The N.C.O. i/c will immediately warn all women in the mending and Folding Rooms. They will leave by the usual exit, if available, otherwise by emergency exit.

   <u>Wash-house.</u> The man i/c No. 3 Washer will unhook the fire hose from the wall and have the coil ready to pass over his machine.

   The man i/c No. 2 Washer will receive the coil from No. 3 and unroll it to its full length on the Laundry floor. He will then run it to the door of the Drying Room and hand the nozzle to the Drying Room attendant stationed there.

   The remainder of the Staff will line up from the Steeping tanks to the Drying Room Door and convey water to the outbreak of the fire by means of the "bucket chain" using the fire buckets provided.

   One man will be detailed to remain in the billet to see that no lights are left unattended there.

   <u>Engine Room.</u> The fireman of the Merryweather Pump will couple up the fire hose, raise full head of steam and await the order "Start pump".

   The fireman of the French Steam Engine will stop all machinery, damp down and then fall in with the "bucket chain" in the wash-house.

   The fireman of the ROBEY Boiler will shut off steam, damp down and then go to the assistance of the fireman of the Merryweather Pump.

   <u>Drying Room.</u> No. 1 will immediately take up his position at the door leading to the wash-house in order to receive the fire nozzle. He will run the hose into the Drying Room and hold the nozzle "ready" to play on the outbreak.

   No. 2 will discharge the water in the fire buckets in the Drying Room on to the outbreak and will then proceed to join the "bucket chain".

   No. 3 will close the hatchway leading to the mending room and then proceed to join the "bucket chain".

   Nos. 4 and 5 will then remove and throw on the floor any clothing from the racks likely to impede the passage of the water.

   Care should be taken NOT to break the windows if it can be avoided.

2. **NIGHT.**
   The guard or night-watchman will proceed to the Merryweather Pump and stoke it up, using, if necessary, the special fuel provided for this purpose.

   The Laundry Staff will assemble in the wash-house (with the exception of one man who will be detailed to remain in the billet to see that no lights are left unattended there) — reaching there by the quickest means — and will line up from the Steeping tanks to the drying room door and convey water to the outbreak of the fire by means of the "bucket chain" using the fire buckets provided.

   The fireman i/c the Merryweather Pump will raise full head of steam and await the order "Start pump". In the absence of the regular fireman the following men will act as his deputy in the order named : Rfn. SIMPSON, Pte. LAMB, Pte. WILLIAMS.

FIRE REGULATIONS FOR CORBIE LAUNDRY - Page 2.

Drying Room. No 1 will proceed to the fire coil over No. 3
Washer in the Wash-house and will unroll it to its full
length on the Laundry floor. He will then carry the
nozzle into the Drying Room and hold it at "ready" to play
on the outbreak of the fire.

        No. 2 will discharge the water in the Drying
Room fire buckets on to the outbreak of the fire and then
proceed into the wash-house to take part in the "bucket
chain".

        No. 3 will close the hatchway to the Mending
Room and then proceed into the wash-house to take part in
the "bucket chain".

        Nos. 4 and 5 will remove and throw on the floor
any clothing from the racks likely to impede the passage
of the water. Care should be taken NOT to break the windows
if it can be avoided.

Mending Room. The Night shift in the mending room will close
the hatchway, extinguish all lights and make their way
through the small hatchway or emergency exit to the Wash-house.

        If a fire occurs in the Mending Room, one man
will sound the Alarm and the remainder will cope with the
fire until assistance arrives.

A.F.Gorvan

Captain R.A.M.C.(T.F.).
Commanding,
33rd. Sanitary Section.

16th. March 1917.

LAUNDRY CORBIE

REGLES EN CAS DE FEU.

1. Sonnez fort l'alarme.
2. Sortez vite mais tranquillement par la porte ou par la SORTIE EN CAS DE FEU.
3. Allez chercher les hommes criant "FA-HIER".
4. Quand les filles sont parties jetez sur le feu (si'l est possible) l'eau qui se trouve dans les seaux.

A. F. Girvan
Captain R.A.M.C.(T.F.).
Commanding,
33rd. Sanitary Section.

16th. March 1917.

War Diary of Captain A.F. SIRVAN. R.A.M.C.(T.F.)
O.C. Sanitary Section 33,
Attached XXII (LIGHT) Division.
Volume 10. Appendix "D"

No. 33
SANITARY
SECTION.

No. S203/17
Date 22/3/17

REPORT

of 33rd. Sanitary Section for
fortnight ending 17/3/17.

This Report is reduced to a minimum on account of present unsettled conditions. All the usual details of inspections, etc. are omitted. The few adverse comments that have been necessary have been made as they arose.

1. The work of the Sanitary Section and attached men has kept the undermentioned concerns in full working order:

    a. Sanitary and Water cart inspections and water point chlorination.
    b. Supervision of working parties for sanitary duties for all the Camps.
    c. Petrol can cleaning for drinking water for the line.
    d. Baths MONTAUBAN.
    e. Baths CORBIE.
    f. Clothing Exchange CARNOY Camp 4.
    g. Blanket disinfection.
    h. Drying Rooms MONTAUBAN.
    i. Disinfection of all clothing for Laundries.
    j. Distribution of disinfectants.
    k. Manufacture and distribution of all anti-trench foot soap and powder.
    l. Disinfection of huts, etc. after all cases of infectious disease.
    m. Divisional Laundry CORBIE.

Taking these in order but as briefly as possible owing to the present changing conditions:-

a. Sanitary and Water cart inspections and water point chlorination.
    This has been carried out precisely as in my last report. During the last week every test of water carts has shewn that chlorination had been properly carried out.

b. Supervision of working parties for sanitary duties at all the Camps.
    The Camps are in an improved state. A great improvement has been effected at the GUILLEMONT Camps and particularly at the Divisional Headquarters at BRIQUETERIE and CARNOY A.2.d.8.7.

c. Petrol can cleaning for front line water.
    All cans leaving GUILLEMONT water point have been boiled out repeatedly till free from smell and then filled with chlorinated water.

1.

d. Baths MONTAUBAN.
The undermentioned units have been bathed and given clean clothing:
Guards Entrenching Battalion.
4th. Field Survey Company.
20th. Division R.F.A.
Salvage Company.
Traffic Police.
Headquarters R.E.
11th. Durham L.I.
12th. R.H. Details.
29th. Divn. Works Battalion.
20th. Division Amm. Col.
61st. Trench Mortar Battery.
59th. Machine Gun Company.
59th. Trench Mortar Battery.
61st. Brigade Details.
6th. K.S.L.I.
15th. Brigade R.H.A.
11th. R.B.
59th. Field Ambulance.
20th. Division Hutting Company.
12th. K.R.R.C.
60th. Trench Mortar Battery.
7th. K.O.Y.L.I.
61st. Machine Gun Company.
Divisional Signal Company.
10th. Rifle Brigade.
29th. Division R.F.A.
11th. K.R.R.C.
60th. Machine Gun Company.
10th. K.R.R.C.
84th. R.E.
59th. Brigade Details.
12th. King's (Liverpool) Regt.
14th. Corps Signals.
4875 men have been bathed.

e. Baths CORBIE.
These have not had much demand. (They have now been handed over to the 33rd. Division - 19/3/17.).

f. Clothing Exchange CARNOY Camp 4.
This has met all demands throughout the period in addition to supplying MONTAUBAN Baths. The hut was badly damaged by the mine explosion but the exchange of clothes was not interrupted. The Exchange has now been shifted to opposite the CARNOY COLISEUM at Camp 5. 32464 clean garments have been exchanged for dirty ones. No Clothing Exchange existed (apart from Baths) until the Division reached the SOMME Area.

h. Drying Rooms MONTAUBAN.
350 dry cleaned articles have been issued.
502 articles have been dried and cleaned.

g. Blanket Disinfection.
The work was interrupted for two days as the huts which were used for the purpose were demolished by the mine explosion in CARNOY Camp 4.
4775 blankets have been disinfected.

i. Disinfection of underclothing for Laundries.
57028 garments have been passed through the Thresh Steam Disinfector.

j, k and l. These require no further explanation.

Laundry CORBIE.
- This is now a going concern employing some 40 men and 10 to 15 women. It does all the washing of the Division.

I suggested the site and made the first designs in the middle of November 1916. The work was carried out by sappers under a succession of R.E. Officers and proceeded slowly in spite of continued efforts to hasten things. The slow arrival of machinery was the principal cause of delay.

The whole place works very well, though bad materials have caused serious defects to show in the fireplaces of the drying room and they will have to be rebuilt as soon as firebricks can be obtained.

4000 garments can be dried in 24 hours.

The Laundry is in charge of Sergeant CAESAR of this Section who is performing his duty admirably

15,791 clean garments have been issued from the Laundry from 8/3/17 (date of opening) to the 17/3/17.

Rough plans are appended.

A.F. Girvan.

Captain R.A.M.C.(T.F.).
Commanding,
33rd. Sanitary Section.

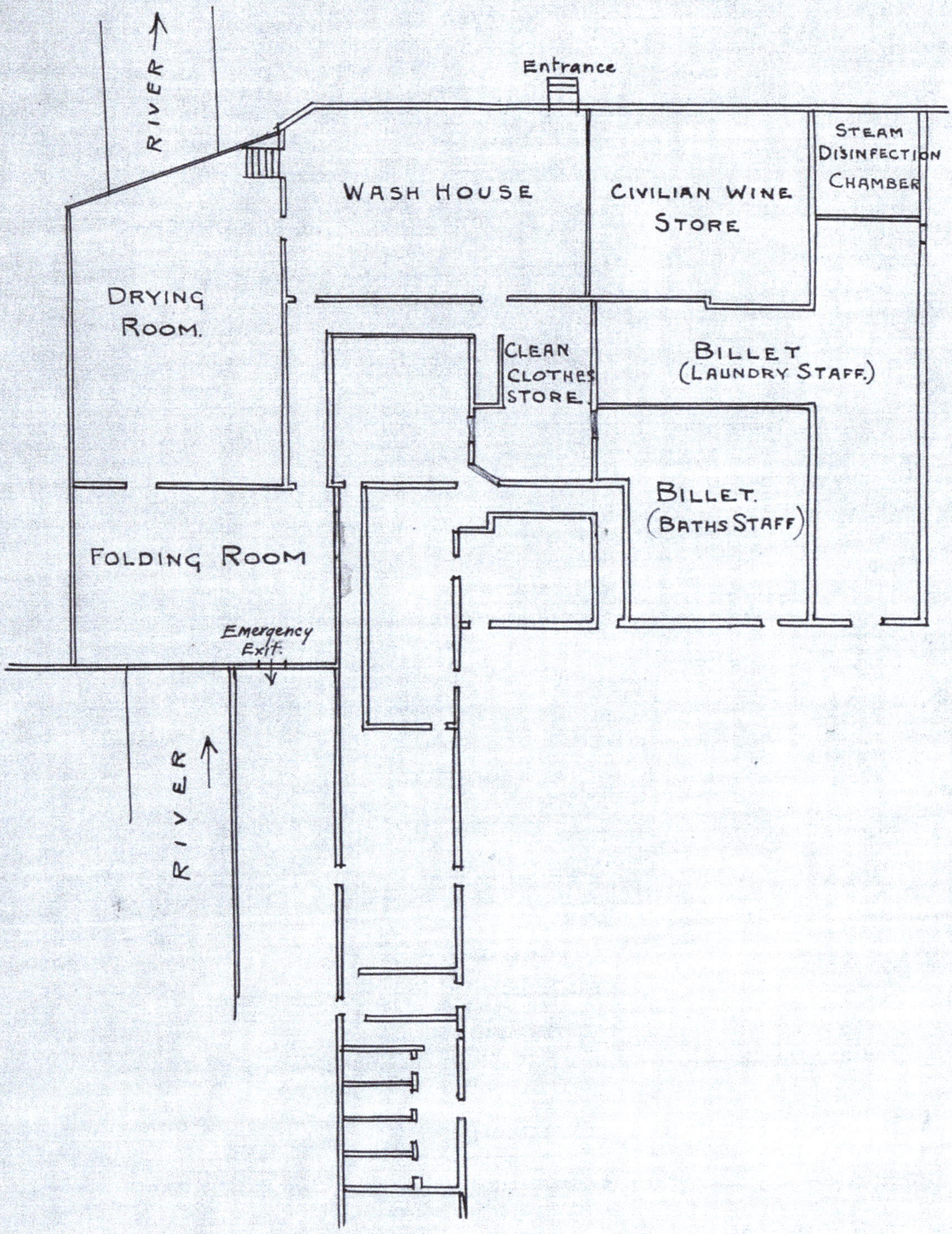

SKETCH PLAN OF LAUNDRY
AT
CORBIE.

A.F. Girvan
Capt.
O.C. 33rd Sanitary Section.

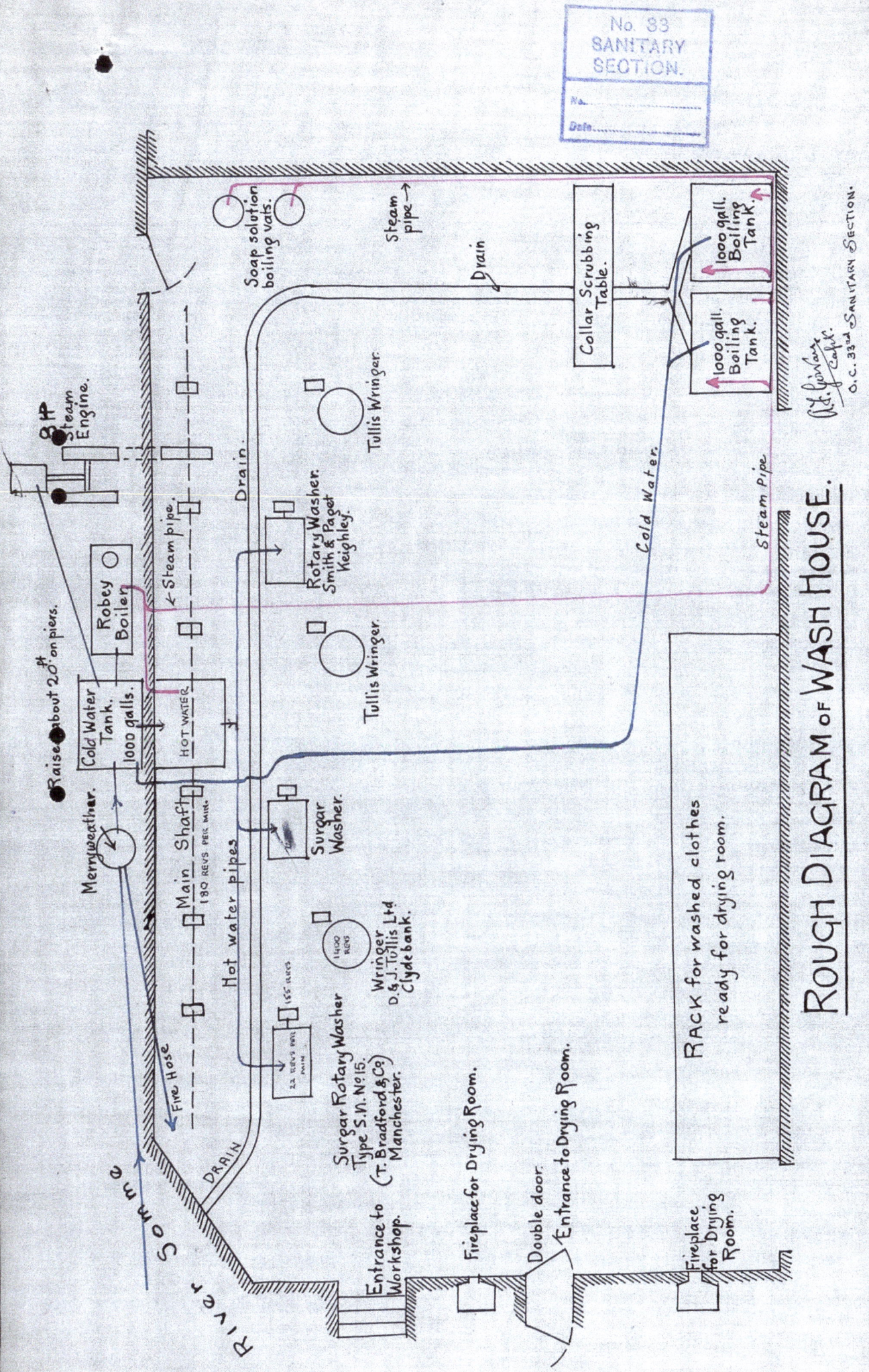

Sketch Plan of Drying Room.

O.C. Sanitary Section 33,
Attached XXth (Light) Division.

War Diary of Captain A.F. SIRVAN. R.A.M.C.(T.F.)

O.C. SANITARY SECTION 33,
ATTACHED XXIII (LIGHT) DIVISION.
Volume 10. Appendix "E".

33rd. Sanitary Section.
No. S198/2/17.

NOTES ON THE USE OF THE POISON TESTING CASE.

HEAVY METALS.

The test for poisonous "Heavy metals" (Mercury, Lead, Copper, etc.) is best carried out by filling two similar test-tubes with the water to within an inch of the top and then adding a couple of drops of sodium sulphide to one of them, the other serving as a comparison tube so that a slight change in tint may be recognised even in an already coloured water. A change in colour which vanishes when a drop of hydrochloric acid is added is merely due to iron, but if it persists a heavy metal is present.
The following table gives an idea as to the tints obtained:

Colour produced.	Concentration of metal present: (Lead, Mercury, Copper, etc.).			
	1 in 10000.	1 in 100000	1 in a million.	1 in 10 million.
	Tube becomes a deep grey or brown and opaque.	Strong brown and opalescent	Distinct brown tint.	Just perceptible to a practised observer.

The colour appears instantly and is best observed before many minutes have elapsed. The tints in the last two columns should be observed by looking downward through the tube and the comparison tube held side by side over a white piece of paper in good daylight.

ARSENIC.

1. The arsenic test as described on the box. (Marsh's Test).
    (a). Never fail to do a "blank" test with the reagents as they are seldom entirely free from arsenic.
    (b). You will often obtain a stain on the porcelain tile but it will not be arsenic or antimony unless it remains in whole or part after a spot of dilute (1 in 10) hydrochloric acid has been applied to it. You will generally find that it vanishes instantly or is not more marked than that obtained from the reagents only.
    Should it persist apply a 1 in 5 solution of bleaching powder; if it now vanishes it is arsenic; if it remains it is antimony. In

either case of course the water is unfit fot use. one ⓠ part of arsenic oxide in 10000 parts of water produced a spot as dark as an ink spot in the a few seconds.

2. An alternative arsenic test which is little known but which I much prefer is carried out as follows:

Put the sample, acid and zinc (only 3 pieces) into a test tube exactly as for the usual test but instead of burning the hydrogen produced put over the mouth of the tube (which is kept upright) a little cap made of a scrap of filter paper (previously moistened in the centre with one minute drop of a saturated solution of Mercuric chloride - Hydrag Perchlor - and then allowed to dry). If a yellow stain appears on the paper arsenic is present. The only disadvantage is that sulphur can also give a similar colour, but it is seldom met with in waters and the result can be confirmed by the Marsh Test. If you <u>don't</u> get a yellow colour Arsenic is absent. If you <u>do</u> get a yellow colour it is as well to do the Marsh Test to confirm the result and to send a sample for further examination.

The following table shows what kind of a colour may be expected:

Concentration of Arsenic expressed as AS_4O_6

	1 in 10000	1 in 100000	1 in million	1 in 10 million	Reagent "Blank."
Time 1 min.	Yellow	-	-	-	-
" 3 mins.	Orange.	Pale yellow.	-	-	-
" 5 mins.	Orange.	Canary yellow.	-	-	-
" 10 mins.	Orange.	Orange.	Very pale yellow.	-	-
" ½ hour.	Vandyk Brown.	Orange Brown.	Pale Yellow.	-	-
" ¾ hour.	"	"	"	-	-
" 1 hour.	"	"	"	-	-

Therefore if no perceptable colour is found after ½ hour there is less than one part of AS_4O_6 per million; i.e. Arsenic may be said to be absent. If a well had been poisoned a much greater amount of arsenic would be expected - probably more than 1 in 10000.

<u>CYANIDES.</u>

The only points to be observed specially are :
(a). Don't add more than the 5 drops of ferrous sulphate.
(b). Boil at least 2 minutes.
(c). Compare the colour produced with that produced

by doing a "blank" test with the reagents only. If only a little cyanide is present the colour will be green not blue. A yellow colour is always produced by the reagents themselves.

Daylight is very desirable for all the tests.
I shall be pleased to supply the pieces of filter paper already treated for the arsenic test as soon as I can obtain suitable paper.
Other reagents are NOT obtainable from me.

A.F. Girvan

Captain R.A.M.C.(T.F.).
Commanding,
33rd. Sanitary Section.

24th. March 1917.

www.ingramcontent.com/pod-product-compliance
Lightning Source LLC
Chambersburg PA
CBHW080810010526
44113CB00013B/2356